MOON CAKES

MOON CAKES

A Novel

ANDREA LOUIE

Ballantine Books

New York

Grateful acknowledgment is made to the following for permission to
reprint previously published material:

The Akron Beacon Journal: Excerpts from "Ancestors Whisper to the Heart"
by Andrea Louie are reprinted by permission of *The Akron Beacon Journal.*

BOA Editions, Ltd: Excerpt from "Persimmons" copyright © 1986 by Li-
Young Lee. Reprinted from *Rose* by Li-Young Lee with the permission of
BOA Editions, Ltd., 92 Park Ave., Brockport, NY 14420.

Cynthia Ning: Translation of the poem "Thoughts on a Quiet Evening"
by Li Bai.

Hal Leonard Corporation: Excerpts from "The Inchworm" by Frank Loesser.
© 1951, 1952 (renewed). FRANK MUSIC CORP. All rights reserved.

Warner Bros. Publications Inc.: Excerpt from "On the Street Where You
Live" by Alan Jay Lerner and Frederick Loewe. Copyright © 1956 by Alan
Jay Lerner and Frederick Loewe (renewed). Chappell & Co., Inc., owner
of publication and allied rights. All rights reserved. Made in USA. Used by
permission of Warner Bros. Publications Inc., Miami, FL 33014.

Louie, Andrea.
Moon cakes: a novel/Andrea Louie.—1st ed.
p. cm.
ISBN 0-345-38554-3
I.   Title.
PS3562.0817M66 1995
813'.54—dc20   94-48115
CIP

Manufactured in the United States of America

First Edition: June 1995

10   9   8   7   6   5   4   3   2   1

To my parents

And in memory
of Ron
who loved beauty

CONTENTS

AUTHOR'S NOTE

This book uses the now standard Pinyin system of transliterating Mandarin Chinese words. For example, what was formerly referred to as the Yangtze and Canton under the Wade-Giles system is in this text spelled Yangze and Guangzhou.

ACKNOWLEDGMENTS

Writing is such a solitary thing that I could not have done it without those around me, both near and far.

With much fondness, I wish to thank:

—Clare Ferraro and Ellen Levine for their expertise and savvy.

—those in the newspaper industry who taught me true grit and the economy of words.

—those with the Freedom Forum in Asian Studies and at the University of Hawaii for giving me the opportunity to fall in love with China.

—Debby Stock for her earnest, meticulous, and good-natured proofreading of the original manuscript—but most importantly for her friendship.

—all the people I love who supported me in more ways than you possibly could know.

—and my dear and true friend, Jen Estes, who saw. (You were right about the water buffalo and so many other things.)

Oh, the feel of the wolftail on the silk,
the strength, the tense
precision in the wrist,
I painted them hundreds of times
eyes closed. These I painted blind.
Some things never leave a person:
scent of the hair of one you love,
the texture of persimmons
in your palm, the ripe weight.

"Persimmons"
—Li-Young Lee

MOON CAKES

PROLOGUE

I WANT TO tell you a love story.

It has no beginning, no end. So I simply must start somewhere in the middle, which is now.

. . .

IMAGINE THAT I am standing on a hill in Shenzhen, a cusp of land that is at the very tip of China, and looking out across the South China Sea. It is nightmarishly hot. Waves of heat rise from the still water, which is blue, blue-green. The sky is the color of ash. The air is heavy and goes thickly into the lungs; it burns.

I stand at the edge of China, which is like being at the end of the Earth. I think of stepping out onto the sea, which looks so thick with salt that it would support the weight of a woman.

Offshore are strange knobs of land that protrude like growths, like lesions, from infested waters. These, too, shimmer in the heat, waver like hallucinations. I want to walk out and push these tiny islands back into the sea, shove them into the shallow waters; I want the water to be like glass, smooth and endless, undisturbed. I want there to be nothing.

In the distance are buildings, hazy in the heat. It is Hong

Kong. We go there tomorrow; for the first time in more than a month, we will set foot on foreign soil.

I stand here and think that, yes, I want to tell you a love story.

But not the kind you think.

. . .

BEFORE I CAME here, I lived in the land of dreams. Everything was real, not real. In my nocturnal world I could not distinguish an old woman on the street from a beggar in my nocturnal world. I felt half asleep during the day hours and most alive in the night. In ancient times a Chinese drum would have tolled the hours: first watch, second. But it was my dreams that punctuated the darkness in those weeks before I left for China—I had crazy, ludicrous visions of skateboarders on top of buses and hot-dog vendors in my bedroom. I dreamed I was in an opera, wearing a beautiful scarlet gown, but missed all my cues because I spent the length of the show backstage, ironing my blood-colored train. I thought I saw sweet red beans in a fountain; I thought I saw an old school friend throw himself out the window of a building.

What was real, what was not? I could not tell the difference because when I was awake in the sunlight, things struck me as bizarre and surreal, fantastical and unbelievable. I saw a couple getting on my bus dressed from head to toe in garish gold lamé. In a downpour I saw a man wearing a pink shower cap pedal a unicycle against the traffic. And once, on a street corner, I spotted a giant vanilla wafer, which did a little tap dance and then paused, waving to me. How could I know that these oddities were not really dreams? How could I know whether I had not mixed up my sense of time and place and actually had seen these things in my sleep?

. . .

I THINK ABOUT this.

But then my thoughts blur and I lose my grasp on them again. My eyes follow the waves of heat in the distance, and soon my mind is not where it was. I look out at the South China Sea and think that this is like no other world. Here, the heat rises from the green lushness of Southeast Asia, rises like a hot flush and floods my cheeks, makes me sweat as I stand here in the air that does not move, that traps me in a time that has no past, no future. I am at the edge of China, which is like being at the end of the Earth. I want to step off the edge. I want to step out into the water, knowing that it will not really support the weight of a woman but instead will envelop me, hold me like the warm, safe embrace of a mother holding her daughter within the inner sea of the body.

I do not think that walking out to sea will be dangerous. I picture myself wearing something white, the color of purity. In the Western world white is for weddings, but in China it is the color of death. In arty foreign films I have seen heroines walking into the sea, and it is ravishing and romantic: The wind buffets her hair and skirts (for some reason the woman always is wearing a lot of skirts and petticoats that fly in the air so beautifully for the camera). The waves are raging upon the shore; the air is gray and tortured and filled with fine mist and sand. You see the woman walking toward the water, into the ragged shallows with the deadly undertow. The salty fingers of water pull at her dress, wetting her skirts, making them dark and heavy. Then the scene cuts discreetly and the woman is merely gone. It is as if she was never there at all, a mere figment of your imagination. You never have to witness the actual unpleasantness of death, the horror. In your mind she is like a soft, transparent jellyfish, billowing in the sea with all her skirts. She simply is transformed into another life-form, lovely and tranquil.

. . .

I HOLD THESE images in my thoughts as I look out at the South China Sea, which is placid, deceiving. The heat is intoxicating. I already feel as if I am part of the sea, salty and wet. Perhaps I really am in the land of dreams: China is so earthy, so close to the ground that I cannot believe it to be real. I have seen a water buffalo in mud up to its ass; I have seen a bus go by with a hundred chickens tied by their feet to the roof, their feathers flapping chaotically in the wind. What is real, what is not? My life in America was not like this. I was the kind of person who, as a child, ate canned fruit cocktail in school cafeterias and thought Mister Rogers was a creep. I bugged my mother to buy me a curling iron and thought Henry Winkler was one hot babe. And now I am standing on a land where generations of emperors had castrated men as servants and tortured all their scholars. . . . I have been in China for barely six weeks, but already I have no concept of America, of what my life was like there. I have no sense of reality, of what is truth or fiction, present or past. All I know is that as I stand here on the edge of the Earth, I can feel that the sea is more real than anything.

. . .

AND HER.

I know that she, too, is real, although she came to me in sleep.

My name is Maya.

Before I came to China, a little girl would come to me in the night, like so many other of my strange and surreal dreamtime visitors. She did not come every night, but every so often. She had come for months, stepping matter-of-factly into my dreams. It was always the same dream, but with different images and new details. I was not frightened. Rather, I was a bit pleased when, in sleep, I spotted the little girl standing in the doorway, like a familiar neighborhood Girl Scout selling Thin Mints.

I had not had recurring dreams since I was a child, when I dreamed that our dining room was filled with snakes. But this dream of the little girl was not frightening and perverse, not twisted. Still, I wonder about it.

The little girl stepped through a screen door, and already I seemed to know a great deal about her, except things that would matter in real life. I didn't know her name or how old she was. But I knew that the little girl did not like things that were pink and was a little bit afraid of dogs. I knew that the girl collected the lint from the dryer, which was soft and rolled off in neat sheets from the filter. I knew that the little girl lived with her parents in a town that had one stoplight. It was summertime.

In this dream the little girl was heading out the front door with a little green knapsack over both shoulders. It was a child's cheerful knapsack, a pint-size one with an appliquéd penguin made of black and white felt. When she was wearing the knapsack, the penguin was always looking at the world backward, as if staring out the rear window of a car.

The little girl was on a mission to find moon cakes. This was very important. The thing was, the little girl had never had a moon cake, so this made things difficult. There was an irrationality that was perfectly acceptable and understandable in dreams, and I sensed this was an urgent endeavor.

Moon cakes are a Chinese sweet popular during the Mid-Autumn Festival in September, when you can buy them in boxes all over any Chinatown. They are round, about the circumference of a good-size orange cut in half. They are brown like the top of a pound cake, but solid, with pretty designs stamped on the top. Inside the best ones are a kind of mashed-up sweetened bean. The more expensive ones contain hard-boiled duck egg yolks, sometimes even two or three. But I always have thought that the yolks seem like a nuisance and leave less room for the bean part, which is better. You eat moon cakes in wedges, sliced with a sharp knife like a baby pie.

For some reason I knew that the little girl was very well equipped as she stood there by the screen door, ready to go out. Maybe she was carrying things in her knapsack that I might have carried as a child going on an adventure. The planning part, I seem to remember, was crucial to any properly executed childhood mission. The little girl had a compass, a red plastic one with a white dial and a black arrow. Sometimes the needle wobbled, as if she was unsure. She also had a small pocket atlas of the world with the different countries printed in yellow and pink and green. She didn't exactly need the atlas right then, but she brought it along just in case. You never know about these things.

She had money in a tiny yellow silk change purse with a white snap. Not very much, maybe two dollars or so. There also was a subway token in the change purse, but she could not use the token in this town because there were no subways. Somehow I knew her father had given her this. He had found it in his wallet when he came back from a meeting someplace where he had to stay overnight in a hotel. Also in the knapsack was a gray stuffed elephant with a white bow around its neck and three Fig Newtons wrapped in a paper napkin. It is very important to bring along provisions when going on an adventure.

It was very sunny outside. You must remember that this was a very idyllic dream in many ways. It was soft, the way dreams often are. The light was very good. Everything was shown from good camera angles. I wonder if perhaps I had been watching too much television.

So in this dream the little girl had on her green knapsack and let someone know that she was going outside to play. Then she went around to the garage and pulled out her red wagon. (Having never seen moon cakes, she didn't know exactly how big they were; she was afraid she might not be able to carry one.) The wagon still was quite shiny. She kept it very well. Unlike the boys on her street, she didn't fill it with rocks or dirt or things that were slimy.

I saw the little girl walking purposefully down the street, pulling the wagon, which made rattling, bumping noises as it hit the spaces in the pavement. She had her black hair in a pigtail on either side of her head, a little dust broom above each ear curving down in a charming angle toward her chin. Her eyes were very dark, and she didn't seem to blink very often. She had on a red cotton jacket with a hood, blue pants, and red tennis shoes. She was a child dressed in primary colors; no indecisive pinks or wan lavenders. In this dream she was a child of conviction.

She decided to visit each store in the town, looking for moon cakes. There were not many stores, because it wasn't a very big town. It was the kind of place people drove through while on their way to someplace else. There were three places that sold food of any kind. There was also a store that reupholstered furniture and a granary, but she didn't bother to stop at either of these shops.

Her first stop was a convenience store, a 7-Eleven or someplace like that. You could buy slushes—ground-up ice with neon syrup injected into it—in bright red or grape or green. It was the kind of thing that you're sure will make you glow in the dark if you drink too many of them. The store also sold candy bars and boxes of overpriced crackers and cigarettes. By the cash register they had all types of spur-of-the-moment items, such as lip balm, nail clippers, and cheap chocolates in the shapes of bunny rabbits or pumpkins, depending on the time of year.

The second store was a mom-and-pop place, half of which was a bakery. They sold glazed doughnuts and cream sticks. The other part was a coffee shop, and people sat down at Formica tables and drank coffee out of olive-colored cups. It was the kind of place that was hot all the time, even in winter. They had candy in the corner, a gumball machine and one that dispensed jawbreakers. You put a penny in the slot and turned the knob around. You had to be very careful when you opened the shiny silver flap door, because the balls always came running out as if they were trying to escape, and sometimes they fell on the floor, which was quite tragic.

The last place was a gas station, where they really didn't have anything except quarts of oil, cigarettes, and chocolate bars. But the little girl thought that she would go there, too, because you never knew.

Although she didn't stay very long in these shops, I sensed—as you can only in dreams—every tiny detail of these places. I knew where everything was, who everyone was.

At each stop the little girl asked if they had any moon cakes.

Oddly, this is where the dream seemed to fast-forward a little. I saw her opening the door to one store, and in an instant the scene changed and she was walking down the street away from another store. The wagon was empty. I felt people smiling indulgently from windows; I saw over the little girl's shoulders, where the felt penguin was riding backward. Her head was down as she stepped over the cracks in the sidewalk. At one point she very deliberately stepped on an anthill built in a crack, flattening the uniform crumbs of dirt into a thin brown crepe on the cement. She did not look back to see the frenzied ants or care that she had rolled over several of them with the wagon.

Her knapsack was very full with things people had given her. They had smiled benevolently when she appeared at their counters, her head barely over the countertops. They seemed to say, Well, no, we really don't have any moon cakes. Are you really sure that's what you want, honey? She was sure. They smiled again, not parting their lips to show their teeth. Well, I'm sorry, sweetheart, but we just don't have anything like that. And when she had appeared crestfallen, they had given her something that they thought would be a reasonable facsimile, something that would do instead.

So inside the knapsack was a croissant, perfectly shaped like the quarter-month moon, carefully wrapped and placed in a small square box with a piece of baker's tissue paper. There were also a round of Swiss cheese from the 7-Eleven and a Moon Pie from the gas station. The Moon Pie was banana-flavored, with marshmallow filling. The little girl had taken care to leave a slight gap in the zipper of her knapsack so that the stuffed elephant could breathe; it was getting very crowded in there.

Although the knapsack was getting heavy, it did not seem to occur to the little girl to put it in the wagon. She just kept pulling it along, empty and rattling over the sidewalk, bumping on clumps of weeds and bits of gravel that had sneaked away from people's driveways.

There were no real voices in this dream, although I could perceive what people were saying and saw them shaking their heads, bemused. They did not think there were such things as moon cakes. What a little darling, they thought. And look at that black hair! But moon cakes, *really*. How quaint.

As I saw the little girl walk sadly down the sidewalk, I realized that I was awake.

It was the morning I left for China.

CHILDHOOD

I DID NOT always live in the land of dreams.

It was quite the opposite: I lived my childhood years intensely, with much passion and love. I did everything with great purpose and intent. As I colored in my coloring books, I wrought grand stories in my head—the slippers I crayoned in were not mere silver but bright, shiny, magical shoes that would take the princess anywhere she wanted with a click of the heels; the forest-green treetops were filled with birds that harvested Froot Loops from special orchards. I spent hours lining up my crayons in appropriate color groupings, a whole swath of them that began with the blackest black and then phased through the rainbow to the whitest white. (Those were the days when I did not associate white with funerals.) I planned elaborate outings for my dolls and stuffed animals, dressing them carefully in old baby clothes and packing wonderful picnics of animal crackers, apple juice, and salt and pepper shakers. We would sit on an old blanket under a tree in the yard and pretend we were on the lawn of King Tut. (Those also were the days when I did not know that Egypt was not renowned for its vast green spaces.) I drew pictures of cats and flowers for my sister and father, both of whom I absolutely adored. It did not occur to me to draw pictures for my mother, probably because she always seemed too busy to react to them.

I loved being a child; I never wanted to grow up. I loved all the trappings of childhood: chocolate milk in little cartons during break time at school, plastic lunchboxes and thermos bottles with pictures of Snoopy and Wonder Woman on them. I loved Golden Rod yellow writing tablets, pink bubble gum that came wrapped in comics, and special "lucky money" in bright red envelopes that my faraway relatives sent me for Chinese New Year. Being a kid seemed to have endless advantages. I didn't want to grow up and learn how to drive because where I grew up, there was nowhere to drive to. And I didn't want to go out on dates because boys seemed more than a little suspect and were gross creatures anyway, especially when they came tearing after you with worms during a rainy recess.

. . .

THE YEAR I turned eleven, I lost a kind of innocence. Sometimes I think I am stuck there forever, battling pimples, a hatred of fractions, and the feeling that I wanted to remain a child forever. It was during my eleventh year that my father, the man of my dreams, vanished inexplicably from my life. He left without telling me he was going, without really saying good-bye. I thought we all had been happy; I thought he had liked his life and had loved me. So it was very hard when he was no longer there to tuck me in at night, to read me a story with much bravado and feeling, then kiss me on the forehead and say, "Good night, sleep tight," with his Chinese accent.

Nothing was the same after he was gone, at least for me. I think I must have stalled out mentally at the age of eleven. My sister, four years older than me, seemed to adapt just fine to our father's absence. And our mother remained exactly the same, too. She never shed a tear, never raised her voice or let on that she might be afraid. To this day she is like a beautiful stone goddess and never blinks, never falters. My mother is an amazing woman, and I regard her with equal measures of reverence, fear, and resentment. Early on, I learned it was wise neither to cross my mother nor to expect too much from her.

So I am moored in the childhood I had had before I turned eleven. I am anchored in the memories of my dear father and in the rootedness of that midwestern landscape, where the trees were sturdy and good for climbing and where daisies and Queen Anne's lace and blue chicory grew on country roadsides. Now that I live in the city I subsist on the memories of roadsides golden with the sun-bright yellow of dandelions, those giant blooms bigger than half dollars that magically transformed themselves into perfect powder-puff seed globes. Breathe on them, whisper to them, and they would release a cloud of promises.

"Look, Maura, look," I would say to my sister as I pulled from behind my back a bouquet of dandelions gone to seed. "Make a wish, Maura." And my sister would close her eyes for a while and think very hard.

"Okay," she would say, opening her eyes. Then she would take a very big breath and *whooosh* . . . she would scatter the little white parachutes into the summer afternoon air.

"So what's your wish?" I would pester her (I was quite good at being annoying, since it was the younger-sister thing to do). "Aren't you going to tell me your wish?"

"Of course not." Maura sniffed in that bigger-sister way. "If I tell you, then it won't come true." Then she would walk off, leaving me with a fistful of ugly, bald dandelion stems.

•

I long for those days before I was eleven, when life was tentative yet seemed whole. The years have smoothed over any hurts I certainly must have had—scraped knees, boo-booed elbows, the late-night hissing of my parents' secretive arguing. In the early days of my childhood years, all was right in the world. I picked white and violet bouquets of wild clover and turned over rocks to look at the soft worms and pill bugs underneath. Grape Popsicles in the high heat of summer turned my lips to purple bruises, cool and sweet. In the coming year I would be in the sixth grade, queen of the hill, a bona fide big kid. I would have a crush on Frank Davis; he would be in my reading group, and I would nearly faint when by chance he would sit next to me.

Those were the days of my endless summer, my wondrous, charmed youth that I have held in my heart like a pearl: smooth and lustrous and whole unto itself.

Once you have known that kind of perfection, nothing else will do. I have spent all these years trying to find it again. I have searched for that kind of ecstasy and comfort and security, and now, finally, I understand that it is lost. The idyllic childhoods we create in our minds are no match for reality.

One day you realize that pearl of youth was made of paste, and it breaks your heart like nothing else.

I was born in the Midwest, where the land is very flat and well kept. The land is divided up neatly, as if it were a square pan of brownies. When settlers first wanted land, it came in sections, each a mile square. Now, more than a hundred and fifty years later, much of it still remains like that—neat patches of land carefully tilled and sown with corn, wheat, or potatoes. These things grow very well there. It is land that produces fundamental food, not crops that might be perceived as silly or inconsequential, like kumquats. It is land that yields wheat for bread and corn that's fed to beef cattle and chickens. It's very basic.

Because it is good land, it's not a place that makes you want to run away. It's not like it is in the desert climates, where people have to move around all the time, following the rain and the washes of green that grow in the water's wake. It is landscape that gives you permanence and roots. There is the comforting thought of all past fields safely harvested, all summer thunderstorms and winter blizzards survived, all ripening crops of bursting tomatoes canned and sealed in their mason jars with rubber rings. It is a land of seasons and cycles, of potato-salad picnics, well-worn softball diamonds, and new socks worn to Sunday school. In a way it is perfect: the ideal mix of a simple life and the chaos of human relations.

· · ·

THIS STRANGE LANDSCAPE and its people are dearer to me than you could possibly know. If I were a young man, a farmer's son, then it would make more sense. It would make sense how I crave this land—these lovely trees that weep at the end of summer and shed their leaves like golden tears; these gentle, endless fields of wheat that flow and whisper in the breeze, moving like an ocean. If I were a farmer's son, this is land I would work with a passion that transcends any bottom line; it would be joyous and hellish to coax life from the earth.

This, however, is not my fate.

I say this like an old woman, like someone shriveled and lined, who has an ill temper and hands destroyed by a lifetime spent in harsh soapy water. If I were an old woman, I would say this while sitting on a front porch, rocking in a chair without getting up all day, just staring at a field gone fallow. I would be waiting only to die because I would have

given up expecting my fate to change, expecting the men I
love to return. Perhaps I would be bitter.

But I am not like that. I am young. My face is unlined,
and my eyes are a little bewildered. Sometimes I catch my
reflection in shop windows and am startled because I look
like I'm trying to find a familiar landmark, even when I'm in
my own neighborhood.

It must sound foolish for me to speak with such resignation, such acquiescence to the cards I have been dealt. But
certain things we can never change: I am not a farmer's son.
And in the part of the Midwest where I was born, there is
little to do if you are not a worker of land.

I am not by nature a wanderer, but I feel that I have become one, cast out from the landscape I cannot possess. Actually, I haven't even traveled very much, but my spirit
drifts. I moved to the city, which is a noisy mess of too many
cars and grit and people. I long to fling open my window to
the sound of birds in flight. I long to be home. Every morning I wake up to the honking of horns and the beeping of
enormous garbage trucks that are backing up to swallow bags
of trash set out at the curb. I wake up every morning and
cannot believe that things are not the way they used to be.
How did this happen? How did my life suddenly change
without my even doing anything?

My mother still lives in the house where I grew up. It is
pretty much the same as it was when I lived there, but now
it is a house of ghosts. There are forbidden memories everywhere—hidden under sheets of newspapers that line the
shelves, inside the imitation blue and white Ming vases on
the end table, behind the brass plate engraved with the word
for happiness that hangs near our door front.

It is a Chinese house.

And, yes, I am a Chinese daughter born in the unlikely
American landscape of farmers' sons.

•

The house I grew up in is made of brick. It stands in a big yard on the outskirts of the town where my parents worked. As a child I loved this house. It is an old colonial, with cream-colored walls and stark white trim. The rooms always seem cool, and in winter are a little bit drafty.

The dining room used to be one of my favorite places in the house because it had a beautiful china cabinet with lovely wooden doors inlaid with glass, so I could look inside at all the pretty dishes. We hardly ever used any of these dishes, and certainly my sister and I were never permitted to play with them. We might borrow a mixing spoon or a few pairs of chopsticks for crafts from the kitchen drawers, but we could never, never touch any of the dishes in the china cabinet. So instead I would go into the dining room, which had a pale green carpet, and stare at all the things behind the glass. The cabinet itself was pretty much standard issue: It was tall and had four shelves and two pairs of glass-paned doors; four solid doors underneath kept cloth napkins and placemats and the stubs of candles out of sight.

But the things behind the glass were wondrous.

There were cloisonné vases the color of green olives inlaid with flowers and birds, sets of blue and white bowls, and crystal wine goblets on precarious stems. On special occasions we ate dinner on blue and white plates and bowls with pictures of dragons on them. We even had a set of ivory chopsticks, probably made in the days when there were more elephants and it was not such a bad thing to kill them. There were crystal candy dishes that were never used and a pair of ugly candlesticks made of pewter that someone had brought my parents from Williamsburg or Philadelphia, someplace with historical significance. My sister and I liked to stand there and stare at all the dishes and dream of all the fancy parties we would have if we ever owned such wonderful things when we grew up.

"I would have Cornish game hens and pâté on little crackers and green beans all lined up on the plate," announced Maura, who had recently started looking through our mother's *Gourmet* magazine. Our mother seldom made anything from this magazine but kept it out on the coffee table.

I did not know what a Cornish game hen was.

"It's a baby chicken," Maura told me with authority. With horror I envisioned little Easter chicks basted with butter.

"Well, I would have wonton soup" (I loved wonton soup) "and giant cheeseburgers with French fries and chocolate-chip cookies."

"You can't have *cheeseburgers* at a dinner party," Maura told me. "That's so gross. You should think of something nicer."

"But I think that cheeseburgers *are* nice," I insisted. "They're the best thing in the whole wide world." I really thought I had come up with the ideal menu, except maybe I would add chocolate cupcakes with little colored sprinkles on top. "It's better than baby chickens," I pointed out. "And isn't pâté just like liverwurst?"

We did not like liverwurst.

"Okay," Maura said. "Then I want to have a wedding cake. I want a big wedding cake with ten layers and roses all over it in icing, and little bowls of those mints."

"But doesn't someone have to get married?" I asked. We recently had been invited to a wedding, which had made quite an impression on both of us. Maura in particular had been stunned by the image of the bride, floating down the aisle in a swirl of white. I had even caught her in her room when she thought no one was looking, walking around with a bath towel draped over her head. I wanted to be a flower girl so I could throw flowers everywhere.

"Rose *petals*," Maura corrected me, exasperated. "The flower girl throws just the petals, not the whole *flower*."

"All right, whatever." I sighed. "But doesn't someone have to get married so you can have a wedding cake?"

"Well, I'll get married," she announced.

"You *will*?" I asked, horrified. I could never imagine getting married. Boys were so weird. "Who are you going to marry?"

"It doesn't really matter *now*," Maura said with continued exasperation. "We're just talking about what we'd have for dinner, right? And I want a wedding cake with a little bride and groom on top. And those pink almonds tied up, do you remember those?"

"Those were gross," I said. "They tasted like chalk."

"They were Jordan almonds," my sister informed me tersely.

"Why can't you have chocolate cupcakes instead?" I asked brightly. "Wouldn't that be good for a wedding?"

. . .

AFTER A WHILE Maura said she was too old to be standing around making-believe what kind of dinner parties she would have with the dishes in the china cabinet, so I would do it by myself. I dreamed of giant turkeys and wontons the size of baseballs. But it wasn't too much fun doing this all by myself, so after a while I didn't do it as much. And after I began having nightmares about snakes in the dining room, I never went in there at all except when I had absolutely nothing to do and there were no other people around.

On the opposite side of the house, far away from the dining room, was the front door. Nearby was a carpeted staircase that led upstairs to our bedrooms. My parents had a big room at one end that was painted cream with white trim like the rest of the house.

My room, however, was yellow, painted that color when I was still unborn and my parents did not know whether I would be a boy or a girl. My sister's room was pink and it had white eyelet curtains. Our rooms are still like they were when we lived in them years ago. It's strange now when we go back for holidays and sleep in those childish rooms, filled with our girlhoods. Open a drawer and we might find anything: old letters from pen pals in faraway lands, a frayed doll with a chunk of blond hair missing, a button from a high school pep rally. At night I sleep in that narrow and slightly lumpy bed, and it's as if all my dolls are rattling the plastic bags in the closet, wanting to come out and play.

When I was a child, I used to barricade myself in bed with a platoon of stuffed animals to protect me from the night. A row of bears, an alligator, and an oddly shaped dog would guard the wall, leaned up against the yellow paint like sentries on the lookout for spiders that might creep down from the ceiling. My more fearsome animals—a large stuffed cat, a stegosaurus with soft scales rising up from its spine, and the Jolly Green Giant (which my aunt got for me by sending in canned-corn labels)—were along the outside edge of the bed, guarding against monsters underneath. I could not sleep if the closet door was open even a crack. Bedtime could be a time of treachery. Things were better though when my father was there and would read me a bedtime story before turning out the light.

When I was a bit older, I used to stay up late at night, reading with a flashlight under the covers. Long past our bedtimes my sister and I would read Nancy Drew mysteries and old copies of *Seventeen* magazine by the light of cheap dime-store flashlights that we had by our nightstands in case we needed to go to the bathroom or the electricity went out or we thought there might be a burglar. Somewhat disappointingly, we never had a burglar. But sometimes I did have to use the flashlight when the electricity went off. It did that a lot in the country during bad thunderstorms. It was very exciting. The dark clouds would roll in from far away; you could see them coming, like a column of dark soldiers on horseback right on the horizon. The thunder was like nothing you knew; the lightning would split open the sky and rain would drive into the earth as if trying to hurt it on purpose.

Most of the time I didn't use the flashlight to find the bathroom. Rather, I liked to feel along the dark hallway, letting my fingertips find the way: across the huge expanse of my room, which was always so much huger in the night than during the light of day. Around the molding of the doorway. To the left, down the hallway where there was some sort of picture hanging (I was so familiar with it, I couldn't even tell you what it was. Birds, I think. Chinese birds—well, they weren't *Chinese* birds, but birds painted by a Chinese artist—and some flowers and a branch). Past the open door of my sister's room. Peek in; can't see anything, just the gray glow from her window with the lightweight curtain drawn over it. Find the molding of the bathroom door. Tiptoe in, feel the cool tiles underfoot. Run for the little pink rug in front of the toilet, the rug that was made of the same cheap material that covered the toilet tank and lid. "Bathroom tank set"; I think they were called that on the package in the store. (My father was always very good about putting the toilet seat down. I did not learn the middle-of-the-night horrors of falling into a toilet with the seat left up until I started keeping the company of men, which didn't happen until I was much, much older.) Once at my destination I had to pee quickly. Put the lid down, flush, then cover my ears so the cascading waters wouldn't be as noisy and someone might know that I had gone to the bathroom in the middle of the night. Make a cursory attempt at hand washing—run hands briefly under water, touch towel with fingertips. Then swiftly back to bed the way I came. Quick!

Quick! Before somebody catches me! Dive into bed, pull the covers over my head.

Mission accomplished.

The daytime was not so rife with distress. It was easy and rather idyllic. My sister and I played house under the dining room table; we had grand tea parties with apple-juice "tea" and vanilla wafers. We washed and braided each other's hair. We staged elaborate weddings where we would marry off chess pieces or Crayola crayons (in color-coordinated ceremonies, Lemon Yellow would wed Midnight Blue or Melon would be betrothed to Cornflower). Sometimes we played Camelot, and I always was stuck being the lady-in-waiting to Maura's queen. When I complained to Maura that I never got to wear the queen's veil (one of my mother's old chiffon scarves), Maura said that it was only right because she was the oldest. But sometimes, in a great show of gratitude to her loyal servant, Maura would bestow on me her Special Queen's Handkerchief, which also had been our mother's, made in Hong Kong and machine-embroidered with flowers.

In addition to my father, my sister was the one other person in the world whom I most adored. As a child I loved her fiercely; it was not hard to love someone who was so lovely and enchanting: her attention seemed like a gift. Maura had a way of drawing you in, of making you believe that to be taken into her confidence was a delicious treat. She had clear, luminous skin, which I envied terribly, and a slim figure. She had small, delicate hands and wore rings well. My sister still has these features, but they have taken on a pleasing womanliness and allure.

It really wasn't hard being her younger sister. I wanted her approval, and she gave it willingly. I was her confidante, her co-conspirator. I worshipped her. I was not as lovely as she, but kinder. I think it must have taken a great deal of her time to be so grand. I was a pretty child, but in the way that children are—fresh and newly minted. I was not as tall as my sister, and never would be. I was perfectly happy being the younger sister; in my eyes it was a perfect position. Nothing was expected of me but to be secondary, a corollary. She had a way of making me think that her praise was mine as well. Only later, when my sister began slipping from my life, did I find childhood awkward and unbearable. When she was not there to define the limits of my personality, I found myself without one. So that even now she is cool, serene, and even, and I am a jumbled mass of insecurities.

I'll never forget the time Maura cussed out Ricky Jones when he pushed me off the merry-go-round at school in the first grade. I wasn't hurt all that badly because I had landed in the sand, but I couldn't stop crying because I had a run in my new white tights and I was so afraid I was going to get into trouble. Not that my mother would ground me or not let me watch TV or anything like that; she'd just *look* at me, and I was terrified of what she *might* do. My sister and I were always frightened into good behavior by the mere thought of angering our mother. There was no such thing as misbehavior; it did not exist.

That afternoon Maura took me to Woolworth's and bought me a new pair of white tights with her own money. Then she dragged me into the slightly dingy bathroom and made me change into them before we got home.

I started crying again in the bathroom stall, and she had to dress me. I felt morbidly guilty.

"Maggie, it's okay," she kept telling me. (Those were the days when I was still called by my given name, before my nickname took hold.) "Here, put your foot through here."

I bawled some more.

"Wha'dif, wha'dif she . . . she . . . she finds out?" I hiccuped.

"She won't find out if you don't say anything. Now here, blow your nose." She held a wad of scratchy toilet paper to my nose, and I blew noisily.

"Now come on."

She washed my hands, brushed off my skirt, wadded up the dirty tights in the Woolworth's bag, and stuffed it into the garbage, burying it halfway in the can and carefully arranging the used paper towels over the top.

When our mother came home from work later, I kept staring at her with wide, frightened eyes. I kept expecting her to take one look at my tights and know instantly that they weren't the same ones that she had bought me.

"Have you been crying?" she asked.

"She fell off the merry-go-round," Maura quickly answered for me. "But she's okay now."

My mother looked at the small scrape on my elbow where I'd landed in the sand and got me a Band-Aid. I stood there mutely. When she left the room, Maura made a circle with her thumb and forefinger: It's okay, kiddo.

After a while I learned that I was one of the few people my sister treated with real kindness. My sister never has been a mean or cruel person, but as I grew older I also realized that she did not necessarily have a heart of gold. It took a while for me to see this; I suppose one never wants to see one's heroines tarnished in any way. But gradually I could not mistake it, for there it was: the snide remark that gave way to a certain haughtiness, the plying of little favors that became true manipulation. Her lovely smile suddenly did not seem so pure. Much later I would one day look into my sister's face and have no idea who this woman was; I would see no connection between the beautiful child I had worshipped and this self-involved, slightly petty woman standing in front of me.

"Really, Maya," she would say to me when I pointed out what I thought was some moral indiscretion on her part, "you can be such a child."

. . .

I REMEMBER WHEN I first noticed a small blemish in my sister's character; we were still children, and for a long time I tried to overlook it.

There used to be a girl in my class who rode our bus. Her name was Beverly. Her hair was long, a nondescript shade of brown, and her clothes clearly were hand-me-downs: polyester skirts that didn't quite fit right, cheaply made blouses that never really matched. She got on the bus after we did. My sister and I took seats across the aisle from each other in the middle of the bus. This was very strategic on our part. We weren't too far in front to be labeled goody-goodies, but we weren't far enough back to be associated with the kids who jumped up and down with the bumps and always got yelled at.

The school year had just started. The bus driver let us sit wherever we wanted for the first week. On the following Monday she would make a chart of where we were sitting that day and those would be our assigned seats for the rest of the year. Every day of that first week Beverly—with her glasses slipping and her nose running slightly—would ask if she could sit with either of us; her question always was directed at Maura.

"Oh, I'm sorry, Beverly," my sister would say, looking sincerely apologetic as she furrowed her brow, "but these seats are saved."

"Why did you say that?" I whispered loudly to Maura the first time; we both knew very well that neither of us was saving the seat for anyone.

"You don't want to sit with *her*, do you?" Maura hissed. Admittedly, I did not.

So Beverly lurched on to the back of the bus as it shifted unwillingly forward. The kids jeered.

"Hey, look, the retard's coming! Don't trip Bev-ver-ly!" some fifth-grader hooted as he carefully planted his foot in the aisle. Beverly stumbled over his blue high-tops and toppled over onto Karen Miller's shoulder.

"Oh, yuuuuck!" Karen whined, recoiling in her seat. "Get your snotty jacket off me! I think I'm gonna puke." Poor Beverly looked around pathetically, trapped and seatless in the back of the bus. Her nose began to run a little more.

Mark Snodgrass jumped up and pointed outside with feigned incredulity. "Hey! Look! It's snowing!" A perpetual class clown, Mark did incredulity quite well.

"Ah, no, I was wrong," he proclaimed, thumping his forehead with the heel of his hand in mock chagrin. "It's just Beverly combing her hair!"

The kids howled. Beverly started to cry. Her nose began running in earnest.

"HEY!" the bus driver thundered. "CUT THAT OUT BACK THERE!"

Nobody listened.

"Beverly! Beverly! Wanna sit here?" Steve Adkins asked. "Well, forget it!" And he scooted over in the seat to prevent Beverly from sitting down. Taking their cue from him, all the other kids with empty seats next to them shifted over in exaggerated terror of having the pitiful Beverly near them.

This continued all week.

On the following Monday Beverly got on the bus. The kids in the backseat began to whine; none of them wanted to be stuck with Beverly the whole year. Maura coolly moved her schoolbag off her lap and slid it surreptitiously onto the seat next to her.

"Sorry, these seats are saved," Maura-with-the-furrowed-brow told Beverly again, patting her schoolbag protectively.

Beverly looked at me.

I shrugged uncomfortably, then nodded. Beverly sat down. Maura gaped at me, utterly aghast. Then she turned quickly to look out the window.

I offered Beverly a Kleenex.

For the remainder of the year Maura would not speak to me the entire time we were on the bus. She would chat as we waited to board the bus or she would say something to me once we got off and neared the school. But Maura would never speak to me if I was within a certain radius of Beverly, even if I asked my sister a direct question. She simply pretended she didn't hear me. For the whole year she had a seat all to herself and would lean her lovely head forward to whisper confidentially to the girl who sat in front of her.

The next year Maura went to high school and had to ride a different bus. Beverly moved away and I never saw her again.

At the time I did not think much about Maura's behavior; I understood it. I felt the same way. But when I was older and looked back on that time, I could see how, even then, she always was concerned about what was hers and how she might acquire a bit more. By the time she became a woman, this had grown into full-blown selfishness. And there was little room left for me.

I think now that my own kindness to Beverly was not so much an act of charity but a way of staving off bad karma. For the life of me I don't know how, as a child, I picked up this decidedly Buddhist way of looking at the world. I don't know how I learned this manner of racking up good deeds to better your chances of a decent lot in your next life—or at least offsetting all the bad deeds and cosmic faux pas that might have been committed by you or those who came before you. I did not do this consciously. I never remember my parents talking about spiritual matters, but a sense of right and wrong in a universal sphere must have seeped into my head somehow. It's true: Sometimes, when you are a child, you think that something you do will haunt you forever.

Once I was told a story in which a twelve-year-old boy drowned in a lake. But people did not find his body for days because his little seven-year-old playmate did not tell anyone where they had been. She did not want to tell that they had been near the water. She was not allowed to play near the water; she had always been told that bad things could happen. So she remained mute, her eyes wide open.

Her family asked her over and over again, Where did you go? Where did you go?

"To the temple," she whispered, her voice barely above a breath. "To the temple."

Alone! Her family gasped.

But what did they do at the temple? Who else was there? When did she notice that the boy was gone? Why did she go home alone? Why didn't she ask someone for help?

Questions. They kept asking her questions.

She shook her head, mute.

Was that "yes"? they asked. Was that "no"? You must tell us, they said. You must say what happened.

She stared at the floor. Then she looked up at them, wide-eyed. They thought she was wide-eyed with innocence, but no, no. She knew too much, and she thought her head would split open and that her brain would fall out; her mind was too full of the truth.

Yet still she remained mute.

Two days later a fisherman found the body of the boy in a lake near the temple. He was dressed in his blue cotton pants and a white shirt that was no longer white, but instead was dredged with the green-gray slime of the bottom of the lake. One of his cloth shoes was missing.

His family wept with grief.

They planned an elaborate funeral, buying a beautiful coffin and paying for a dozen professional mourners, who wailed and cried as if their intestines were being pulled out and strewn about in slick garlands behind them. The father hired a funeral band with gongs and drums and high-pitched flutes. The procession wound its way through the streets of the village with much sobbing and fanfare, so there would be no mistaking how bereaved this family was: their only son, dead. No one left to carry on the family name. They wailed and wept some more and beat the little girl behind closed doors.

He was your responsibility, they told her, even though she was so much younger. That boy who drowned in the lake had been her brother and they blamed her for letting him die.

You've brought nothing but misfortune to this house, they told her.

Later, the girl's father took on a younger, second wife, who was not much older than the girl herself. This second wife gave birth to a son, and the family did not want anything bad to happen to him. So they sent their daughter away before she could jinx the new baby any more than she might have already.

Her parents sold her to a rich man to be his concubine. They did not care if she became a concubine because they already thought she was worth nothing.

So a palanquin came for her, and she was carried off to a distant village. She was thirteen. She was not draped in red, and there was no wedding band with gongs and drums and high-pitched flutes. The girl really did not mind that too much, as she thought wedding bands sounded too much like ones for funerals.

She never saw her family again.

At her new home the girl learned quickly how to be a very good concubine and won all the favors of the rich man. She did not particularly like the rich man; he had a brooding manner and a nose that was too broad. But she smiled prettily just the same because she was not stupid; she knew what she was doing. The rich man bought her everything she wanted and ignored the pleadings of his first wife. Sometimes, when the first wife went out for rides or to visit relatives, the concubine would pretend to be tired or ill and stay home. Then she would sneak into the first wife's bedroom and take her pearls and jade pendants. She bribed the servants and told them nasty stories about the first wife. But to the first wife's face the concubine was sweet and loving and always thoughtful. She brought the first wife a flower from the garden or sweets and fruits that she was known to favor. As second mistress the concubine brushed the first wife's hair and called her dear older sister.

. . .

THAT IS SUPPOSED to be the end of the story. But not exactly.

That little girl who became a concubine was my grandmother, a long time ago in China. My mother told my sister and me this story at bedtime when we were very small. It seemed to be a strange and slightly scary story. After she finished telling it, my mother took my sister and me to our rooms. My sister and I lay awake in our separate beds for quite a while after our mother had turned out our lights. We could not sleep. I crept down to my sister's room and we held hands, staring into the darkness.

I was very frightened.

Although I knew our family was Chinese, I did not know where China was. We lived in Ohio, and if we got in the car and drove for a while, we could see farms and cows that were black and white and sometimes brown. I knew milk shakes were made from cows, and intuitively I knew that milk shakes were not a very Chinese thing.

"Where's China?" I whispered to my sister.

"It's really far away," she whispered back. "It's on the other side of the Earth."

Maybe, I thought, if we drove for three days, then finally we would be in China. I wondered whether there were any cows in China.

For many years after that I vowed never to play near water. I tried to be good, but I still got into trouble. Sometimes my mother was very harsh. She did not beat me, but she became so cold that I thought I was being stung by a bitter wind. I began to wonder if I was being punished for the bad things that my grandmother had done. Every time I was reprimanded for not putting away my toys, leaving the faucet dripping, not picking up my clothes, or not eating a corner of my toast, I wondered if I was getting punished double for something I did not do. Later, when I learned what karma meant, I took it to heart: That must explain it, I thought. That must be why bad things happen.

It did not occur to me until I was much older that my mother—in telling that story—had casually imparted something quite crucial about herself: She was the daughter of a concubine, a woman who had bought her whole worth through her beauty, charms, and cunning. My grandmother (who died in China before I was born) had been a woman who had no money or social standing in the world outside the favors of the man who was not even really her husband. She was less than a wife. And, worse yet, she had borne no sons, so all her charms and beauty were not enough to push her to a higher standing. I often have wondered what she told my mother about how to live one's life. But my mother doesn't talk of such things. Instead, the story she spins of her youth is grand and exotic: She says she is the daughter of a rich merchant in Shanghai, a man who made his fortune by exporting beautiful jade figurines, ivory carvings, and teak furniture; she says her mother was regal and one of the most beautiful women in Shanghai. All this is probably true. But my mother does not say that she is the daughter of a concubine, that by Western standards she is a bastard child.

I have wondered whether this is why my mother is a cruel woman. This is somewhat difficult for me to say, and I resent even having to admit it. In my imagination, in my heart, my mother is kind; she is a warm woman who gave me sour plum candy when I was a child, who bathed me and wrapped me up in soft towels. But she was not. Is not.

I have a vivid imagination.

My mother is not an evil woman, a person who beat me, who locked me in closets or threw me in clothes dryers and turned them on. (There is a mother who did this. I read about it in a newspaper. Her children died finally. Blessedly, after all that torture.)

No, my mother did not starve me or deny me juice or milk. Rather, she showed my sister and me little love. She measured it out in stingy teaspoonfuls, as if she were afraid that if she gave too much away, she would shrivel up, that all the blossom in her cheeks would drain away. Her parenting consisted mostly of a certain indifference. I have marveled at how other mothers—some of them my friends with babies of their own—seem to delight in their children. These mothers take their children onto their laps and read to them, tickle them silly, suck on their tiny toes. My mother treated us more like plants, to be watered and then left alone. It was easy to turn to my father, with his easy affability and affection. One did not have to buy his attention with good behavior or a clean room. In the childhood of my memory, my mother is hardly there. Instead, she was someone to keep quiet around, to not disturb as she worked in her study.

Is it a crime for a mother not to love her children? Actually, my mother did love us, but she squandered most of her love on herself, to make herself strong and willful.

Everything about my mother is very cool. Her skin, even in the heat of summer, is dry and cool like a nectarine that has been in the cellar. Her temperament is serene and unruffled. She is like the jade pendant she wears, that doughnut-shaped piece of green, smooth and worn down like a flat Life Saver, seamless and exquisite. She wears it on a gold chain, hung slightly beneath her breastbone. She never touches or fiddles with it.

She is a college administrator in the town where I grew up. Even-tempered, gracious, and proper, she is very good at her job. The men—and there are many men at her university, as in all institutions of higher learning—are slightly in awe of her. My mother is very beautiful, and in that town very exotic. Her hair is very black and twisted into a neat and artful chignon at the base of her neck. Her clothes are well cut and made of floating materials in the colors of the sea: sandy beige, foam green, steel blue. She wears linen jackets and silk blouses and lots of drifty scarves that she keeps in check with gold clips.

My mother smiles on all the appropriate occasions and is utterly ruthless.

I only have one photo of my mother that was taken when she was still in Asia. It is a passport photo that was taken in Hong Kong before she came to America.

In it my mother is very young, perhaps seventeen. Her hair is pulled back with a fashionable curl above her forehead, movie-starlike. She is wearing a gray cheongsam with a stiff collar that reaches halfway up her delicate neck. There is a rib of white rickrack that traces its way around the bodice. My mother is not smiling, but her lips are soft, at ease. Her skin is flawless, gliding over high cheekbones and a nose that is a little too long. Her eyes and nostrils are very dark.

Although my mother is in repose, I can imagine her sitting on the edge of a small stool in the studio, on the brink of her womanhood.

Six years before this photo was taken, the Japanese had seized Shanghai and my mother's family fled to the south. They do not know what happened to their home, to the green celadon vases, the twelve wooden figures of the animal zodiac, the paintings of the nine immortals. They do not know what happened to all the photo albums, with the snapshots of my mother and her sister pasted on the black pages with cardboard black corners. My mother's beautiful silk New Year's dress, the turquoise one embroidered with the flying phoenixes, is gone.

The only thing my mother knows for sure is that as the Japanese came into Shanghai, the amah let the cats go into the street and they bolted into the darkness.

When I was very small, I did not think it was strange to have such a family history. After all, it was what I was accustomed to. But as I got a little bit older, I noticed that we had a slightly different past. We did not have ancestors who fled potato famines or religious persecution. And even though my sister and I went to the same school as everybody else and lived in a house that pretty much looked like other people's houses, I began to realize that we were . . . different. We were not born in that county or were even from there. We did not have a lot of relatives around us except for a distant cousin of my father's, who lived in Columbus. We did not go to church. We did not eat meatloaf and mashed potatoes; instead we seemed to eat an inordinate amount of rice. Both my parents worked and people thought we were rich, but this was not really so. So, sometime during elementary school, I decided that my family was definitely strange.

We were not a family that went on a lot of outings together. I remember being amazed at neighbors who would take their children to ball games, amusement parks, and the circus. Parents always seemed to be shuttling kids to ballet, piano, and soccer practice; they even would drive hours to go to a zoo and see animals locked up in cages. I think now that it didn't occur to my parents to get us involved in any of these things. My mother in particular always was completely absorbed in her own work at the university.

"Why doesn't Mommy like me?" I had wept piteously to my father one day after my mother had scolded me for interrupting her with one small request or another. Was it so terrible that I wanted a cookie or for her to look at a picture I had colored?

My father had patted my little shoulder.

"Ai, Maggie-ah." He had sighed. "It's not that Mommy doesn't like you. Mommy's very busy. You have to be patient with her."

He had paused.

"I had to learn to be patient with her, too. But it's okay. Your mama is just like that."

"But *why*?" I had wailed. I didn't *want* to be patient.

· · ·

SO I ALWAYS was a little frightened and envious of other children whose blond-haired mothers would come and help out in the classroom, cutting snowflakes out of folded typing paper or passing out homemade cupcakes at break time. Who *were* these mothers, anyway? They seemed like fairy-tale mothers, with Band-Aids and fruit-flavored Life Savers in their purses.

The only mother who wasn't like that was Beverly's. Here was a mother who wore no makeup, had a bad complexion, and kept her long hair in a ponytail with a rubber band. She wore an ugly, orange winter coat that had annoying little orange pills all over it. Beverly's mother came only once to our class (unlike my mother, who never came). But the peevish woman quickly grew tired of helping us color in maps of the United States.

"Fuck this shit," she said. "I need a cigarette." She grabbed her dirty macramé purse and headed outside, lighting up on the way. Our teacher, Mrs. Robertson, paled. When Beverly's mother came back in, coughing, Mrs. Robertson took her arm and whispered something to her. Beverly's mother snatched her arm away.

"Hey, look, lady. I don't even have to be here," she snapped, grabbing her coat. "I've got better things to do than hang out with you and a bunch of shit-faced brats." She flew out the classroom door, struggling with her dreadful, lumpy coat and looking like some sort of horrible pumpkin witch. We stared at her retreating figure in amazement; then, as if on cue, all our heads swiveled to Beverly and we gaped at her in disbelief. This was Beverly's *mother*? Grown-ups didn't do that sort of thing, did they? Beverly dropped her head, and her lips began to twitch.

After that episode I decided that my family was not the weirdest; thankfully, there were other people who were even stranger. I felt a little bad for Beverly, though. But at least she saved me from being the oddball queen of the universe, and for that I was grateful.

. . .

BUT WRETCHED BEVERLY—the one who made everyone raise their eyebrows and snigger disapprovingly—seemed to be the exception. All of the other families seemed seamlessly normal, with station wagons full of Boy Scouts, a hamster in a plastic cage, and a never-ending subscription to *Reader's Digest* in bathrooms painted baby blue. They brought Jell-O molds (sometimes in an appalling concoction of lime gelatin embedded with sliced celery and "iced" with mayonnaise) to potluck suppers and stared at my mother's chow mein with suspicion. "Oh!" they commented, poking at a water chestnut as if to see if it would move. "Pretty interesting!" (Except they pronounced it "inner-resting.")

I suppose my family seemed odd, like a perplexing but unthreatening novelty. Every now and then strangers would stop us in grocery stores and look intently into our faces.

"Are you Japanese?" they would ask in low, excited voices. "We find the Orient simply *fascinating*. Do you know karate?" No, my parents would say politely. We are not Japanese. We do not know karate.

Sometimes, others' curiosity was not so benign. When Maura and I were very small, a few cars stopped on separate occasions and young men would lean out, jabbing their middle fingers in the air and yell, "Fucking Vietnamese! Fucking VC!"

My mother would keep walking, staring straight ahead. But when I looked at her, I could see her jaw clench. My father would frown.

"But we're not Vietnamese," he would say. "We don't even look Vietnamese. I just don't understand."

"Daddy," I would say. "What's a fuck in D.C.?"

But no one would answer.

Most of the time, though, no one said anything to us. They just smiled and left us alone.

In those days I did not think of our family as Chinese. Different, yes, but not necessarily Chinese. I did not really know what that meant because there were no other Asians where we lived, and I had nothing to compare us to. And for the most part it didn't seem to be something to be bothered about. There were games to be played, pictures to be drawn, storybooks to be read. I had another agenda.

As a little girl, I liked to pretend that I was Spanish. I wanted to have long, wavy dark hair, huge eyes, and olive skin. I wanted to ride a horse in a big parade. I coveted a big skirt with a crinoline and castanets at my fingertips. At ten, I insisted that I be called Maya, after some great ancient people I had read about in an encyclopedia while doing a report for social studies. The name stuck; hardly anybody calls me by my real name, Maggie, because almost no one knows it. And only my mother uses my Chinese name, and that is usually in anger.

After school, before my parents got home, I would dress up in a wide, poofy skirt that had a lot of layers and a white blouse with puffed sleeves and ruffles around the neck. My parents had Bizet's *Carmen* on an ancient LP, and I would whirl around the living room with old bottle caps Scotch-taped to my fingertips so that I could tap them together high above my head. Then I'd grab up my skirt in huge handfuls and trill my tongue, "Ya ha llrrrrrrr!" to the toreador's march. I'd spin around and around, twirling my way out of reality.

As soon as I could, I took Spanish at school, in the eighth grade. I loved the way the sounds rolled off my tongue: *mi amor, la cucaracha, quesadilla.* My love, cockroach, cheese pie. I bought a phrase book and learned completely ridiculous phrases such as "Let us prepare for an earthquake" and "Where is the American embassy?" and said them with zest. Later, I would whisper Spanish endearments into the ears of lovers because I thought I sounded more romantic.

As a child I never was terribly gregarious, but as I slipped into my adolescence, I don't know what happened. Simple things began to terrify me. I worried that, on the freeway, things would fall off the backs of trucks and hit the car I was in. I had fearful images of new automobiles rolling off those precariously stacked semis and crashing into me; I thought that enormous rolls of blue steel would fly off flatbed trucks and crush me where I sat. I also worried that I would be snatched away as I got off the school bus. Or worse, I feared that I would simply vanish—that one day I would fail to appear on Earth and no one would notice. In that Wonder bread world of Middle America, I saw nothing of myself reflected in that comfortable expanse. And when I did not see myself, I began to doubt my own reality.

My sister had vanished into high school, and without her around to be my point of reference, I found I had no center of gravity, no sense of direction. I had no sense of boundaries, of where my body ended and the rest of the world began. I felt lost in a kind of space and clung to the backs of rooms, the sides of hallways; I liked walking near rows and rows of lockers at school because their expanse of gray metal always told me where I was.

In the miserable vacuum of my father's absence, my sister had the nerve to thrive and blossom. She was always at school, in rehearsals, in debates. She was no longer around long enough for me to check my presence in relation to her response to me.

"Maura, I baked some chocolate-chip cookies," I would say lamely. "Do you want some?"

"I'm so incredibly late," she would say without appearing to have heard me. "I've got to go research Blackmun's opinions. I hope the library doesn't close early tonight. Do you know where my coral sweater is? Oh, here it is. Never mind," she would continue, half out the door. "Tell Mom I'll be late."

In a whirl she would be gone, her sweater tucked under her arm. I would eat a handful of chocolate-chip cookies and take the rest to the busboys at the Chinese restaurant where I sometimes worked on weekends.

And then, before I had quite grasped the situation, my sister was gone altogether. She had packed a trunk full of plaid skirts and virgin-wool sweaters in crayon-box colors like green and maize and had sailed off for Yale, the mythic land of the chosen, the blessed. I tiptoed around the house, wearing darker and darker colors until I was sure that I seeped into the shadows. Like a relic from the seventies, I wore my hair straight and long, parted in the middle. In the summer I kept it pulled back with a plain brown barrette. And forget the wool crew-neck sweaters and oxford-cloth shirts worn by my classmates. In contrast, I wore tons of black and donned dark sunglasses in glamorous shapes like those Marilyn Monroe wore. One pair even had three tiny faux diamonds at each cat-eye corner. I never spent a great deal of time on my nails but kept a mirror on the inside of my locker door, stuck there with duct tape. I am ashamed to say that I chewed a lot of gum, mostly out of an ever-present nervousness. I felt so strange, so out of place. Makeup tips that I tried in teen magazines ("For a Sweet-n-Natural You!") always left me looking like some kind of maudlin harlequin because eye-shadow instructions always assumed you had eyelid folds.

My insecurity probably had something to do with having an extremely fashionable mother. Now that I look back on it, my mother was exceptionally chic for our small-town community. No floral housecoats or polyester pull-up shorts in pastels during the summer months. Now that I live in the city, I go into Chinatown and am visually accosted by the normal uniform of Chinese ladies: polyester blouses in rather awful prints over pants with elastic waists. Shoes fashioned out of some kind of synthetic material that strongly resembles Naugahyde sofas. When I look at these women, I begin to think that my mother is really the strange one; no one else outside of broadcasting looks like her.

So there I was in high school, the misplaced Chinese kid in a sea of white faces. On a dare I tried out for cheerleading but didn't make it because I couldn't do splits and was too slow when climbing on top of the other girls to make pyramids. So I joined the Pep Club instead and painted big posters in green and yellow; at football games I waved pom-

poms on sticks and, even then, never fully grasped the concept of "downs."

I still liked to draw and decided to become an Angst-Ridden Teenage Artist; I thought it would fit in with my general sense of being askew from the rest of my peers. I carried a sketchbook with me and penciled in moody renderings of mailboxes and ketchup bottles. I drew the baby shark suspended in formaldehyde in the biology room and the maple tree outside the foreign language room that was dying of some sort of disease.

My attempts to become an artistic radical were not altogether successful, however; I was a little weak on my darker vices. I simply could not acquire a taste for beer. I tried to learn how to smoke in the girls' bathroom but could not stop coughing; the smoke made my eyes tear, sending mascara running down my face in a very uncool manner.

I did not have a whole lot of success with boys, either. Some guys made feeble attempts at groping under my shirt behind the gym during school dances, but then I would get ticklish and start giggling uncontrollably, which did not lend itself to romance. Maybe I wasn't such a hot catch, anyway; there weren't that many boys who asked me out (I liked to attribute this to my general oddness), and those who did seemed to give up on me pretty soon. Guys, I decided, hadn't changed all that much since the days when they were throwing worms at us girls during recess.

But one time a guy frightened me quite a bit. He kept pushing too hard, kissing me roughly until I finally broke away and found the safety of some girlfriends near the punchbowl, which was filled with some sort of greenish beverage in honor of St. Patrick's Day. I could not stop trembling. When he came back into the gym, he acted as if nothing had happened. In fact, he behaved like quite the gentleman, bringing me punch and a folding chair.

"Well, she seems all right," I heard his mother say to another chaperone at the dance. "But I hope Brad doesn't get attached to . . . you know . . . an Oriental. Not that I have anything against them, of course."

"Oh, of course not." The other chaperone nodded sympathetically. "They're fine people."

"It's just that Brad has so much going for him," his mother said.

"Absolutely," the other chaperone agreed. "He's such a fine boy."

"And an Oriental, you know, well . . . at least . . ." His mother looked around, then dropped her voice. "At least she's not . . . you know . . . black."

I suddenly felt sick.

I looked around, trying to find some kind of escape. Could one of my girlfriends drive me home? I asked the chaperones. No, no, Brad should stay, I told them. I'm sorry, but couldn't Stacey drive me home instead?

. . .

BY THE END of my senior year I was sick of Pep Club and Spanish Club. I was tired of school, period. I didn't get voted "Best Dressed" or "Most Artistic"—those honors went to kids with more conventional tastes. And I certainly didn't get "Most Likely to Succeed" because no one seemed very sure what I was suited for; even marriage seemed a bit outlandish. Four years earlier Maura had been voted one of the "Most Likely to Succeed," and for once that was not a curse. Unlike other students who seemed fated to sink into oblivion, Maura had gone on to Yale. And then I came bumbling into high school only a summer after my sister had swirled away amidst pomp, circumstance, and National Merit Scholarship money. At first I missed her horribly. But soon Maura's hovering successes irritated me. People stopped mentioning my name in the same breath as hers;

probably so as not to taint Maura. But in the end I survived high school well enough, moderately unfashionable and depressed. My grades were mediocre, and my test scores were a hairline or two above the "remedial work needed" range.

So as Maura entered medical school with a fresh glow on that still-perfect skin and commendations from the governor on a luminous undergraduate career at Yale, I staggered into a state school with two duffel bags crammed with black clothes, a glass bowl that held three fat goldfish, and a sense of finely honed purposelessness.

I was leaving the house of ghosts.

WOMANHOOD

MY PASSAGE FROM youth was neither distinct nor significant. I cannot point to one particular incident and say, "This was a turning point. This was the event that changed me forever." No, instead, the years since I left home have fused together in a continuum of perplexity. I have wished for a conviction-filled and passionate spirit, but to no avail. And now that I am no longer a child, I am disappointed that I did not evolve into a woman of exceptional character, a person who does good. When I was young, I had a certain hope: I desperately believed in the story of the ugly duckling, the awkward and mottled thing that one day is transformed into a creature of beauty and grace, drawing in admiration simply on her own strength of being.

But it hasn't happened. And finally I have realized that I've spent far too much time shirking reality for anything out of the ordinary to happen. So I've adjusted. I've simply learned to accept indistinction and mediocrity—because I've also learned that I'm simply too lazy to do anything to change. Years of inactivity have made my spirit lax.

. . .

IN MY EARLY days at college I drifted through an unhinged curriculum of my own design, like some sort of free-range chicken that never put on any academic weight. I took courses in transcendentalism, cubism, and feminism. On a lark I actually took a class in basket weaving that was offered out of the fine arts continuing-education program. (I still have the basket I made; it's quite nice, if I do say so myself. I keep yarn in it.) I taught myself to drink coffee and hung out at bohemian coffee shops, taking in spontaneous and moderately bad poetry readings.

Still, I always felt stunned by the swirl of students, striding about with their backpacks. I saw tables of them in the cafeteria, loudly downing slices of pizza and big paper cups of Coke, and I was completely intimidated. Their raucous beer parties at frat houses sent me into spasms of nervousness, and I would dart past their front yards, hurrying to the library, where I would find an empty study carrel in the deserted reaches of the Spanish literature section. Gabriel Garcia Márquez demanded nothing of me, and for this I was thankful.

. . .

I LET MY hair grow very long and got a spiral perm that was supposed to be very tight and curly. But because my hair is so thick and coarse, it ended up a bit looser; at last I had my Latina hair, or at least something that I thought looked Latin-American. After so many years of wearing dreary colors, I suddenly hated looking funereal all the time. I totally switched styles and shades. I went through a phase when everything I wore was in muted shades of the same color groupings. I had a pumpkin outfit with ocher hose, a dark brown skirt, an orange blouse, and an orange-rust blazer. Another day I would wear entirely blue, right down to a pair of blue suede shoes, which I thought were extremely witty. I amused myself by frequenting secondhand shops and had a good eye for outfits that looked outrageously expensive but weren't. (My sister also had great clothes, but she's always been much more sophisticated than I am. Who has time to iron linen? Then again, now that she's a doctor, she can afford all that dry cleaning.)

At parties my roommate, Lynne, always introduced me as "Maya, my neo-hippie-Chinese-Latin-American-fashion-plate friend."

"Hi," I would say.

Then I'd be stumped for further conversation, and people who initially thought I'd be fascinating abandoned me to find someone more verbal.

I did have friends, but not too many and none too close. These were quasifriendships that were accidental; I did not have to make small talk or reach out to them in any way because we were acquaintances really, who lived in the same dorm and who were merely thrown together by the student housing authority. These were kids with whom I hung out in hallways after dark, nursing open containers and bound by our misguided notions of doom and the Cold War.

I found little solace in romance. I had gone out with a few men: an anguished poet who wrote everything in the same cadence as "Annabell Lee . . . Annabell Lee . . . in her sepulcher there by the sea"; a chemical-engineering student who kept spiny lizards in a glass cage; and a medical student who was beginning to think he hated speaking to people. My love life seemed incredibly unnotable and dissatisfying and, worse yet, seemed destined to remain that way.

I think my college days actually began during my sophomore year, when things took a turn for the brighter. It was then that I met Lance, who was to become the first boy I loved, the one who whisked me away. He was tall and beautiful, and lived with a sense of daring and irresponsibility that I found exciting and intoxicating. Our acquaintance was short, but it opened up a space in me where loneliness grew after he left: I had learned what it was like to have someone near, and for some time afterward I was bereft in his absence.

But somehow I managed to build a precarious comrade-ship with other students as we were forced to eat unidentifiable college cafeteria food and continued to cope with having to do laundry on a quasiregular basis. Lynne tried to show me how to smoke pot and make decent conversation so we could rush for some sorority or other, but I chickened out in the end.

By this time Maura somehow had orbited completely out of my life. She lived on the East Coast, seldom calling and never writing. Sometimes I saw her at Thanksgiving or Christmas, sometimes not. For the first time this seemed all right, this life without Maura. No one at school knew my beautiful, brilliant older sister. True, I could not ride in the swell of her brightness, but neither was I forced to drown in it.

. . .

I ENDED UP stumbling upon my major totally by accident. I had wanted to take an art history class about abstract expressionism, but it was closed. The only thing open during that time slot was something called the History of Chinese Painting I. What the heck? I thought. Anything to avoid being forced to take my more loathsome and technical requirements.

Finally, it seemed, I liked school. I liked art history. It was pleasantly womblike in those lecture halls, where I would sit in the dark for hours, staring at slides of paintings hundreds of years old that were thrown against the wall, larger than life. In those rooms nothing was real, nothing was pressing. All mistakes in war and love had already been committed; there were no decisions to be made. I simply could sit there and nod with appreciation or dismay. If I had pulled an all-nighter, I even could sleep in there, lulled by the steady voice of my instructor.

"Now, note the placing of the figures, how the women look as if they're suspended in thin air," my professor would say narcotically as my head began to droop. "Note how there is only this small tree and this rock to denote that these women are in the garden. Otherwise, they could be any-where—inside the house, in space, even. . . ."

My eyes would close and my mind would drift. Images of court ladies playing flutes danced in my head. (Oh, ladies playing flutes. . . . In that repressive Chinese court society, what a salacious, sexual picture the image of a lady playing a flute could connote. . . .) I dreamed of Buddhas gazing down from the walls of caves; massive horses full of spirit dancing on their hind legs, their slender ankles looking as if they were about to break. Album leaves would fall open to reveal little scenes of rivers and delicate plants, scholars strolling by a stream or a willow tree casting all its sorrows into the wind.

A classmate and I always joked about the names of Chi-nese paintings, which seemed to be combinations of the same words: *Travelers on a Mountain Pass, Travelers Among Streams and Mountains, Taoist Retreat in Mountain and Stream.*

· · ·

AT TIMES I would wonder why I had decided to study some-thing as inherently pointless as Chinese art; it was so obscure, virtually useless at dinner parties, where those who knew anything about art were versed in Renoir and Monet, Klee and Pollack. They had never heard of Tung Yuan and his soft, wet brushwork that evoked rivers in the mist. They did not know Fan Kuan, who painted a cosmic mountain. So at parties I bit my tongue. To be honest, I didn't find the Chi-nese works as aesthetically pleasing as, say, Japanese art, with its lovely muted subtlety.

But in the darkness the stories would come alive. As a child I had grown up with the stories of Snow White and Little Red Riding Hood. I did not know about the emperor who had fled into blue-green mountains and the Queen of the Western Skies who had nothing whatsoever to do with Dorothy.

It is said that the brush stroke is everything. In a single stroke must be life and energy and movement. There is shadow and light, sadness and gaiety. Simplicity is deceptive. There is only ink. The ancient Chinese painters did not talk about acrylics, oils, or egg tempera. They couldn't scratch off a mistake with a razor blade. Once the brush was committed to silk or paper, that was it. No second chances.

There is a vividness in black ink that doesn't come across very well in color. With shades of gray everything is left to the imagination; the mind must fill in the pink in the peony, the green-black of the distant horizon. I remember standing in the art-supply store once, fingering all the bamboo brushes with their horsehair tips and the smooth, black ink-stones, heavy and cool. I would stand there for a long time, wondering how artists were blessed with that kind of vision.

. . .

"IF YOU EVER go to China," my teacher had said as he stood in front of an enormous image of a landscape painting thrown on the wall, "you're going to be amazed. You'll see that the landscape looks like this. But not precisely, because there isn't exactly a scene like this one; this is a landscape of the mind. This is how the scholar-painter expressed himself. And sometimes these paintings were extremely political.

"Now look at this painting. What do you see here? There's a mountain, obviously, and here, up here"—my professor tapped the wall with his pointer—"you see a pavil-ion perched on this outcropping. And very small, inside the pavilion, you see a man, probably a scholar, practicing callig-raphy on a small table. So, you say. Very nice. Quite attrac-tive. Interesting brushwork. But that's not all. This is not merely a pretty picture of a man practicing calligraphy in the great outdoors, and other scholar-painters would know that.

There's the hidden message that this is how the scholar felt, metaphorically exiled in the wilderness as China fell into political chaos."

In the lull of the professor's voice, you could hear the steady scratching of pens in notebooks. Across the aisle from me someone had given up on alertness altogether and was slumped forward on the desk, his head buried in his arms.

"Now, let's go on to this painting," the professor said as he advanced the projector. "This is a very interesting piece, once again of the mountains. . . ."

. . .

Some of this was a little too obtuse, a little too fantastical. Still, to me, the mountains were my favorite; they were like magic. And as I sat there in those dark lecture halls, I would be lured away, lured back into a time and culture that seemed at once ancient yet familiar. Older than history itself, the mountains told stories from long ago, long before I was born.

The mountains evoked a time when China still had emperors and court ladies with painfully small feet, when people traveled by boat and by water buffalo. In those days it was perceived that the universe had a splendid order: There was the Earth, and on Earth lived man; above the Earth was heaven. The emperor was the son of heaven, a man who was more than simply a mortal, and everyone had to obey him, respect him. If no one challenged this divine order, then all would be good in the universe. If men and women and children did not question their place, their fate or lot in the mortal world, then all was as it should be. And so there would be peace. There would be no droughts, no famine, no flood. The ancestors would be happy; your wives would become plump with children, and your sons would grow up fat and prosperous. This was the way of the universe. This was how it was perceived when there was no knowledge of any other worlds, when China was considered the center of everything.

One of these stories began when a man saw a mountain and painted it, using nothing but black pinesoot and water. He saw another mountain and painted that one, too. Then he spied an ass pulling a cart with men walking alongside it. These he put in the picture, very small; you could hardly see them in the picture. Most of it was mountain. A very large, cosmic mountain.

I have seen this painting, or at least pictures of it in books. It never occurred to me that one day I might actually see this mountain with my own eyes.

In those years my life was filled with beauty.

I became enchanted with a world on paper that was incredibly lovely—the landscape of a place I never had seen, the renderings of birds and flowers that were too exquisite to be real. I would look into those images and be taken away into mystical forests and down rivers of dreams; I had clear passage into mountain pavilions and imperial courtyards. In this world of brush and ink, everything was so neat, so complete. There were no loose ends to be tidied up, no crises to be solved by me personally.

My life then was also beautiful because I was in love again. I met Alex during my final year, and in his presence everything took on the color and nature of soft fruit—everything was sweet and succulent. I thought I only needed air and him to survive. Love, I suppose, will do that. For a sliver of time all was right in the world, and it made me think that those ancient Chinese had it all figured out: There was the Earth, there was me and the one I loved, and there was heaven, holy and benevolent. Love made me feel immortal. I had a sense that time went on forever, that from that point on nothing bad ever would happen again.

I moved in with Alex, and together we set up an intimacy

that was both soothing and safe. I knew what kind of shaving cream he used; Alex could go to the grocery store when I was ill and buy the kind of instant pudding he knew would comfort me. He was a painter, and I liked to sit and watch him work; I liked to be near him and witness his vision as it blossomed on blank paper. Although he liked to paint landscapes, they were not traditional. There was something slightly harsh about them, something about those strokes that spoke not of the thirteenth century but of our own; his was a reality seen through a far different prism than that possessed by ancient scholar-painters in seclusion.

But gradually things began slipping out of joint for Alex and me. It was as if I tried to hold on to a bundle of contradictions, and one by one they kept falling out of my arms; after a while I could not keep a grasp on anything at all. Eleven months after my graduation from college, Alex decided to leave. I did not seem able even to breathe. I became melodramatic, and in a kind of blindness I ran away.

I moved to New York to be with my sister, and for years I could not see anything at all. Several years vanished as I remained cloaked in that opaque haze.

When I first got to the city four years ago, I was a mess. I went through a stage of sheer delirium, when I ate nothing but orange food—Chee•tos, generic macaroni and cheese, and bottles of neon orange drink that came in little plastic containers shaped like barrels—and did nothing but watch massive amounts of horrible television after coming home from one dreadful temporary secretarial job after another.

I lived with my sister for about a month, then got one of those microscopic Manhattan studio apartments, which I can barely pay for with the meager salary I now get as a receptionist in Midtown. "Hello, Roth Publications," I intone a hundred times a day. "How may I direct your call?" There are only three other people in that windowless office besides me, and the boss makes me say that so that people calling in will think we're a big company. But I don't know who he thinks he's fooling.

My years in the city have blended together; I have had no sense of time. I have spent a great deal of energy trying to do as little as possible. And in the meantime I suppose I really have lost four years of my life. But I have been blessed with a kind of amnesia: I cannot remember much of these years at all, so sometimes I try to convince myself that I have not really lost that much time at all.

I have found it too exhausting to make friends; it seems to take so much effort to be *nice*. I suppose my best friend is Candy (I know, I can't believe her name is really that, either), who grew up on Long Island and wants to be a bass player in a rock band. Problem is, she has no musical sense whatsoever and has trouble keeping time. Sometimes I help her when she's practicing by tapping a chopstick against her lamp like a human metronome, but it's no use. She's a lost cause. Besides, Candy gets on my nerves a lot, anyway. At the age of twenty-nine she still snaps her gum and is always worrying about cellulite.

"Am I getting fat? Tell me I'm not getting fat," she keeps saying, turning around to look at herself in the mirror for the umpteenth time. "Do these pants make my hips look big?" So I've been steering clear of her for a while. Just for a breather.

. . .

My sister has given up trying to be nice to me, especially when I slump into my dyspeptic mode and mope for weeks, gnawing on animal crackers. It's usually around Alex's birthday (October 21) or the day I drove to New York (April 29).

"It's been four years," my sister tells me. "Snap out of it already, okay?"

But I can't seem to snap out of it. Maybe I can't snap because I feel so rubbery and formless; I have no backbone, nothing crisp or brittle enough to break apart so I can step out of myself and move on. I have no spirit. One day oozes into another, I seem to have no control over anything that transpires. I make a little money; I spend it on something to set on a shelf in my apartment. I watch people rush by on the street and wonder where they are going.

I live year-round in the city—through those disgusting, sticky summer months when it is so humid that exhaust fumes will adhere to your skin and through damp winters when those bitter winds are rushing so strongly down the avenues that you almost have to cling to lampposts for support. I hate the city but seem unable to leave it. My sister has tried to get me to go away with her and her boyfriend when they spend summer weekends out in the Hamptons or fly away to St. Martin in the dead of January. But I never go. I just stay in the city, perpetually uncomfortable, eternally at the wrong temperature, like some sort of Chinese bagel that refuses to rise. I miss the Midwest and its sense of space. I miss the quiet, the trees that let one know the earth is near. I miss the small kindnesses of people there, their openness. But I have been nearly inert in the city, somehow incapable of doing anything or changing anything.

My sister, however, managed to leave our childhood home without looking back and without remorse. She came to the city years ago, to go to school, and had seized Manhattan as if it were a luscious crystal fruit ripened for her alone. She took on all its affectations and its sleek appearance. And somehow from the start, even when she was in medical school and had no money, she collected all its accouterments—the clothes, the style, the sharp edge. Perhaps my sister and the city always have been very much alike, stunning and somewhat heartless. I followed Maura here hoping that her nearness would give me solace. But it has not, and her town and I have been a wary and uneasy match.

For a long time I have needed to get out of that state of mind; I'm not sure how this happened, how I went from one who loved beauty to one who found it almost painful. I started having strange dreams. Small things started to irritate me, and I quickly became peevish. I became hypersensitive to sounds, which is bad in New York, where it seems that something or someone is always beeping, honking, or yelling. I never wanted to go outside, even to see the tulips at the botanical garden in spring or to catch a special exhibit at a museum.

The oddest thing was that, at some strange level, being a woman began to annoy me. Not that I wanted to be a man, but there were just things I despised about womanhood. First, I resented pantyhose and painful shoes. Then I became incensed at doormen who said hello to me with voices that seemed a little too meaningful. Finally, I raged at all manner of issues—rapes and glass ceilings and the lack of family leave. I fumed at not being able to walk alone down a sidewalk at night without fear. I raged at getting my period.

I remember one bizarre instance quite clearly.

I got up to flush the toilet and saw the blood ooze through the water, turning it red and violent.

I flushed quickly, watching as the clear, pure water swirled in from the sides, sending the repellent redness away.

For years I had menstruated and thought nothing of it. It's a natural bodily function that has its moments of annoyance and inconvenience. My mother explained it to me when I was ten. Actually, she gave me a set of free pamphlets that she had sent away for (forget my mother's doctorate in biochemistry; when it came to personal matters, she was just as silent as most mothers): *You and Your Menstrual Period, You and Dating, Marriage and Sex*. They were pink, lavender, and

blue, respectively, and had innocuous ink drawings of flowers and smiling girls in them. A year later, when I had my
first period, my mother showed me where the Kotex was
kept in the bathroom cupboard.

That was it. No trauma, no confusion about womanhood
or anything like that at all. For fifteen years every month, I
had bled without thinking. There had been the occasional
horror of being trapped in a public place without a tampon
in my purse, the usual nuisance of having to scrub out stains
from panties and sometimes a bed sheet. But I had accepted
it all as a matter of course.

But suddenly one day I hated it. I resented the dull pain
and hated the sight of my blood. Nothing made sense, and it
made me angry. Bizarrely, my nights became filled with
strange dreams; it was as if my subconscious was being operated by an autopilot on 'ludes. I dreamed I sang in the opera;
I dreamed that I threw sweet red beans instead of coins into
a fountain. I could not tell what was real, what was not, because during the day I kept happening upon odd personalities on the streets—a couple dressed from head to toe in gold
lamé, a dancing vanilla wafer, a man who lectured while
standing next to the garbage bags. "Seize the moment!" he
yelled to us passersby. "You are the master of your destiny!"

Everything seemed irrational.

In my sister's eyes I'm the one who's irrational; I'm the one
who is misguided. She sees me as the one with the horrible
job, the horrible apartment, and no diamond ring. The thing
is, I'm not sure I could tell you anything in defense of my
own character. It's true. I think everything went downhill
after puberty. What can I say? It's always so difficult to say
anything about yourself. It's like when you meet someone in
a club or at a party, and everyone is trying to make small
talk. And half the time everyone is trying to figure out what
everyone else does for a living and if they're rich. I know

too many women whose eyes just glaze over when they learn that some guy is a bartender or something but just get so interested when they meet someone who is a stockbroker, as if he was the answer to all their dreams. Well, maybe he is, so who am I to say? My sister is marrying a lawyer. And she's marrying him because of that. She might have married a doctor, but she didn't want two doctors in the family.

I really don't think I'm that interesting. I don't have any exotic hobbies or interests and can't hold long and lucid conversations about Proust or the effects of Western colonialism on present-day Third World countries. I don't like to travel. And although I like to cook, I'm not very good at it. I used to be able to cook pretty well, but now I can't seem to get all the ingredients together at once: I'll have the sweet but not the sour or bacon but no eggs. It all seems to take more thinking than I can stand to do these days.

I hate exercise in all forms and have never belonged to a gym, although that seems to be such the "in" thing. (Paying to be miserable and sweaty just seems like a colossal waste to me.) I also find most activities suspect when the exercise is hidden, like volleyball or tennis. You're still moving around and sweating and cursing, so what's the point? But I do admit that some of my fear of sports stems from horrible gym-class experiences as a child; it's not hard to figure out that I always was the last kid picked for dodgeball. (What kind of a game is dodgeball, anyway? Line kids up and have them hurl objects at one another with intent to harm and maim? Hardly an activity for children, I say. No wonder we have world wars.)

I'm also bad with all things mechanical—cars, computers, microwaves, and digital clock-radios included. Unfortunately, I'm also not very good with directions, either the written or verbal. Or polar for that matter: I couldn't tell north from east to save my life and am intimidated by maps. All of these drawbacks make me a very sedentary and home-oriented person, I suppose. I figure my way around and stick to it. Even going into a strange supermarket can be stressful if I'm unable to locate the peanut butter. (I love peanut butter and am very particular about it. Peanut butter is one of those foods that must be difficult to categorize, because I've found it everywhere from the cookie aisle to somewhere over by diapers. I just don't understand. Why don't they put it next to bread?)

Ever since a girl in college taught me how to knit, I've kept up with it. Sometimes I can't seem to stop—I'll knit on the bus, the trains, on my lunch hour at work. I've wondered if I'm like that boy in the book that was named after him; I think it was something about a kid who couldn't stop washing his hands? I hope I'm not psycho or whatever. In any case, I am actually quite good at knitting. I have tons of sweaters because I love yarn and can't resist both buying and making woolly things. All those fuzzy skeins are so charming and comforting somehow. I've often thought they would make good pets.

I also love boxes. Little boxes you can put things in. I have them everywhere, on every available horizontal surface—end tables and bureau tops, the ledge on my stove, on the toilet tank, even the radiator. (One time I made the mistake of putting this adorable set of plastic children's boxes on the radiator, and during one particularly cold snap in the winter they melted. It was quite a mess.) I love the fact that you can hide little things in there, like matchbooks or buttons or safety pins from the dry cleaners. I have paper boxes covered with beautiful papers and carved or painted wooden boxes. I have a few made of stone—a thin, white alabaster one is one of my favorites. It's so pure, like milk that's been frozen into a shape. I don't have anything in that box; I like to keep it filled with nothing but air, to keep it chaste.

I didn't arrive in New York with so many possessions but accumulated them over time. It was rather pathological, I suppose: I hated having empty space. I wanted to fill my small room to the ceiling with things, any sort of things. A stretch of space on my walls suddenly seemed very stressful. I hated to look at it, that emptiness. I bought another picture at a flea market, another cigar box from a thrift shop; three dollars here, five there. I spent little bits at a time and it all added up, filling my room to the very seams. And finally I liked it in there. It is crowded, too cramped. Maybe, if someone looked in, they wouldn't even find me.

Unfortunately, I hate to clean. It is truly my least favorite thing. But for a person who doesn't like to clean, I have a very sophisticated vacuum cleaner—probably because I need a miracle worker by the time I force myself to attack the dust. It takes me hours to vacuum around all my little boxes and everything else, but thank goodness the machine has great little attachments. Because dust bunnies the size of real rabbits grow under my sofa. It's frightening.

Maura doesn't like to come over to my apartment. She says it's too small, too cluttered with junk.

"Really, Maya," she would say to me. "You're such a pack rat. This place is a wreck. Why don't you clean it once in a while?"

She was always afraid to sit down because she didn't want cat hair on her clothes. So after a while she stopped coming over altogether, which really was fine with me. I was getting tired of her getting on my case all the time.

Maura and I have been having problems for a while now. Things have never been as good as they were when we were kids, but I suppose that is a sad part of growing up.

My sister particularly gets on my nerves these days because she is getting married soon, to John, the attorney. I've seen it happen a hundred times to my girlfriends: A perfectly rational woman simply flips out when she starts planning the Day of Her Dreams. Suddenly her speech gets all screwed up. She starts talking sweetheart necklines, 100-pound card stock, freesias and Jordan almonds. It's enough to make a liberated woman puke. And I don't have the heart to tell my sister that I hate her gown because it makes her look like Princess Di and look what happened to her.

I'm going to be Maura's maid of honor, but I don't feel very honored about the whole thing. Somehow, I think she asked me because she took pity on me or felt obligated. It's very tacky if your only sister isn't there dabbing away tears of joy with a silk handkerchief, I guess. John's sister is bridesmaid No. 1. And then there are six of Maura's girlfriends, none of whom have their natural hair color. John rounded up eight of his lawyer/racquetball buddies who were willing to rent tuxedoes and wear silver-blue cummerbunds. They probably agreed to do the gig because they knew they'd get free champagne; just because they're rich doesn't mean they're not cheap.

Par for the course for a bride-to-be-who-has-lost-all-sense-of-reality, Maura has picked hideous bridesmaid dresses. We're all going to look like Glenda the Good Witch from *The Wizard of Oz*. The dresses are kind of a dark slate-blue color. They have plunging necklines, lace collars, and enormous bows that sit right above your rear. None of us has the right chest for this dress; we're either so small that the top keeps flapping open or so large that any heaving bosoms are going to pop out. The waist drops down to a huge, tea-length poofy skirt that makes all of us look like we have seventy-inch hips. The satin shoes are dyed silver (what else?), with killer pointed toes and three-inch spikes. My sister is going to kill us all.

"But it will be wonderful," Maura promises me. "The fois gras at the reception alone is costing us an absolute *fortune*." The wedding will be in a giant cathedral in Midtown, which really is very beautiful. (I've been wondering if Maura deliberately hunted down some guy who was Catholic just so she could get married in a cathedral. Maybe it's spiteful of me, but I wouldn't put it past her.) My sister is paying more for flowers than I have seen in two years of paychecks; I think it has something to do with the imported tea roses. The reception promises to be excessive—an elaborate banquet at one of the glittery hotels where they have real towels in the bathrooms instead of the disposable paper variety. And already Maura's friends, co-workers, and in-laws have set up three bridal showers and a bachelorette party among them. There will be limos, white gloves, and crème brûlée.

. . .

RECENTLY, SHE AND John registered at three department and specialty stores. I was over at their place when they showed me the printouts, which I read with horror.

12 six-piece place settings china. Rosemont Pattern. $347 each.

12 five-piece place settings silverware. Susan Pattern. $225 each.

12 pairs chopsticks. Lotus Empress. $115 pair.

"A hundred and fifteen bucks for a pair of chopsticks!" I gagged. "Maura, what *is* this?"

"Oh, they're *fabulous*," Maura gushed. This whole wedding thing made her gush a lot in general, which was really beginning to annoy me. "They're just gorgeous," she went on. "You won't believe it."

"I don't believe it now," I told her. "Didn't anyone tell you that you can get ten chopsticks for a buck down in Chinatown?"

This was ridiculous, I thought. My sister was turning into

a Chinese Martha Stewart. If she started making wonton wrappers by hand, I would know she truly had lost her mind.

"Maya, really," she said, picking up a Tiffany's catalog from the coffee table. "They're a very good investment."

"What are these things made out of, anyway?" I demanded. "Jade? Gold? Ivory? Are you guys going to kill a bunch of elephants just so you can brag to all your friends about how you have chopsticks crafted from an endangered species?"

"They're made of silver," Maura informed me, somewhat snootily. She absently leafed through the catalog. "They're very intricately carved and have a delicate chain at the top. They really are fabulous. John thinks so, too, don't you, dear?" She patted his knee, which was next to hers on the couch.

"Huh? What, babe? I wasn't listening." He clicked the remote a couple of times.

"Aren't the chopsticks we picked out great?"

"Oh, yeah, babe. The best." He flipped through two more channels and stopped at a tennis match on ESPN. He leaned back on the sofa, raked a hand through his perfectly cut blond hair, and put his arms behind his head, still holding the remote. "'Tis the season to be jolly, so might as well ask Santa for the best, huh?" He winked. I hated it when he winked.

"But isn't this excessive?" I turned page after page of the registry printout. "A mixer for four hundred and seventy-nine dollars? With dough hooks? Since when did you guys start making bread?"

"Maya, when you get married, you can do whatever you want, but this is our decision, okay?" Maura said. She was being irritatingly rational about this, but I pressed on.

"It's your decision to scalp your friends for a ninety-eight-dollar sauté pan and . . . and . . ."—I scanned the pages quickly—"and a sterling silver garlic press? A *garlic press*? You guys don't even cook!"

"Look, we're both in very competitive fields," John said, his voice easing into a soothing litigator tone as he lined up his fingertips on either side of the remote. God, he was such a creep, I thought. "We have clients, associates. It's important to us professionally to uphold a certain image that's expected of us, that's all."

Maura sniffed. "Besides, I've certainly spent *my* dues on wedding gifts. When our friends Lena and Mark got married, they even registered a crystal lamp fixture for their dining room. I think it's about time we had some nice things. I'm sick of living like a student."

"Yeah, like students can afford a two-bedroom apartment on Park Avenue," I sniped. "You guys don't even eat at home together."

"We will be expected to entertain," Maura said coldly. She got up and tossed the Tiffany's catalog onto the coffee table. John didn't budge. She took her glass from the coffee table. "I really don't want to discuss this anymore."

She walked toward the kitchen. "John, do you want more iced tea?" I noticed she wasn't offering me any.

"Yeah, thanks." John zapped the TV to a bad beach movie, then switched back to the tennis tournament and leaned forward, staring intently at the television.

"Hey, babe!" he yelled after Maura, not taking his eyes from the match. "Can you find anything to eat in there? I'm starving."

I threw the registry printout on the coffee table and got up to go home. This, I could tell, was a marriage made in heaven.

As I walked downtown on Park Avenue, the massive apartment buildings rising up on either side of me were soothing in their coldness and silence. I knew I should have been more understanding about the bridal registry, but I just couldn't be. The whole affair just seemed to emphasize that she was getting married and that I was not.

It was around this time that I decided to go to China. Soon after our run-in over the bridal registry, I got a brochure in the mail from the American Institute of Asian Studies. I had heard of them. They offered lectures and language lessons, and were announcing that a tour of China would be taken in summer. In the pamphlet there was a slightly fuzzy picture of someone standing by a temple. "A cultural experience of a lifetime," the text read. It had never occurred to me to go to China, but why not? I thought. What did I have to lose? I certainly wasn't accomplishing anything here. And I was sick of Maura and her impending wedding, which was coming on like a case of the flu. I filled out the application immediately, writing my credit card number in the little boxes provided. Two weeks later I got a confirmation letter in the mail and had to figure out how to go about getting a passport.

So before I really had time to think about it, I was bound for China with a new backpack, a Mandarin phrase book, bug repellent, and a stash of chocolate-covered maltballs. I also had stowed a few packets of Chee•tos, like the ones that are included in schoolchildren's lunchboxes. Just in case.

"The mountains," I babbled when I told my disbelieving sister. "I'm going to see the mountains."

Maura gaped at me. "But what about my wedding?" she demanded. "You're my maid of honor. You have responsibilities."

Yeah, for what, learning how to pin her train up into a bustle? Forget it.

"Sorry, Maura, but you know I'm no good at that kind of stuff, anyway," I told her, trying to be diplomatic. (This was actually very true.) "Why don't you just get Nina or someone else to be your maid of honor? They're really into all that wedding stuff."

Maura knew I had a point. She said she would think about it.

"Well, have a good time," she said. "Don't drink the water." Maura herself had no real desire to visit China. "There are so many places I'd rather go first," she said. "People say the food is so bad there."

I think I decided to go to China out of desperation. I have found it amazing that a broken heart can drive one to a rashness I never dreamed possible; my grief that Alex is gone still shocks me sometimes, as though I expected to wake one morning and find that he had not really left and everything had been a dream.

I used to read about how some people totally lost their minds over unrequited love or a case of mistaken identity. I read how people took their own children hostage, then fired a gun through their husband's or wife's head and ultimately shot themselves. I saw on television how teenagers would lie down during the night on train tracks and country roads, directly in the paths of enormous oncoming vehicles that could not stop until it was too late.

"I never saw them," these drivers would say, stunned. "I didn't know they were there. I just didn't know."

But I now understand the blindness that overcomes you so that you cannot see or hear. I understand how—in a fit of delirium—a woman could be seized by an emotion she did not know she possessed and could smash an expensive wineglass on a table. Or fling a cat against the wall. Or strike her child. There is no excuse for such things. But I think I understand where it comes from. In my case I decided to travel overseas, which was bizarre enough behavior according to everyone. I did not have to maim anyone to shock the people I knew.

. . .

WHEN I DECIDED to go on this trip, I had to have someone take care of my cats; I knew Maura wouldn't do it. I have three cats. Marlowe is gray with white paws and very unsociable; he steps around my apartment as if it is a hardship to share that space with any other living thing. Fitzpatrick is a tabby and gloriously chummy. He even pays attention when cat-food commercials come on the television. I inherited Thelma from a next-door neighbor who was leaving the country to join the Peace Corps. They are good animals, but they shed a lot, and I am constantly defuzzing my clothes with a sticky lint roller.

I finally decided to ask my neighbor to feed my cats. I left directions—two and a half pages worth written in tiny cursive—for Renee, a good-hearted transvestite who lives two doors down from me. She's actually going to have the operation next year to become fully female.

"Don't you worry about a thing, honey," Renee said to me, folding my cat instructions in half and carefully creasing the seam with perfect nails painted with Honey Rose enamel.

Renee followed me into the kitchen, and I showed her where the cat food was stored.

"I have it written down, but Marlowe doesn't like the tuna flavor," I said, shuffling boxes around in the cupboard. "I have, like, four boxes of Seafood Blend, but if you need more, go ahead and buy it. I'll pay you back."

Renee stood staring at the clippings on my refrigerator, all the while running her fingernails down the crease of the cat instructions, *zip, zip, zip*.

"So this is your itinerary, huh?" she asked while peering at a sheaf of papers stuck to the fridge with a magnet shaped like a miniature box of macaroni and cheese (a freebie from the days when I ate a lot of it). "Oh, it just sounds all exotic, honey. Inner Mongolia and Beijing and the Great Wall and everything."

Renee's hair is long and dyed a blondish color. It's a kind of long shag, and that day she was wearing a T-shirt. It's strange, but despite her femininity I think her elbows give her away. They're too strong or something, too lean.

"Will you do something for me?" Renee said suddenly.

"Sure," I said. "What do you want?" I hoped she didn't want me to bring her back something heavy and unreasonable, like a piece of lava I once was forced to lug home from Hawaii for a friend who had a rock garden; I was terrified that I would be struck down at any moment by the volcano goddess, who frowns upon such pilfering.

"Here," she said, giving me a tiny photograph of herself. It was hardly bigger than a matchbook. "I want you to take this with you when you go on your trip. And then you can take it out every so often and say, 'Here, Renee, this is the Great Wall!' and 'Here are those terra-cotta statues you saw in *National Geographic*!' " We laughed. I looked at her face in the small picture; she looked so young.

"Sounds pretty sappy, huh?" Renee said. "But I don't know." She stared blankly at the countertop and smiled. "I probably won't be getting to China anytime soon. When you're young, you think you're going to go everywhere— Africa, Europe, the Caribbean. You're going to do everything. And then after a while you realize you aren't really going to go anyplace at all."

"But you can still travel, Renee. My God, it's not like you're near death or anything."

"I know," she said, absently picking up a box of cat food. "But I'm not going to be traveling much, I don't think. It's too much hassle. And I don't deal with change very well." She laughed at her own irony. "Sounds pretty funny, right?

Anyway, since I'm not going to China, you'll just have to show me around just so I can say I've been there. In the spirit, you know?"

I found myself lining up the cat-food boxes carefully so that each corner matched the adjacent one exactly.

"When I was little, we used to dig to China in the back-yard," Renee said. "The crabgrass sloped off into a ravine filled with broken bottles and tires and shit, and we used to dig around in there all the time. One time we dug up this huge hole. I mean, it was huge. We were sure that any day we'd just break through the crust on the other side of the Earth and out we'd pop. A bunch of snot-faced little kids in the land of chop suey."

FROM THE
WILLOWS

WE LIFT OFF from New York, and the city is a jewel. From this height there is no filth, no sorrow, no heartbreak. It is the top of the Golden Mountain; make a wish, then send it off like a kiss, and it will come back to you, fulfilled. The city is ablaze, each window a gem. This is the promised land. This is where fortunes are made and happiness grows on trees like succulent fruits that you can pick as you walk along the street.

Briefly, the plane is over the sea; I can look out the window and watch it—an eternal stretch of blueness. Today is very clear; there are no clouds. No interruptions. Just the sea, which is like a vast calmness between worlds.

The air outside must be cold, bracing, unbreathable. Yet I feel I am near the kingdom of heaven. The light from the sun is golden, and the sky is exquisite.

We move toward China, flying between heaven and sea. I am going toward a world like no other, but I know it in my heart. I feel it. The dust of China is in my soul; it drifts, it clouds my vision.

. . .

BESIDE ME IS a little old lady. She reminds me of those old women in Chinatown who tell fortunes: tiny, tiny, bent women who sit at candy-red plastic tables and chairs made for children. Their bamboo canisters of fortunetelling joss sticks are on one side of the absurdly low table; a bunch of tiny, chubby bananas—no bigger than your hand—is on the other. These little old ladies are always sitting, always talking. They take a banana, no longer than their fingers, peel it, eat the miniature fruit in two bites.

This woman is a talker, too. Chatter, chatter, chatter: Where are you going? China! I go there, too. Why you live so far from your parents? You have good job? Make good money? Good, good! You can take care of your parents when they old like me, ha ha!

I can't believe that I have to ride on the plane all the way to China with this woman. She will drive me insane. I look out the window and guess we are somewhere over New Jersey; a million more miles to go and I'm stuck next to an incessant chatterbox. She rummages in her brown plastic purse, pulls out a packet of tissues, and offers me one. I decline. Then she pulls out a little bottle of Tiger Balm and rubs the all-purpose ointment on her temples.

She wrinkles her nose.

"So dry," she says. "Air on plane always so dry." I nod.

She drones on, something about her son. I nod again, make some sort of sympathetic noise. I look out the window at the clouds, the patches of houses and trees. I look at the pattern of roads cutting through trees and fields. We fly over some sort of town, and the buildings are so tiny, like matchboxes set on a thread of road. It's hard to imagine that there really are people living down there, with mortgages and dentist appointments and birthday parties; from up in the sky it all looks like a land of "let's pretend," of play cars and play supermarkets. Suddenly, I realize that the old woman is saying something about America, America the beautiful. And gradually I drift into consciousness. I listen to what she is saying.

. . .

HAVE YOUR BABIES here, and they grow up fat with their good fortune. Here in America your children eat oranges all year 'round; in China oranges are luxury. Drive car, buy television, get multispeed food processor, house with three bedrooms and automatic garage-door opener. Get dog, cat, but keep it as pet, not main course. Send your children to school; soon they learn English and become doctor, marry and give you grandchildren.

Yes, yes, this is promised land! The Christian say there was place called Eden, beautiful garden. I say, this America must be like that, place with no sorrow, no heartbreak.

Ai, but things not so easy.

Here in city, there are no trees, no fruits that grow on them. And, yes, you get oranges all time, but they trick oranges! They look so big and round like sun, but peel and wah! Skin is so thick; fruit small, dry, have no taste. Car costs so much. You buy these other things, so much money! Have to pay rent, and so many bills and bills. Get dog and get in trouble because it go wee-wee on your neighbor geranium plant and bark too much and plays too rough with little boy next door so you have to kill it. Vet does it, though. No cutting throat in alley.

Your children, your grandchildren! So little joy and so much worry. My daughter, their mother, work very hard. Work all time; she sew in big factory. But grandchildren, they get fat. So lazy! Play video game all day. Good hand-eye co-or-nation, they say. But for what, for what, I say? No big plane, no big tank come chase-chase in America, no machine have to shoot bum-bum-bum in hallway. Waste of time, waste of time. Aiya!

Then they go sleep with boyfriend, girlfriend (they think I don't know this, but I know this), but no marriage, no children, no good. They just watch TV, go shopping, go sleep. I come to America for this?

Grandchildren go out all time, go to party, go to movie, go out on date. Waste so much money! "Oh, Grandma, need a dress!" Why you need dress, I say. You have plenty dress. Open closet, so many dress right there. In China, in war, I have one dress, only one! We run away from Japanese, no time take anything, so that all I have—just one dress, on me, that all!

One time, my granddaughter have party at home, all her friend come. So many people, so much food. Very nice, very nice party. But friend bring too much beer, they all drink so much. Not so good, I think. I look at all my granddaughter friend, and it very strange. . . . They all look Chinese, I think. Very beautiful, very nice dress, shirt. All very smart. Go college, right? Very smart. But all speak English! No Chinese at all! I ask my granddaughter, Why don't you speak Chinese? She just laugh, say, "Oh, Grandma, don't be so see-ly." But I think very strange, wah. Room filled with Chinese girls, Chinese boys, but they not seem so Chinese. In heart, you know. Not so Chinese.

When you come to America, you want to be *American*.

But you don't know, when you American, you no longer Chinese, at least one hundred percent. And this hard. Sometimes you can't stop being Chinese, even if want to. Like birthmark; don't go away. You rub and rub and rub, but it always there. Put makeup on to hide, but still there, underneath.

We so sorry when children try to forget to be Chinese. But maybe we foolish, no, we old women? "American" means new thing, new person, more braver, ready to take over world. Children tell me they, wah, "straddle fence" between Chinese side and American side. Hard on their bottoms to sit there all time, easy slide off, fall down, lose face, break your heart.

Ai, how we know these things when we left China? Times were not so good then, you know? Japanese, Communists, everybody fighting. So people put idea in your head, idea you never had before. Soon, you hear and hear it, believe it true, believe that it right for you. "Go to America! Go to America!" So, yes, yes! You dream America is bigger than rest of world, bigger than China, bigger than ocean. Everybody rich. Nobody hungry. That good, that good, you think, right? Nobody hungry? For long time in China everybody hungry, people die all time. So no hungry is good.

I don't know. It very hard here. Not so easy, ah?

No, just break your heart. Who say there no sorrow on Golden Mountain? In China big river called Sorrow of China because flood in bad year. But you have warning, right? Here, you have no warning, no nothing. And there plenty sorrow here. Sorrow like river, flowing down street.

Nah, you good girl, going to China. My grandchildren won't go to China. They say "Too far, no time, what's in China?" And what can I tell them? China not like Las Vegas vacation, right? Not like big video game with lights, big fun all time. You don't have grandma? Too bad, too bad. She proud of you.

Aiya, I talk too much, too much. You sleep now, okay? Sleep, sleep, and when you wake up, you in China.

· · ·

SHE PATS MY hand.

Then she folds her own hands in her lap across her brown plastic purse and shuts her eyes. I watch her, still amazed at her rush of words. In less than a minute her breathing is even. And when she wakes she will be in China, the land where all her hopes were born.

Opening scene in China.

Airport. Flat. Is that the air traffic control tower? My God, it looks like a joke. Why is everything so beige? Wait. Beige implies color. There is no color. Everything is just the same tinge of dinginess. I am delirious from fatigue, hours on different planes. The little old lady had patted my arm when we got off the plane; now she has disappeared. Maybe she wasn't even real; I can't tell at this point.

Nothing is real.

Line up. Go through immigration. Thin, unsmiling Chinese men in uniforms stamp our passports. Are these guys Communists? They must be, right? If they work for the government? I wonder if they carry guns. But they're sitting down; I can't see anything. Linoleum. Bad fluorescent lights. I want to sit down. No, I want to keel over.

A small man is greeting us, smiling a lot. He says his name is Jim; he is our guide. Welcome to China, he says, welcome to our country. Smiles some more; I wish he'd stop. Short-sleeved pale blue shirt. Dark slacks. I look around. Nearly every man is dressed like this. A herd of Taiwanese tourists moves by; their guide is waving a little triangular flag, leading the way to a minibus parked outside. I hope we don't have a flag; it looks ridiculous.

Our group looks dazed. Night of the living dead. Somehow, we get our luggage. Line it up on the floor. Some guy in a uniform heaves our bags onto a cart, heads outside. A man wearing a short-sleeved military jacket and a police hat blows a whistle and directs traffic.

The door opens.

The heat hits us, a full body blast. We have been on planes so long that we forgot about heat, about life outside climatically controlled airspaces. The sky is gray, but the sun is shining, hurts our eyes. Why is the sun so bright? We wince. God, it's hot. We're sweating already. I have to go to the bathroom. I want to lie down. I think I'm getting a headache.

A bus roars by. It seems obnoxiously loud. There are cars

everywhere, little white and gray cars. I feel as if I've walked onto a movie set from 1953. The man in the white uniform blows his whistle again, waves his arms furiously. Suddenly it dawns on me: I can't understand what people are saying. I feel deaf. A voice shoots out of the public address system; it is a woman's voice, flat and bored. She speaks fast and in a monotone "So-that-it-all-sounds-like-one-word. Thank you."

Thank you. *"Xie xie."* I understand that.

My God, I think. I'm in China.

I have said before that I am not, by nature, a wanderer.

I believe this is true. I think that I am akin to things that grow close to the ground, in the shade. Like mushrooms, perhaps, soft and brown, that shrivel up in the sunlight. Mushrooms are very grounded; you don't think of them darting and running about, loose and untethered. I have never heard of a militant mushroom; there are no tabloid accounts of "Rampant Fungi Overtakes Italian Villa" or some such thing. Porcine mushrooms are not subjected to metal detectors.

So that is why I think I'm out of my element, here on the road, here traipsing across China with an oversized knapsack and a point-and-shoot camera. I was slow to welcome newness or change of any kind. When I was a child, I even found it traumatic to start a new spiral-bound notebook in the middle of the term: all those blank pages, clean and crisp. All those things I was still expected to learn.

In light of this intolerance to even the most minor of fluctuations, it truly is odd to find me in Asia, where I must wash out my dirty socks and underwear in the sink each night, where I must perform the daily ritual of cooling boiled water from the hotel room thermoses before filling my own cheap plastic water bottles. Hot boiled water sits around my hotel room in every available container, like offerings to low-rent gods who don't demand that expensive oranges be laid out for them.

. . .

MY TOUR GROUP is a rather madcap bunch. I was rather fond of them immediately, in the way that one is drawn to animals in a pet store. "How adorable!" you think. "So charming!" I suspect that by the end of this trip the novelty will have long worn off. I'm actually a little worried. When I signed up for this thing, it somehow never occurred to me that I'd be on a tour group with other *people*. (Stupid, I know, but these things often seem to escape me.) I mean, I've been hibernating for years. My friend, Candy (as in the gum-chewing bass player with no sense of rhythm), hardly qualifies as contact with the real world. And now I'm stranded in China for *weeks* with a bunch of people I've never met in my life. Well, it's too late now, I suppose.

This is a tour sponsored by the American Institute of Asian Studies, so not everyone in the group is interested in China per se but in Asia in general.

There is a retired couple, the Barclays, who are originally from England and are somewhat picky, Mrs. Barclay in particular.

"Barclay, as in the bank," she pointed out to us when we all were introduced. "Of course, you have heard of the bank?" I have never really heard Mr. Barclay speak, but I assume he does. I mean, he wasn't introduced as "Mr. Barclay, who uses sign language" or anything like that.

There are three older women traveling together. Mrs. Petersen and Mrs. Yamamoto have rich husbands, whom they left at home. "You know how it is," Mrs. Petersen told us. "Our husbands would just be miserable. They never want to do anything but watch football, and it's not even football season. So we just decided to go by ourselves. It's so much better that way. But I had to spend two weeks freezing my husband enough dinners. Two weeks, can you imagine that? Silly man, he won't think to eat a thing if it's not already in the house. Not a thing." The third member of their triumvirate, Mrs. Edward, is a Chinese woman who had married a man from Connecticut and is now a widow. She seems rather sweet and is the quietest of the three.

A college professor, Dr. Theodore, brought along his son, Marcus, who was adopted from Korea. Dr. Theodore is rather dashing, with dark hair and that rugged, adventurer look. He wears an Indiana Jones–type hat and has one of those photographer's vests with a lot of little pockets. I think he must actually take pictures, though, because he seems to have quite a bit of equipment. Then, again, the people who have the best equipment are seldom the best at whatever, whether it's taking pictures or playing in a band, so who knows. I believe Dr. Theodore is an anthropologist of some kind.

His son, Marcus, seems quite precocious. He is nine. Marcus carries a little knapsack (which must be expensive because although it's small it has leather trim). Quite proudly, Marcus shows me what he has brought along: a pair of binoculars ("They even work underwater"), a penknife with all sorts of tools, a metal canteen, a glass jar ("For specimens"), a thick guidebook, a field log book with grid pages, and a portable compact disc player. He also shows me his watch, which is guaranteed to keep working even if three miles underwater. It also keeps time in five countries simultaneously, has an alarm clock and an address book built right in. I give Marcus my phone number in New York, and he earnestly types it in.

"That's quite a lot of stuff," I tell him. "Looks like you're prepared for anything."

"Well, let me and my dad know if you need something,"

Marcus says amiably. "My dad has a water purifier in his suitcase."

I promise that I will notify him the moment my supply of potable water reaches a dangerously low level.

Also in the group are three graduate students, two of whom seem wildly brilliant and lively. I feel like shrinking my head in between my shoulders when they ask me what I do for a living; it's not much fun admitting you're a failed academic. So I tell them I am in publishing, which is not altogether untrue.

"Oh, that must be so fascinating," they say. "It must be exhilarating to be right at the forefront of new literature."

I say it pays the bills. (Which is more true than they could possibly know.)

One of the graduate students, Robert, speaks flawless Mandarin, much better than mine. Robert also speaks Japanese and Russian. He is charming and delightful and wonderful to look at. He is also, I suspect, gay. Rats. (Why do I always fall for men who have no interest whatsoever in women?) The second graduate student, Chad, claims to speak Thai, but I suspect that it is bad because he doesn't seem very verbal to begin with. ("Yo, dudes, howzit going? We ready to do the China thing or what?" he says by way of introduction.) He hails from Long Beach, California, and obviously has an Asian-woman fetish. He often just stands there, dreamily looking at me and Joyce, the other graduate student. We do our best to imagine that he is a slug, a train of thought that I really think won't be all that difficult to sustain.

Joyce and I are assigned as roommates.

Annoyingly, Chad immediately dubs us the China Babe Doublemint Twins. I am beginning to realize that this trip could be very long. Very long, indeed.

As it turns out, Joyce is a journalism student and is forever scribbling down notes for some huge story she plans to write after the trip. She started her project the minute we landed at the Beijing airport.

"I want to sell a piece to the *Washington Post Sunday Magazine*," she tells me.

I nod.

"The whole aspect of multiculturalism is very hot these days, very hot," she goes on. "Of course, it's only right. People of color have been repressed in America for two centuries with no voice, *absolutely no voice*, and really, it's high time that the white male establishment understands—I mean, *really understands*—about diversity in all its facets. Don't you agree?"

I nod some more. This trip suddenly looms interminably.

The leader of our group is Mr. Wong, a retired chemical engineer and a member of the Asian Institute. He is supposed to be the spokesman for our group and help out our national tour guide, Jim. Unfortunately, Mr. Wong seems to be a dead ringer for the absentminded professor type. Twice, he thought he had misplaced our passports and then our plane tickets, only to find them in his left coat pocket instead of his right.

"China is a very interesting country, very interesting," Mr. Wong tells us as he fumbles around for his glasses. He finds them, puts them on. "But you must remember that you are not in America anymore. You must learn to be very understanding, very understanding."

I wonder if he always repeats everything twice. He takes off his glasses and puts them back in his pocket.

So this is our tour group. Some old, some young. Half of our group is white; the remaining portion of us are Asians of assorted descents. Obviously, I belong ethnically to the second group, but other than that I'm not sure where I stand. Maybe it's nowhere. There are no other people in this group with temperaments resembling mushrooms. They are not shy. They are all avid travelers, even the little boy, Marcus, who likes to read aloud portions of his guidebook at odd and inconvenient moments, like when we were gathering around Jim to get our room keys at the hotel.

"Absolutely essential is a good pair of sunglasses, particularly in the Xinjiang desert or the high altitudes of Tibet," he informs us from the *Lonely Planet* guide, even though we are going nowhere near Tibet.

Everyone is so terribly excited to be in China; they've all read so much.

"I've been wanting to come for so long," Mrs. Yamamoto tells me, "ever since Nixon came."

"How did you choose this particular tour?" Mrs. Edward asks me.

I tell her it was an accident.

"We even took language lessons before we came," Mrs. Petersen remarks on behalf of herself and Mrs. Yamamoto. "Nee how, nee how," she parrots with a somewhat toneless and mildly dreadful accent. "It's so helpful to know a little of the language," she goes on. "That way, you can communicate with the natives."

Somehow, I think, I am beyond communicating with anyone.

It is our second morning in Beijing.

I can't sleep. I roll over and peer into my travel alarm clock: It is barely five in the morning. Joyce is sleeping soundly, her notebook and pen finally at rest on the little nightstand, on top of a book of Mao's speeches that have been translated into English. I try to fall back to sleep but can't; I am inexplicably awake, which is annoying since I couldn't fall asleep last night. Jet lag, I guess. But I feel restless, so I dress quickly and take the hotel room key, jotting a note on Joyce's pad: "Went for a walk. Back soon."

It's 5:17.

In the hallway by the elevator the bellhop on duty looks up suddenly when I appear and nods. I nod back. There are bellhops on each floor, sometimes four or five during the day. They fetch boiled water or carry bags, but most of the time they just sit around, reading newspapers or playing cards. Sure there's no unemployment in China—just hundreds of people doing pointless jobs that could easily be handled by ten. I smile at the bellhop when the elevator dings and step into the red-carpeted cubicle.

We are staying at an excessively nice hotel with a gaudy chandelier and a lot of carpet in the lobby. We didn't like this at first, being sheltered and pampered like rich American tourists (which I suppose we are), but after our first day of touring around Beijing in the heat and dust, the nice shower, flush toilet, and individually controlled air-conditioning sure seemed nice.

My brain has been dead since I got here. I have no reaction to anything, it seems, no emotion, no anything. We went to a museum near Tiananmen Square yesterday, and I stared into the badly lit cases holding ancient bronze vessels as if these objects were as mundane as cans of orange juice. Nothing is registering. Maybe it's because I can't sleep.

It's cool outside. Even the early morning air is gray in Beijing; this city is so colorless that it makes New York in the fog look like a box of crayons.

I walk.

Gray dust blows around in the streets, collects in the windowsills. It must be all the grit from the city, from the smoke that belches out from the stacks. In China there are no laws against pollution; there is no EPA, so the air is caustic. By midmorning it burns your throat so it feels dry and raw.

Even before dawn there have been women out on the streets with giant brooms made of some kind of straw, sweeping. The world is quieter now; the air is cleaner. The stillness seems pure and chaste. Stars pierce the sky, cold and sharp; they are pinpoints of light that slowly disappear as the glow of daytime appears on the horizon and swallows up the darkness. The women, with kerchiefs tied around their lower faces, sweep the street, moving in platoons down the wide, laneless avenues.

Ssup, ssup, ssup, say the brooms. The brooms look like ones that witches ride on Halloween but without the handles. The women just hold the knot of straw above where it is fastened together.

Ssup, ssup, ssup down the streets at 5:30 in the morning. The street sweepers probably have been up for hours already, preparing for the day.

Ssup, ssup, ssup. Piles of dust so fine it is like soft flour. Where does it come from? Within hours it will all be blown back by the harsh, dry, caustic winds.

The breakfast vendors are out with their metal carts and giant tureens of "jook," or white rice porridge, which is thick and luminous in the dawn. People sit on their haunches in the street around the vendor, slurping up the jook out of enormous enamel bowls. Long, fried doughnuts lie in piles on the vendors' carts. These donuts are not sweet, but bland. Foot-long and golden, they are broken up and eaten with the porridge. The Chinese call them "oil-fried demons." Are these enemies or friends one has for breakfast? Do they swallow the devil each dawn?

The light creeps up without my knowing it. Suddenly, I look around and the white and bluish glow of daytime has arrived. A faint sliver of the moon remains, high in the sky. A lonely star shines persistently overhead. The cars are more numerous. The stream of bicycles thickens.

People stand in the side streets outside their homes, brushing their teeth with some kind of toothpaste that makes them foam at the mouth like mad dogs. They spit into the street, rinsing their mouths with water from white enamel cups that have poorly printed pictures of red flowers on them.

Carts pulled by weary donkeys are coming into the city from the surrounding farms. They are piled high with cabbages, irregularly shaped beans, purple Chinese eggplant (which is longer and narrower than Western eggplant), and bundles of greens. The wooden wheels creak and groan on the road; the donkeys shake off the flies gathering about their eyes. The farmers are dried and sinewy under their large, umbrellalike hats. Their feet are rough and ruined in their worn rubber sandals. As the daylight takes hold, the carts roll toward the marketplace; these are the stragglers, the ones who, for reasons unknown, got a late start. Others have been there for hours already, coming in from the countryside in the dark, even before the street sweepers began.

Traffic thickens. The stream of cyclists has turned into a steady, slow-moving tide that stops for nothing. Amazingly, no one ever seems to get killed. Just step into the flow and be taken along. The masses will protect you. The women are fresh in their dresses, their hair pulled back. Their high-heeled shoes are scuffed and discolored but worn with clean anklets trimmed with schoolgirl lace.

Everyone rides with the same dispassionate face. The face that everyone in Beijing seems to have: completely serene and utterly blank. Look at a thousand faces this morning and not a single one will give away what anyone is thinking. They all simply pedal along, riding the swell on their tinny bicycles, leaving little puffs of dust in their wake.

They look at me, these Beijing residents. They stare at me, so obviously a foreigner, but not so strange as someone who is white or African-American. They look at me straight on, then pass on their way. No one says anything. I feel odd in my shorts and T-shirt and sneakers, out of place. Only children dress like this here.

It is 7:30, and already the dust hangs invisibly in the air. The heat is rising, thick and oppressive. I wipe my face, which is sweating a bit.

The street sweepers have disappeared, and I realize I must hurry back to meet the others for breakfast.

Today we go to the Forbidden City; its very name is evocative of intrigue, sedition, and general misconduct of the highest caliber. You can see the rooftops of the massive compound from a distance. First we climb a nearby hill, which was artificially constructed with the soil excavated for the palace moat, in Coal Hill Park to a pavilion. Round a corner and suddenly there it is: a vast expanse of the Forbidden City's yellow roof tiles and low-slung buildings, all long and rectangular, with the eaves curving toward heaven. Everything else is straight, perpendicular. The Forbidden City is not a world of circles. It was never a gentle world, but one that was totally grand, repressive, and unnatural. It was where the Ming and Qing dynasty emperors would live and rule, carrying out their mandates of heaven. Curvatures were not necessarily found in architecture but in forms of misdeed and ill intent, of currying favor and greasing palms.

We climb down from Coal Hill Park and enter the Forbidden City. Even with all the tourists the pathways seem immense and cold. The walls are high and unyielding. At each doorway is a tall step that must be stepped over.

Our guide Jim looks at his watch.

"Hello, hello! We only have one and a half hours here," he tells us. "So we do not have time to see everything. The Forbidden City is very large." He waves his arm behind him in a show of the compound's expansiveness. "So we will only see part of it today."

And then we are off, hiking through the place at a sprint-like pace. We zoom through the Meridian Gate and head for the Three Great Halls, which make up the heart of the palace grounds. We dart toward the Hall of Supreme Harmony and peer over others' heads to see the Dragon Throne, where the emperor would preside. The throne is opulent and gilded and looks terribly uncomfortable, I think. We pass by the Hall of Middle Harmony and the Hall of Preserving Harmony in a blur.

"Can't we slow down?" Mrs. Barclay asks peevishly. "We don't have time to see anything. I came all the way to China to see this, and we don't have time to look at anything."

"Sorry, sorry, no time," Jim informs her. "Please, please, step this way."

My eyes start to glaze over.

I feel the walls closing in on me, shutting out the light. I start to notice ridiculous, meaningless things: the peeling ox blood–red paint, the weeds sprouting up between the crevices of the stone pathways. The sun is shining, but I feel suddenly chilled in the shade.

We go down a narrow passageway that suddenly opens up into yet another courtyard. I have lost all sense of direction. These, Jim tells us, are the Western Palaces, where the empress and some of the emperors' concubines lived.

My interest is piqued.

We peer into the row of rooms, dark and small. Some of the rooms actually are quite well appointed: one has a bed with a beautiful blue-silver silk spread, embroidered with flowers. The dressing table is made of carved rosewood; on top sits an elaborate standing mirror, made of silver. There are little bottles of scent, a tray of combs. So this was the best that a concubine could aspire to, I think to myself: to be the consort of the emperor, to have access to power like no other woman could. We walk down the row of rooms, looking at each one, looking briefly into what the life was of someone at some time.

"Please, please, step this way," Jim says. And we are off again. We go to the Nine Dragon Screen, which is made of glazed tiles. Colorful yellow and blue and purple dragons dance along the length of a wall, their tongues and tails all in motion. The creatures are multilimbed, their peculiar arms and feet all tangled with their bodies. Each one is perched on the crest of a foamy, pale green wave. The tiles are in relief and are wonderfully textured. I want to reach out and touch the glazed scales, the sharp nails on each foot, the steady, gentle curve of the water. But there is a low, metal fence that keeps us away from the wall. We lean on the railing; we are tired and watch our shadows on the pavement.

I have decided that I do not like the Forbidden City.

A harshness seems to seep from the walls, from the muted yellow roof tiles. Fearful gargoyles with gaping mouths and horrible eyes perch on each roof corner. And then I realize that there is so much stone here—stone pathways and stone walls and stone corridors. There are no living things, no trees or plants that blossom and soften the harshness. There is nothing living except the errant weeds growing up through unused pathways, which probably did not exist years ago, when the Forbidden City was a brimming compound. In the near distance I see the hill that we had climbed earlier; the temple is there, rising above a line of trees. The gentle curves of its eaves reach toward the sky.

So this is what it must have been like.

To live your life here, cradled in this tomb of heaven, and only get a glimpse beyond its walls of where the living world breathed and went on without you.

. . .

THAT NIGHT WE are driven somewhere to have the famous Beijing duck.

" 'Your meal starts at one of the agricultural communes around Beijing, where the duck is pumped full of grain and soya bean paste to fatten it up.' " Marcus reads from his guidebook in the van.

"That sounds disgusting," says Joyce, whom we have discovered is a vegetarian.

" 'The ripe duck is lacquered with molasses, pumped with air, filled with boiling water, dried, and then roasted over a fruitwood fire.' " Marcus pauses. "Gee, I guess they've killed the duck by then, right? It sounds pretty awesome."

"Absolutely not," Joyce snaps. "It sounds positively inhumane."

A few minutes later we are led into a hotel, supposedly renowned for its Beijing duck. (Of course, they could have taken us to the Chuck E. Cheese of Beijing duck establishments and none of us would have known better. I am relieved to know that I am not the only one who has lost a total sense of direction.)

Our party takes up two round banquet tables. Bottles of warm orange soda and beer appear.

"All right, sports fans, let the games begin!" Chad exclaims exuberantly as he reaches for a bottle of beer. He fills his glass and passes the bottle around.

Much fuss is made as a waiter presents the duck (which really does look quite tasty) on a platter. Then he walks out with it.

"Why did he take our duck away?" Marcus asks, quite worried. We are all thinking the same thing.

A few minutes later the duck reappears, all cut up and boned, with its crispy skin. Waitresses set down little dishes of scallions, plum sauce, and crêpes.

"How do we know it's the same duck?" Mrs. Petersen whispers loudly.

"Don't ask, just eat," Mrs. Yamamoto whispers back, pouring some orange soda for her companion.

The waiter shows us how to spread some plum sauce on the crêpe, put some meat on it, and add the scallions. He rolls it up expertly and proudly presents it to Joyce, who cringes and shoves her plate at Robert.

In Mandarin Robert explains to the slightly put-off waiter that Joyce does not eat meat. The waiter raises his eyebrows and shakes his head. He must think Americans are nuts. The waitresses are tittering, pretending to hide their giggles behind their hands.

"Here," Robert says, reaching for a plate of white buns. "Have a roll, Joyce."

The rest of us dig in enthusiastically. Joyce, who looks a bit ill, nibbles on a plain crêpe. We eat ravenously, although it seems we only had lunch a little while ago.

"Well, that was simply splendid," Mrs. Barclay exclaims as she leans back in her chair and sips some tea. "China is simply a wonderful country, don't you agree?"

. . .

ON OUR THIRD day in Beijing our tour group goes to see an opera.

Drums beat.

They beat in the distance, a steady, insistent pulse that throbs in the air, in the make-believe trees, down fictitious mountain passages. It pulses through the delicate branches of willows, waving like vaporous silk in the breeze.

Closer, closer, down from the heavens, down from the hills. You hear them coming like an imminent storm. Like magic for a wedding, for a wake. Red banners and silk robes for the bride; white veils for the dead. Closer and closer! It's coming, it's coming, it's coming. . . .

Flutes whine. Strange stringed instruments seize our ears and scream high-pitched and dissonant melodies into their tender, soft inner parts. Cymbals clang urgently, going faster and faster and faster, as if trying to outrun the rest of the symphonic gathering.

Now there is no running away.

We're surrounded by the drums that seem to flog our bones. The flutes are screaming; the stringed instruments are shrill and unrelenting, wrapping sound around our skulls. The cymbals buffet our bodies, our equilibrium. *Chang, chang, chang, chang . . . chang, chang, chang, CHANG, chang chang . . . CHANG CHANG CHANGCHANGCHANG*. People are whirling about onstage in fantastic costumes, in bolts of silk in yellow and red and turquoise; they brandish swords and silk scarves and frightful face paints. I do not understand the story, but this story seems like all other stories—good against evil, and save the kingdom. Voices whine. The spoken words are exaggerated and pompous. Then the music picks up again, louder and louder, the screaming of the flutes and strings pierces the air. Now everyone is onstage; there is a tremendous battle with swords and soldiers vaulting into the air. A maiden is slain; she dies splendidly. This sends the cymbals into a fit of sound; they are furious at her death.

In this ecstasy of sound and color we want to be released from this passion play, this operatic fury. Yet we want it to go on forever, to be lost in this frenzy of noise and dissonance and chaos.

Without warning, it stops.

The air still vibrates, and the silence is excruciating.

We clench our eyes shut, breathe deeply with mouths open. Spent, we clap politely. The overseas Chinese tourists are standing up, applauding furiously, whistling. We blink as the houselights come on, suddenly and without warning.

The grand theater is over.

Offstage, face paints are wiped off, revealing tired and dull faces. Gaudy silk robes are put on their hangers, frayed hems dragging on the floor.

We rise, unsteadily, to our feet. Follow the crowd down sticky aisles to the lobby, overwhelming in its earthiness. Fluorescent lights burn our eyes. The cracked linoleum seems particularly ugly and offensive. The hum of voices around us is too loud, although the buzz of their voices is mostly lost to the burning hollows in our ears, which feel torn and bleeding. The crowd is expelled into the hot summer streets. The light is mostly gone and the gray darkness is cooling. Outside the theater is a fountain that has no water. People are sitting on its circular edge, eating dried watermelon seeds and spitting the hulls onto the road. They are laughing. A child eats a frozen-fruit Popsicle.

We climb into the van and say nothing. We are exhausted. The driver pulls into the street, honking his horn loudly and obnoxiously; a wave of cyclists parts momentarily and the van slips into the stream of traffic.

It's time to go home.

. . .

IT IS OUR last day in Beijing, and I am still restless. My feet seem itchy; I hop from one foot to another, look around, hop again. I want to go somewhere, but I don't know where. We have been touring the city nonstop, herded about from breakfast to museum to lunch to the Ming Tombs and back. And still I'm restless. Exhausted and restless. I am tired of eating all the time. I am beginning to feel like a pig being fattened up for someone else's feast at the end of the trip.

Ever since we arrived here I've been waiting for something to happen. People say you're supposed to feel more Chinese when going to China, but I do not. But what did I expect? Did I think that one day I would wake up, look into a mirror, and see another me? Did I expect suddenly to find my skin and face transformed, a modern-day version of a Tang Dynasty figure with my hair piled up and silk robes draping from my shoulders? Of course not.

But still I look. And wait. For what exactly, I have no idea.

I think it began the moment we arrived. I started taking down observations in my head as if I were Joyce, scribbling in a little notebook. I've been looking for something ever since our plane broke through the clouds over Chinese airspace and I first glimpsed the browned and greened patches of farmland. But nothing. I heard nothing, felt nothing. Just a kind of emptiness where I thought a sureness certainly should have grown.

I have walked down the streets of Beijing and they have been silent to me, despite the steady stream of cars, bicycles, buses, and pedestrians. I looked into piles of bananas, a display of canvas shoes, a wok filled with dumplings dancing in oil; I looked into these things as if I expected the answers to my unarticulated questions to spring suddenly from their centers.

I stood in Tiananmen Square on a hazy, hot summer evening, looking for blood on the pavement, ghosts calling from the stones. But still, nothing. The expanse of concrete squares seemed vast, stretching from a heroic-looking statue of revolutionaries near one end to that famous portrait of Chairman Mao at the other. He stares out over the square; the painting is smaller than one thinks it would be, but still, there it is: Mao in the green suit that bears his name, his benevolent dumpling face peering out above the tight collar. At this end of the square are little card tables, scattered across the pavement.

"Picture! Picture!" the men call to me and the others, waving their arms at the tables. Beside each table is an easel on which photographs are taped: smiling children and parents, lovers shyly standing close to each other, all with Mao beaming in the distance behind them. "Picture, want picture?" a man asks again. He pretends to hold up a camera in his hands and clicks the shutter. "Picture?"

I smile at him and shake my head.

I thought I would feel something as we filed past the well-pickled body of Mao Zedong in his mausoleum, lying there with almost obscenely red cheeks. We had waited forever in line, even though we foreigners got to bypass all the Chinese tourists, queued up for seemingly miles in neat, straight rows. But I felt no emotion as we walked past the eminent corpse; the hushed silence only seemed to press into my ears painfully. The whole affair seemed a bit maudlin; it was more impressive to me that so many people waited patiently to do this. We were told to be quiet as we entered the hall, told not to take pictures. And then, before we knew it, we were outside again, staring at the lines of people waiting to get in.

. . .

AND ULTIMATELY I had wanted joy or exhilaration when I visited the Great Wall. This, after all, was the only structure built by people that could be seen from the moon; it was an incredible feat of architecture and sheer labor. I fingered the names of some of the millions who had carved their names into the Great Wall like a Chinese version of "Kilroy Was Here"; it was odd to see Chinese characters scraped into the blocks. This shocked me; idiotically, I had thought graffiti appeared only in English. Did these Chinese say what English speakers would have said? Did these words mean the equivalent of "George was here" and "Debbie Luvs John 4ever"? I touched the stones, and they were hot from the sun. But the mountains, the massive stone structure, all of it still remained silent to me.

The graduate students, Marcus, and I had hiked all the way to the end of the rebuilt portion of the wall that lies north of Beijing. It had been an arduous, uphill climb, and terribly hot. The wind was stiff. And with all the vendors hawking T-shirts, junk jewelry, and cheap paper fans near the entrance to the wall, it was hard to imagine Mongols thundering down from the north on horseback. Still, the view at the end was magnificent. We took turns looking through Marcus's binoculars, gazing into the hazy distance where the terrain became more rugged and inhospitable. The original wall was still there, crumbling and only a fraction of the height of the rebuilt section. We mugged for photos ("Look, Mom, we're on the Great Wall!"); we cheered as a woman from Shanghai took our picture. We rested a bit, steadying ourselves for the walk back through seven watch towers. Joyce scribbled in her notebook. Chad tried to start up a conversation with the woman from Shanghai, but she laughed, shook her head, and walked away.

. . .

I THOUGHT TODAY might have been a good day for an epiphany of some sort.

The day dawned on our fifth morning as if God had spoken, unleashing a splendor over Beijing, which had thus far been hidden in a smoggy, dirty haze. It was a brilliant sunrise that filled the huge expanse of sky with reds and blues and creamy clouds. Beijing itself was glowing, bathed in a warm, golden light that gladdened hearts and pulled the corners of grim mouths into laughter. In this light even the mist rising over the cesspool near our hotel was enchanting. This splendid sky seemed to reach to forever, an immense display that filled the heavens and pushed at the thin seam of the distant, earthly horizon. This, then, was the mythic China, grand and vibrant and impervious to human folly.

I waited for the strike of lightning. The moment of enlightenment.

I waited to hear the voices everywhere, the wordless whispers from the soul of China. We walked through the Summer Palace, a colorful delight with all the good that lives: the squeals of little children, the gentle banter of people at leisure, the rush of wind through willows and fantastic rocks. The grand scale of China at her most opulent and richest, from gilded dressing table to the little boy eating a sausage, was here.

But still, nothing.

I don't know what I'm looking for, and I don't know whether to be disappointed or not.

. . .

IT OCCURS TO me that I have been transported into a China that for me is suspended in time. Nothing ever seems to change here. I would guess that the markets sell the same kinds of vegetables they have been selling for centuries, that the food stalls hawking tureens of rice porridge at dawn have been there since the beginning of history. It all seems timeless, even the steam and the rivers and the water, the mud clinging to the legs and backs of water buffalos. In the China of my mind it always has been this way: This China is unscathed by momentum; it is frozen in time.

We are going to Inner Mongolia, and this prospect excites me; maybe I'll calm down when we're out of the city, away from all these people. We get off the tour van, scurry over to the huge, dirty, uncolored train station. I have to step over a puddle of vomit. I am unfazed.

The train station is chaotic. It is not like Grand Central Station in New York, which—despite all its flurry of people dashing about—somehow still has a semblance of order and intent. The Beijing station is like nothing I have seen. It is crowded with people, but in addition to suitcases there are baskets of leafy green vegetables and watermelons in mesh bags. A woman is standing there with a crate of brown ducks, which peck at the wooden spindles. There are long lines that seem to lead nowhere but into more long lines. A few men are lying on the cement floor, sleeping peacefully. All the seats are old and wooden and filled with more people and all their parcels. Our tour group stands close together, looking and feeling unbearably foreign. Mrs. Barclay wrinkles her nose, but even she has been stunned into speechlessness. Mr. Wong and Jim are somewhere getting our train tickets. At one corner is a snack-food stand, selling provisions: rice crackers and packages of cookies, plastic containers of dried seaweed, and bags of peanuts and sunflower seeds. A crackling announcement booms over the loudspeakers, which sets some in the room scurrying for their luggage. Two babies start wailing, one at each end of the room. We stand and sweat.

Suddenly Jim emerges from out of nowhere with our train tickets. An old man loads our luggage onto a metal cart. We are led out onto a platform where a massive train sits, steaming in the heat. It's just like the movies, I think. Several cars down stands the enormous black engine, which hisses and puffs. The Chinese word for train literally means "fire car," and now I fully understand what it means, for this monster truly looks like a dragon waiting to spring.

We climb up into the train and are shown pleasant, first-class compartments. In each there are four beds, two on each side. The beds are covered with starched, white sheets with blue piping trim and ruffled hems. A little table is bolted underneath the window, which stands open. Joyce and I must share our compartment with Robert and Chad.

"Oh, this is really rather charming," Joyce exclaims, fingering the ruffled sheets. "It's so cute."

Chad hits his head while trying to sit in the lower bunk.

"I think I'll take the top," he says, and climbs the little ladder. But the ceiling is too low for him to sit completely upright, so he stretches out, his boots soiling the crisp, white sheets. "Hey, this is awesome," he says, bending down to look out the window. "But look at those dudes over there. They probably, like, hate us, right?"

We all look outside. On the other track is another train, and we find ourselves staring into the third-class, "hard seat" compartments, which are nothing more than wooden booths like those in a restaurant. Whole families of six or eight or more are crammed into a space smaller than ours. They are already eating, peeling pears with a small knife, breaking open steamed meat buns wrapped in newspaper. Their windows are open as well, and we can hear someone coughing in their car. They stare at us openly, then laugh among themselves.

Our trains start to pull away in opposite directions. "Hello!" They smile and wave. "Hello, hello!" We wave back. They seem to think this is very funny.

Chad settles in for a nap, but the rest of us sit on the bottom bunks and stare out the window. The train pulls out from the station; I can hear the engine hissing, see the trail of smoke it belches from the stack. The back sides of houses are ugly as we move slowly past; Beijing is in a gray haze again. I suppose like anywhere else, real estate near the train tracks is not a hot commodity. The homes are pieced together from bits of wood and corrugated metal. A shallow gutter of waste water and mud runs near their perimeter. Children stand near the tracks, holding hands and waving at the trains. For whatever reason none of us waves back.

Chad breathes heavily, like a child.

. . .

AFTER AN HOUR or so, the urban landscape gradually thins. Soon we are out in the countryside. We spot a water buffalo and people in wide, straw hats. On this overnight train to Inner Mongolia, we sometimes pass another train, heading toward Beijing. I look at the faces that peer from the hard-seat-compartment cars whooshing by in that passing train; the faces are tired from travel, numb to the sights. I see a white light that glows from behind the silhouetted mountains; it is the sun falling, slipping below the horizon. A faint orange afterglow remains. Then this, too, fades. It seeps into the blueness of night, and then there is nothing.

I have never seen such darkness.

Now it is 6:56 A.M. on the Orient Express.

It is more beautiful here than I expected. We are headed toward Hohhot, the capital of Inner Mongolia. The mountains are ever present on the horizon, with a stretch of flatlands reaching to their foot.

Despite my unsteady sleep I am rested and calm. Chinese radio comes fuzzily over the speaker; on it the saucy voice wants you to believe that some pretty young thing is behind the little box. Joyce, Robert, and Chad are playing poker on the floor of our compartment, using sunflower seeds and peanuts as chips, but I do not join them. Our door is open. Next door I can hear Mrs. Barclay telling Mrs. Petersen and Mrs. Yamamoto about her trip to Poland two years ago. Out in the passageway Marcus is reading aloud something about Kublai Kahn and then asks for sesame crackers. For some reason all this activity around me makes me even more still, more calm within myself.

The local Chinese who walk through the passageway on their way to the bathroom don't disturb me at all because they demand nothing of me. No attention, no speech, no interest. I am glad to be around them, these men in their undershirts who violently clear their throats and spit.

I look at these men. None of them looks like my father. These men all seem bonier, tougher. Some have liver spots scattered across their faces; they look as if they were caught in a dark rain that stained their skin.

. . .

SUDDENLY MY CALMNESS leaves. I stare out the window from my top bunk. The endless, monotonous landscape feels as if it is closing in; the sound of the steel wheels on the tracks grows loud and harsh in my head. My thoughts start jumping around. I cannot stop them:

These men do not look like my father, who liked the Chinese opera. My father once gave me five cents for a brand-new piggy bank that my aunt had sent me from far away. I used to shake that glass bank, shake and shake it with the five pennies inside so that it was like an internal tambourine, clanging in time to the opera music.

I have worked so hard at not thinking about anything in recent years, especially about my father. I rather liked that numbness, that deadening of my senses. But now I cannot stop all these thoughts that come back in a rush. These images come from the past, haunting like ghosts rushing down the cold, cold passageways of a palace where no one lives.

I try to take a deep breath, slow down. Calm down.

I fix my attention on a corner of the bunk opposite me. I stare at the line where the metal bars come together to form a right angle. I try to make my mind blank again. But still, my father creeps into my thoughts, stealthily, like a foot soldier among trees, seemingly erratic but with some destination in mind.

. . .

WHY DO I think of him, then? He who went away and did not come back, who did not say good-bye even. After he left I found a basket of his unwashed shirts in the basement and nearly lost my mind with grief. One day the shirts were gone. Missing. Did someone take them away? Were they given to old tramps on the street, in the alleys, under a metal bridge on the river? But wait, there was no river by my home. And there were no tramps, no homeless men.

My father had undershirts like the ones the men on this train are wearing: short-sleeved and kept folded in the top drawer of his bureau. What is it about men's shirts that can pull at a woman's heart? I think of other shirts that belonged to other men. There used to be nothing better than putting on the shirt of the man I loved, slipping it through my arms and wrapping it around me like a robe. Walking around the room with nothing on but that big shirt, feeling sensual and indulgent and blissfully slothful all at the same time.

And I remember laundry, stacks of Fruit of the Looms warm from the dryer. Peeling the soft lint from the screen trap and rolling it up like sushi. New underwear, fresh and white and warm, soft like a cloth diaper.

The thoughts keep rolling in my head, rising like brackish water that slowly eats up the shore, inch by inch. I close my eyes, give in. Feel the wash of memory flood my senses.

Yes, none of these men looks like my father, yet each one reminds me of him.

FATHER

I LEARNED EARLY on that memories could be a tricky thing.

It began with my father, who had no past, no childhood. Or at least one that he cared to share. I do not know if his youth in China was filled with pain or hunger or blitzed with wartime fears. I do not know if, as an adult, the slow wail of an air-raid siren in a war movie made him clench for a moment before he realized that no, he was not in danger. I don't know which filled his youth more, happiness or horror; he simply would not say.

As a result, my sister and I never were regaled with those "Well, when *I* was a kid" hardship stories that other children heard from their parents—we never heard how cold it was in the winter, how far one had to walk uphill to school in ill-fitting shoes, how there wasn't television, or how hard it was to work in the meat-packing factory, making ham loaf. Maura and I wanted to know about these things.

"Daddy, what did you do when you didn't have a TV, huh? Were you so bored you thought you'd die? Huh, Daddy? Were you?" My sister and I could not imagine life without *Little House on the Prairie*. Laura Ingalls was our hero.

"What was it like when you were a kid, Daddy?" we would pester him. "Was it like the Stone Age?" Giggle, giggle.

"Well, it was a long time ago," my father would admit. "Ancient history, right? You don't want to know about that."

And that would be that. We never got anything out of him.

It was as if my father had deliberately misplaced his past when he was fourteen, as if he had left his boyhood on some San Francisco side street and never gone back to get it.

He smiled and then he forgot.

It's not so difficult, he had said, to forget. You can make yourself do it. And then, after a while, it's as if nothing ever happened. It's not so bad. Your life can be unblemished this way. It's easier to live with. Memories can bring you so much grief.

. . .

HE WAS THE first man I loved.

My father, the man who was so calm and funny and smelled of peppermint and hand soap, the man who married my mother. At times I have wondered if he owed her something, if that was why such a gentle man would choose a woman of iron. But I will never know this. My father died with all his secrets, and my mother lives unpartingly with hers.

Unlike my father, I have remembered my past.

Sometimes I think I have kept too much. I collect memories like knickknacks, and I also have too many of those. But I like details; they are like shiny little baubles to me, precious little trinkets to be stowed away in a safe place, like in a special tin, then taken out later and looked at in secret.

I had a tin like that when I was a child. It was square, red and blue, with a picture of a Chinese woman on it. She was wrapped in silk, scarves dripping and flowing from her wrists. Her face was oval and perfect in the way that women in pictures always are. A full, creamy moon hung low in the horizon behind her. This tin originally had held moon cakes for the Mid-Autumn Festival. Four of the pastries had fit neatly in the box; they were round and pretty and perfect with their sweetness inside.

I kept all sorts of things in this box: letters from my pen pal in California (her name was Sarah, and she only wrote me twice, but I kept her letters very carefully; she told me about her cat and how their house had cacti growing in the front yard); four baseball cards from losing teams and a stick of cardboardlike pink gum; a plastic hibiscus from a Hawaiian costume I'd worn for Halloween; and three marbles, including my favorite, which was green like seawater and so clear that I thought by looking through it I could see all the way to where the stars began. There was a stub of a red pencil in this tin, too, and a matchbook that said "1–800–TAX–HELP." Silly, meaningless things were in there, which somehow had taken on great significance.

I loved this moon-cake tin, and over time the things that I kept in it changed. I took the baseball cards out and put in a plastic mirror. The hibiscus gave way to a book of daily devotions that had been distributed on a street corner. My fancies changed. As I grew up, what was once so important did not seem so vital anymore.

. . .

I STARTED COLLECTING memories when we went to my Great-aunt Bertha's house. I was there for one week after she died, and I have no memories before then that remain as vivid.

I was very small, perhaps not even much taller than the height of a dining room table. I know this because I was in the second grade, taken from our home to California, where my parents had gone to bury Aunt Bertha, the one who had raised my father after he came to America. My sister was not with us. I don't remember what the reason was for her remaining at the home of a neighbor.

I do not remember very much about this house except that it was nondescript. It was not a beautiful house. But as I sat in that living room, looking at the petrified tangerines on the teak tables—leftover offerings to ancestors—I began storing thoughts in a mental hope chest. I put away the heavy smell of sesame-seed oil after a meal and the slippery feeling of rosewood under my fingertips. I put away the patterns of seat cushions and the inlay of silver carvings. I remembered lingering cigar smoke and the residual dust of incense long extinguished. I absorbed the patterns and colors of fine silk thread, and the way that white paperboard boxes were tied up with red string when cakes were brought home from Chinatown. I found a place in my head where I could keep the way the light shone through a curtain of gauze and where I could remember the feel of the textured, silky red and gold couch I slept on at night.

The house seemed very dark all the time and had a closed, unused smell. I think this was because my Uncle Aldolphus had died a long time ago and Aunt Bertha had been in the hospital a great deal, going about the business of dying. But their house was still a fantasy to me, filled with things that were both strange and comfortingly familiar. There was a painted-glass Buddha, the laughing one who held a peach and was surrounded by children. There was the black and white photograph of my Uncle Aldolphus in a silver frame, and another of him and Aunt Bertha in their youth, with full cheeks and looks of alarm on their faces (from real fear or surprise at the camera flash, I'll never know). There were vases that never held flowers and carved ivory cities with footpaths that led nowhere. Later my parents got these things; they are now in the house of ghosts, where my mother lives.

I do not remember the layout of the house. For some reason I don't remember any other rooms except the living room. All I can remember are two things: the living room and an image of my carrying a stack of silk stockings in pretty red boxes through the house, helping to pick up the house after my great-aunt died. I thought this was a lot of fun, this picking up of the house.

My father and mother thought I didn't understand that someone had died.

But the thing was, I did know. I looked at my great-aunt in her coffin, where she lay like a mannequin with a dime between her lips. I thought the dime was very interesting; it looked silly there in her mouth where it didn't belong. I think it was supposed to symbolize that she was to have wealth in the afterlife, that she would be well provided for. But a dime, how foolish; that would hardly do, because it didn't even buy you a candy bar.

Still, Aunt Bertha and Uncle Aldolphus held no meaning to me as real people, as loved ones to be mourned in loss. My father had never told me anything about them except that Uncle Aldolphus was part owner of a laundry (what else) near Chinatown. And now they both were dead, these mystery people of my father's unknown past. They could have been a prince and princess in China; they could have grown up in an enormous house with a lot of servants and a stable of magnificent horses. But now I would never know for sure.

So the only thing that was real and tangible to me as a child was their house, filled with wondrous things. I thought the house wanted me to remember it long after it had been sold to someone else. I believed it wanted me to remember that my great-aunt and great-uncle had lived there, that they had shared a life and helped to raise a boy, even if he wasn't their own son. Perhaps I thought I had to remember because I knew that after that week, after everyone had divided up the jewelry and dishes and pictures, they would go home and forget everything. Deliberately. Even children have a way of knowing these things sometimes.

What I find worrisome, though, is what *I* have forgotten.

I don't remember what anyone said during that week. I have no recollection of important family conversations or vital bits of information carelessly tossed out about my father's life. All I remember are strange, useless things—like my mother and my aunt, arguing over who should get a particularly nice jade pendant and a string of freshwater pearls (my mother won out, saying that she should have them for her daughters; but my mother has kept them in her velvet-lined jewelry case, and Maura and I never have been allowed to borrow either one). I recall my father, gazing out the dining room window, absently eating handful after handful of soft boiled peanuts. And I remember the image of me as a little girl, sitting alone in the dark living room and looking at a bowl of tangerines that long ago had dried to the hardness of stones.

. . .

WHAT I DO know about my father has been pieced together from stray conversations in ensuing years. My father left his family in China when he was fourteen years old. It was 1948, the year before the Communists took over. His parents wanted him to be a doctor, and China was troubled, not a good place for a young boy. My grandmother didn't want to leave Canton, so she and my grandfather stayed behind and sent my father to live with his Aunt Bertha and Uncle Aldolphus in America. Later my grandparents were sent to reeducation camps after the Hundred Flowers Campaign in 1957. "Let a hundred flowers bloom," Mao had decreed. Let all open their minds and let out their opinions about China, he said in such a fatherly way. It sounded so lovely, so noble. Later, many of those who had spoken out were taken away and sent to prisons or work camps in the countryside. Most did not return. My grandparents were among them.

This all happened before my sister and I were born. My father never spoke of his life before San Francisco; it was as if America was the only reality he knew.

"Oh, that was a long time ago," my father said when we asked him anything about his boyhood. "That was ancient history. You don't want to know about that." He smiled and seemed to remember nothing.

. . .

AND THE MORE he seemed to forget, the more I tried to store up everything I knew about him, especially after he left us without warning, without notice. My father was the first man I loved, a man who belongs only to my childhood. So in my mind he is perfection. We never argued about curfews, mysterious dents and scratches in the car, dubious boys whom I dated. Those discussions belonged to my mother and me.

Instead, my father filled my childhood with charm and wonderment. He was the one who gave me peppermint candies when I went to visit him in his office. I watered his plants and helped the receptionist, Carol, file records. I always loved how the colored tabs matched up: whole sections of blue and green and red. I glued tongue depressors together into log cabins; I stole cotton balls and cotton swabs with the long wooden handles and kept them hidden in my underwear drawer at home. I liked feeling decadent when I cleaned my ears with the overlong Q-Tips, those stolen treasures from my father's office.

I thought him a knight. He treated my mother with grace—opening doors, pulling out chairs, buying her flowers on all the appropriate occasions. They had met while in graduate school. I am not so sure why my father chose to marry my mother. Certainly she was beautiful, bright, and glowing, like a gem. But I would have thought my father a more careful man than to marry for mere appearance. Perhaps he found her aloofness alluring; perhaps he thought he could warm her heart with his. Perhaps she was simply his weakness. I suppose that fathers, however good we think them to be, make mistakes.

My mother probably married my father because he was one of the very few Chinese students she knew and because he was soft. Like water, he slid around all her sharp edges. He would never hold her back, never interfere. In return, she played the part of the perfect doctor's wife at all the requisite clinic functions.

· · ·

As CHILDREN, MY sister and I would sit on the bed and watch her dress for these affairs—her lovely silk dresses that hung just so, the pearl stud earrings with the tiny diamonds, and just the right amount of scent dabbed at her wrists and neck. We would take turns brushing her hair. But Maura always got to go first to unloosen the tangles. I was not good with tangles and made my mother grimace in pain.

"*Aiya!* Maggie!" she would scold, using my given name. "Watch what you're doing! *Bei* Maura go first, la." Let Maura go first.

And so I would watch while Maura took the brush and worked through the lower reaches of our mother's hair, which fell past her shoulders one length of a child's hand. Maura would brush and brush, going up higher toward our mother's crown each time. When at last the hair fell in a smooth, black curtain, Maura would hand the brush to me, and I would draw the brush through the inky thickness with great satisfaction. But my mother would not sit still long for this extraneous grooming; once the business of disentanglement was taken care of, she was eager to move on.

"That's enough," she would say crisply, holding a hand out for the brush. I always was reluctant to relinquish the brush and would take a few more, furtive sweeps through her hair.

"Come on," my mother would say, waving her upturned fingers at me. "That's enough."

Slowly I would place the brush in her palm. She would pull the stray hairs from the brush and place it on her dressing table. My mother is the only person I have known to have one of those matching silver brush and mirror sets that you see women in movies using. She even had a silver tray on which both were kept. The back of the mirror was carved with the swirl of a mythical bird and its handle was made of pale jade. I loved this mirror and brush; I loved my mother's dressing table, a gleaming piece of rosewood furniture with a large mirror that framed my mother's face like a portrait. There were little drawers on either side that held a splendid assortment of little bottles and powders and brushes. A lacquered jewelry box sat on the left; it was lined in purple velvet and sectioned off in compartments for rings and clips and necklaces. My sister and I were not permitted in my parents' room when they weren't there, so the times we watched my mother dress were secret and wondrous, a glimpse into the mysterious world of womanhood and all its glimmering accompaniments.

Sometimes, after my mother had taken her brush back, I would stay awhile and watch her roll up her hair expertly in a smooth chignon right above her slender neck. She would pin it in place, then reach for a nail file and begin working on her hands. I did not find this as interesting, so I would wander down the hall to watch my father shave in the bathroom mirror or, better yet, follow him into the kitchen to see him iron his shirts.

My father was very meticulous about his shirts and spent a great deal of time pressing the collar and the creases of his sleeves. When he was a boy, he had to help out in Uncle Al-dolphus's laundry. My father had gone to the steamy shop every day after school and ironed men's dress shirts and then boxed them up in cartons. I'm surprised that my father ironed anything at all after all those years of pressing button-downs in a Chinatown store window, but he did not seem to mind it. In fact, he seemed to enjoy ironing his own shirts and pants as a kind of meditation. He would switch on a small tape player plugged in by the ironing board and hum aimlessly along with the high-pitched wailing of a Cantonese opera. I do not know where my father got these tapes; I think there were only two of them in any case. I hated that awful whining sound, that nerve-racking clanging of cym-bals and the gong. I would squish up my face and put my hands over my ears.

"Daaaad," I complained. "Do you have to listen to that music?"

My father would not answer but would merely look up and smile at me.

I'd pace around with my hands clamped onto the sides of my head. My father kept ironing. Finally, worn down, I would have to resign myself to the fact that the music would not stop. So I leaned with my elbows on the kitchen counter with my fingers in my ears, watching my father navigate the steam iron around buttons and up side seams. He was an efficient worker, but he also took his time, occa-sionally humming a few stray, atonal notes or tapping his fingertips on the ironing board in time to the neurotic op-eratic percussion. He would stand there in an old pair of trousers and his undershirt; the iron would hiss when he lifted it up. I watched him, not with the awe and amaze-ment I had when gazing at my mother at her dressing table, but with more of an easy companionship. There was less ceremony in my father's preparation for an evening out, less of a show. He ironed his shirt and pants every evening for the next workday anyway; for a dinner party he simply pressed a different shirt.

My father seldom talked during this domestic routine; hence its meditative quality, I suppose. Actually, he was a man of few words altogether, but he seemed to turn more inward at the ironing board, humming absently to the raucous wailings about invading armies and unrequited love. Finally he would be finished. With the pants and shirt hanging neatly on a hanger, he would unplug the iron and switch off the tape player. Then he would leave to dress.

Later my parents would emerge neatly pressed and beautiful. They would say good-bye and my father would help my mother into the car. Maura and I would watch them drive away, waving at them out of the picture window.

One time, when they were away, I took my father's Cantonese opera cassettes into my room and pulled out all the ribbon until they were in a shiny brown heap at my feet. That, I thought, would put an end to that racket. But then I thought about how sad my father would be (and how furious my mother would turn), so I took a pen and wound the cassettes up again. They seemed no worse for the wear, for the wailing emerged from the tape player as robustly as ever the next day when my father pressed a white shirt and hummed.

. . .

I MUST NOT have learned anything from watching my father iron. I cannot iron to save my life. I don't know, there's just something about the coordination of fabric and board and steam that I cannot seem to master. Somehow, things I have ironed don't necessarily look better; but occasionally I do it just so I can say I have ironed a better dress to go in out or whatever. This is another reason I like sweaters: They are hardly ever wrinkled. When one of my first boyfriends asked me to iron his shirts, I stared at him as if he were mad.

"Don't you know how?" I asked. It never occurred to me that a man could not iron a shirt; after all, my father could do this.

"Well, my mother always did it," my boyfriend said unapologetically. "Here." He flung four shirts from his closet across the room at me, and I caught them. "You can do it, right?" he said. "Isn't it a woman thing?" He did not say this cruelly, but in those days I did not know better, so I ironed the shirts.

"These look like shit," he told me when I gave him the finished shirts, hung on four hangers as I had seen my father do. "Didn't your mother teach you anything?"

No, I wanted to say. She did not.

Instead I looked away.

Even now, years later, there are days that my father still seems unaccounted for. I get the sensation that he is merely missing, that a police officer will come to the door and tell me, "Your father has been found. Everything is all right." And then I would grab my coat and rush out the door, driving crazily to Arizona or Florida or Massachusetts, wherever he has been all this time.

Oh, Daddy, I would say. I've missed you. Where have you been?

For some reason there are times that I half expect him to call; I pick up the telephone absently and suddenly, when I realize his voice is not at the other end, I am disappointed. It's silly, I know. But then I get angry, furious that he will never call, that he is absent from my life.

A fine father you are, I fume in my head. Where are you when I need you? You're supposed to be here, checking to make sure I'm okay. Well, I'm not okay, what are you going to do about it?

I curse his memory. And then, a moment later, I am sad that I did.

. . .

THESE FEELINGS ARE strongest whenever I go home for one holiday or another and stay in my childhood home. I will round a corner in the hallway and think I sense my father's presence in the next room. But then I will look in there and see nothing but the emptiness of that space, with shafts of dusty light coming through filmy curtains. Or I will wake up suddenly in the morning, thinking I have heard his voice downstairs; but I never know what I thought I heard him saying because everything is quiet except for the ticking of an old Snoopy alarm clock on my bureau.

This is why I say that my mother lives in a house of ghosts.

But I do not think my mother hears anything, senses anything. She is not the type of person who would. Once I asked my sister if she felt anything peculiar when she visited our old house.

"I don't like going back there," my sister said, curling her lips slightly in distaste. "It's so provincial. I can't live anywhere where they don't have a double espresso." Then she laughed at herself and walked away.

So I'm the only one who's afraid of walking into the living room. I'll suddenly think that my father is sitting in his reclining chair, eating an enormous bowl of caramel-pecan-praline ice cream.

"What are you doing here?" I would gasp.

"What?" he would say, lifting the spoon to his mouth. "Where did you think I'd be? Want some ice cream?"

No, I would say. I don't like ice cream anymore.

. . .

DURING THE COURSE of his life my father must have eaten bathtubs full of ice cream. When he still lived in that house with us, my sister and I would ride with him in the car whenever he went to buy it. He drove miles, even in the dead of winter, to a special ice cream parlor in a neighboring town. He would buy two gallons of premier caramel-pecan-praline, chockful of little candy and nut clusters that were so sweet your teeth would hurt just thinking about it. Even Maura and I would not touch it.

Two gallons of caramel-pecan-praline ice cream lasted approximately nine days.

"Want to go to Patti's?" my father would ask us. We seldom turned down the offer to go to the ice cream parlor. When we arrived at the door, the workers would begin packing his ice cream right away while Maura and I clung to the freezer cases and stared at all the different flavors.

"Hello, Dr. Li," the waitress would say. "Glad to see you here on such a cold day." My father would smile and nod.

My father would buy Maura and me treats to eat while we waited, but he wouldn't get anything for himself. He simply would sit with us in a red vinyl booth while my sister and I slurped happily at our desserts. Despite all the time we spent staring into the freezer cases, rolling the names of all the wonderful flavors around on our tongues, my sister and I were creatures of habit: Maura always ordered vanilla in a fluted silver dish and I got a double-chocolate-fudge cone with rainbow sprinkles. By the time we had finished, the waitresses behind the counter would have my father's order ready to go. The women in their pink uniforms and white frilly aprons would smile and hand the brown paper bags to Maura and me, and we would hug the chilly parcels to the car.

"Bye, girls, see you next week," they would call, waving to us. "Don't eat that all at once." They winked at our father.

"It's not for *us*," Maura and I would chime week after week. "We don't *like* praline." We would squish up our faces in utter disgust and run out to the car while our father paid.

I do not know where my father acquired the taste for caramel-praline. He was not known for having a particularly sweet tooth otherwise. In general, foreign-born Chinese do not like things that are too sweet; they simply are not used to it. And, as a whole, Chinese desserts are mediocre at best; in my opinion Europeans win hands down in the confection-ery department. After dinner Chinese might have a piece of fruit, a bowl of sweetened red bean soup, or perhaps a bun with sweetened black-bean-paste filling. But that's about it.

"No, no, too sweet," my father would say, turning down a chocolate bonbon or a piece of carrot cake that was offered to him.

But then, every night before going to bed, we would hear him clattering in the kitchen, getting out an enormous soup bowl from the cupboard and opening the freezer compart-ment. He would scoop out a huge portion of caramel-pecan-praline, then sit down with it in the living room while watching the ten o'clock news. He ate the ice cream very slowly, savoring each creamy spoonful and every crunchy pecan. When at last he had raised the bowl to his lips and drained the remaining ice cream "milk" at the bot-tom, the half-hour news show would be nearly over. He would set the bowl aside, watch the final happy news fea-ture, then switch off the television. We could hear the water tap go on as my father washed his bowl and spoon and set them in the dishrack.

This signaled the end of the day.

My father then would make the rounds of the house, locking the doors and turning off the lights. Usually my mother's light in the study would still be on for another half hour or so. Then she, too, would go to sleep.

My father was a man of simple passions: He liked to eat and he liked to grow things for eating. Unlike many of the other doctors and lawyers and so-called professionals in our community, he did not belong to the Rotary or the country club. He did not play golf or tennis or bridge. His colleagues did a good bit of entertaining, though, and my father dutifully brought my mother to those affairs, where perfectly matched couples would sit out on decks in the summertime, sipping cool drinks and grilling large pieces of meat.

In general, my father preferred the solitude of the garden. After a day of listening to peevish patients, he appreciated the silence of a plant, which did not flinch or whine when it was snipped or tied to a stick to make it grow upright. Much of his spare time during the warmer months was spent out in our backyard, weeding and pruning. My father made a rather silly sight outside because he didn't have any leisure clothes. He simply would put on an old pair of office trousers and tuck in an old white shirt. He would slip on a pair of rubber thongs, roll up his sleeves, and set to work. In the spring my father paid a neighborhood boy to come with his dad's rototiller; in a single afternoon the young man would turn our backyard into an open field. My father would stand at the back door, nodding with approval as the soil was turned over, fresh and ready for his hoe.

"It's good to feel the earth under your feet," my father would say as he hosed off his feet and rubber thongs after working in his garden. "A good feeling, good feeling."

My mother did not like to garden and looked upon my father's activity with thinly veiled disapproval. "Look at him, he looks ridiculous," she would say, shaking her head as she watched him in his old office trousers and shirt squatting between rows of blooming melon vines. "He should wear a hat; he looks like a peasant." My mother did not like to stay out in the sun and always wore a wide-brimmed hat to shield her face whenever she did have to go into the yard. Later I realized it must have been her Shanghai upbringing that made her shy away from the sun so; the northern Chinese women in particular have always been vain about their fair skin, white as pale jade.

"Just make sure that dirt doesn't come into the house," she would tell my father as he cleaned up. "I don't want that dirt on the carpet. Shake out all your clothes." My father never tracked anything in; he kept his gardening clothes hung up neatly in the back hallway. And all his vegetables were freshly washed and shining before he brought them into the house in big plastic tubs. Despite her distaste for gardening, my mother did not complain about the fresh vegetables, which indisputably were better than anything that could be purchased in a store.

We did not have a big yard, but it was amazing what my father could get out of it: bushels of zucchini and yellow squash, enormous tomatoes, bunches of scallions and cilantro. Every year my father would have his cousin in San Francisco send him packets of seeds from Chinatown. By midsummer the garden would be growing thick with Chinese vegetables: wrinkled bitter melons and the pleasantly green summer melon, tight bundles of napa cabbage and sprays of watercress. The delicate vines of snow peas would wend up trellises and the long white radishes would grow thick under the soil.

I do not believe that my father's work at the clinic was one of his great passions, but this did not seem to bother him. He was a general practitioner just when general practitioners were losing esteem; although those in the field kept saying that the good, old-fashioned hometown doctor was a physician of merit, patients kept flocking to specialists hours away, paying vast sums for the availability of shiny, new whiz-bang machines that blipped and beeped and were terribly impressive. There was little glamour in dealing with some strep throat here and a bit of acid indigestion there.

But I think there was a predictability in his work that my father rather liked. There were few traumas and cases of emergency. His hours were fairly regular, all things considered. And in his white lab coat with the stethoscope looped around his neck, he was Dr. Li, GP: He had his place in the world and had done his part to further the notion of the American immigrant dream. What more could he want?

So he was perfectly content to tinker about at home in his off hours, digging in his garden. I often would wander out into the backyard during those summer evenings, watching my father.

"Here, see this?" he would say, showing me a tuft of crabgrass that had sneaked into the garden. "If you see something like this, pull it out. No good, no good. Takes away all the nice food for the vegetable." We spent many hours this way, in close proximity, weeding out stray clover and dandelions and tenacious crabgrass.

"Growing things," he told me, "is good for the heart." He patted his chest. "Not just how it beats—thump-thump, thump-thump, too fast or too slow—but how it feels. This is also important."

In that fading light of summer after the solstice, it was easy for our hearts to feel good. We did not talk much, my father and I, but it was pleasing to be out there together, feeling the earth under our hands and feet. I think that it was there, in that little patch of green, that I truly learned to love that midwestern landscape. My father was happiest when he was in his garden: In my form of logic, if a small plot could bring a person so much joy, then surely a tilled expanse of sixty acres should bring that much more happiness.

Together we watched the plants bud and produce lovely little white flowers or big yellow blossoms. It was sad to see these fade, but in their shriveled wakes would be the tiny, hard beginnings of their fruits. With water and sun these swelled and grew heavy. When we finally picked the melons and tomatoes, they still would be warm with the daylight, and we washed them clean with the garden hose until they gleamed.

"Very nice, very nice," my mother would say when she inspected the brimming tubs. "But here, take this outside," she would say, handing my father a particularly red and ripe tomato, which had a spot in the side. "It has a worm in it."

I would follow my father as he took a small kitchen knife and went outside onto the back step. He would carefully cut out the section with the blemish and toss it in the compost pile. Then he would slice the rest of the tomato. We would sit on the step and eat it together, wedge by wedge.

"You know this is the best tomato," my father would tell me, "because the worm knows. It always picks the best one." He would hand me another wedge on the blade of the knife. As I ate it, I believed there was nothing sweeter in the world; the warm juice filled my mouth and dripped down my chin, so I would have to wipe it away with my hand.

· · ·

MY FATHER ALSO cooked a great deal of what he grew. We had wonderful platters of stir-fried vegetables in the summer, amazing pots of clear summer melon soup, just cooled to pleasant. In the winter my father took to glancing through my mother's *Gourmet* magazines. He tried one recipe, then another. Soon, on the weekends, he was cooking up pots of savory stews from Tuscany and a delicate Greek spinach pie wrapped in layers of phyllo. We ate duck in red wine and fettuccine in heavy cream sauces; he ordered wild mushrooms from a catalog and learned how to make his own sun-dried tomatoes. By the time I was ten, my father did virtually all of the cooking, much of it on the weekend and heated up during the workweek. Ironically, the only time my mother cooked was when we had dinner parties; then my father was made sous chef, and he merely minced and chopped vegetables or boiled rice.

"You're one lucky fellow," the men would tell my father, thumping him on the back. "You eat like this all the time, right?"

"And he's getting fat," my mother would say, frowning oh-so-well in jest. "He likes to eat too much."

But it was true. My father loved food. He loved growing it and preparing it. Eating was only a happy end result of all his work, but he undertook it earnestly, as he did all things.

I loved my father more than anyone, even more than Maura, whom I worshipped. He called me his "little plum" in Mandarin, my mother's dialect. *"Wo xiao Li."* A play on our last name. They are the only words I ever heard him speak in my mother's native tongue; otherwise he always spoke English or Cantonese to us. I especially loved my father because, very simply, he was not my mother; he was my best refuge from what I perceived as her indifference. In my mother's presence I always felt as if something in me was lacking: I was too slow, not bright enough, not pretty enough. I had not been quiet when she was trying to work. I was asking too many questions. I had missed rinsing a bit of dirt from the vegetables. I had tracked in some mud after playing outside. I do not really know anymore if my mother was a harsh person or if I merely felt she was in the absence of any warmth from her. Once, when I was about ten, my mother caught me sketching a trellis that my father had rigged up in the garden for his beans.

"What are you doing?" she asked, appearing silently from nowhere.

I snapped the notebook shut.

"Nothing," I said, twisting the pencil in my hands.

"Come on now," my mother said. "What were you doing? Were you writing something? Let's see."

Finally I opened the notebook. She took it from my hands and leafed through the pages.

"Hmm," she said, looking at the trellis, a picture of a horse, a mountain in the clouds—all of them simple, childish renderings. But I had signed and dated each picture elaborately in the lower-right-hand corner.

"Well, it's a good thing you don't want to be an artist because these need a lot of work," my mother said briskly. "You should concentrate on your math."

She handed the notebook back to me. "Don't you have any homework?" she asked, turning to go back into the house. "Don't you have anything better to do than just sit outside? Why don't you do your homework, like Maura?"

As I watched her go into the house, I felt my heart well up in my throat; I thought it would explode.

But I would not cry. I was not going to cry.

Very calmly, I stood up and collected myself, tried to steady my heaving breaths. I primly held the notebook between my fingertips and walked back to the house. I bit my lips to stop them from shaking.

When I got inside, my mother was in the kitchen making tea. She only glanced at me briefly as I walked past her and up the stairs. I went to my room and shut the door. Then, in a violence that surprised me, I ripped every picture out of the notebook, tearing them out so hard that the wire spiral strained and bent out of shape. I ripped and ripped, with tears streaming down my cheeks. I did not care. I ripped each page out, even the ones that were blank, and then began shredding them, three and four sheets at a time. I accidentally ripped off part of one fingernail and the pain was excruciating, but I did not care. The blood smeared on the pages, but I did not stop. I tore the cardboard covers into little pieces and stretched the spiral out straight. Finally I stopped. I got a garbage can and systematically swept everything in. My fingertip had stopped bleeding, but it was crusted in drying rust-blood and was beginning to swell. I went into the bathroom and washed my hands and face. I got a Band-Aid for my finger, which was beginning to throb.

I did not draw again for many years and then I did it without my mother knowing. I don't know why everything she said affected me so, seemed so devastating. But she had a way of crushing me with her sheer offhandedness.

I had never said that I didn't want to be an artist.

"Oh, look at this!" my father had exclaimed just the week before when I showed him a picture of his tomato plant. "You drew this, ah?" We were sitting in a red vinyl booth at the ice cream parlor. He didn't say anything else, but when the waitress came to give us our bill, he showed her my picture.

"See"—my father pointed—"my daughter drew this."

"Oh, that's very nice!" She beamed. "You have a very smart little girl, Dr. Li! You must be very proud of her."

Maura rolled her eyes and sighed.

My father didn't say anything but smiled and paid the bill. "Come on, girls." He motioned to us and handed the picture back to me. "Time to go."

My father had a reliability about him that I loved dearly. Everything he did was measured and predictable. When he got up in the morning, the first thing he did was pad down to the kitchen and make coffee. He ended each dinner by saying, "Ah, excellent, very good, very good," regardless of who cooked it. Every night he ate his caramel-pecan-praline ice cream. Every spring he planted his garden, and each autumn he cleaned and put away his tools. There was an evenness to his pace and a steadiness to his manner that never seemed to change. He never raised his voice or lost his temper; he was never curt. Year after year everything was the same. He was my father, and life with him had a pleasing rhythm, a comforting pattern. My childhood with him was like a favorite bedtime story that was read and read again and never grew tiresome.

. . .

EVERY YEAR DURING the Mid-Autumn Festival my father would insist that we all sit down and eat a single moon cake together. That was one old Chinese custom that was very important to him, and the Chinese are big on food metaphors. The moon cake symbolized wholeness and roundness and completeness. The family. China. The universe.

"We must share a moon cake," my father said every year. "It's very important." I remember the Mid-Autumn Festival of my eleventh year very clearly. I can see the four of us sitting around the coffee table in the living room. My sister and I were sitting on either side of my father on the sofa; my mother was seated in her wingback chair. Maura was fidgety; I could see her with her legs crossed, watching her foot as she bounced it up and down. She was fifteen. She had better things to do than sit around eating a moon cake with her family.

I remember my eyes turning to my father as he took one moon cake from the box and unwrapped the cellophane very carefully. He set the cake on a plate that had a doily on it. Then he took a clean, sharp knife and cut the moon cake in quarters.

We watched.

I held my breath in rapt attention as he made two precise cuts perpendicular to each other through the center.

My father passed the plate around: first, to me, the youngest. Then Maura and my mother. My father took the one that was left. I stared at my piece. It was so precise, such a perfect quarter. There was a dragon imprinted on the top of this moon cake; I had chosen the slice with the head, and the dragon's eyes peered out crookedly and ferociously at me. I used to think that it was a good thing that we didn't have more people in our family because then we each would have to have a smaller piece. What if we had had five children, like the Chens, who ran the Chinese laundry in the next town? I tried to figure out how one could slice a moon cake into seven slices equitably.

My father raised his slice of moon cake like a champagne glass.

"To happiness," he said, smiling. "To family."

Then he took a bite. We followed, chewing silently. The black-bean paste was heavy and thick, sweet but not too sweet.

We swallowed. We took our last morsels, put them into our mouths, ate silently.

There was a long, silent pause. Out of the corner of my eye I could see Maura's foot moving, tapping to her own urgent, internal rhythm.

"I have to do my homework," she said finally, staring at her paper napkin. Her foot stopped. "Can I go now?"

"Yes," my mother answered without hesitation, without glancing at my father. "I have some exams to grade myself." She got up and dusted some nonexistent crumbs from her lap. "Thank you," she said to my father. "That was very good."

Maura nearly ran to her room, and my mother followed her down the hall to her own study in the spare bedroom.

My father sat there looking at the empty plate. There was a grease spot on the doily where the moon cake had been.

"Well, since it's just you and me, how about another piece?" My father winked conspiratorially, unwrapping another moon cake. I grinned and nodded, asking if I could do the honors. He smiled and handed me the knife.

At that moment I loved him almost more than I ever had before—completely and innocently, with the unblemished adoration of a youngest daughter who was the apple of her father's eye, his little plum, his little bit of heart.

And then he died. All of a sudden, two weeks later. He collapsed of a massive heart attack after seeing a patient. (Ever courteous, it makes sense that he would die after all his patients were gone; no need to keep anyone waiting that afternoon.)

It was a Thursday. He had had breakfast with us girls. Oatmeal. Hot coffee that he brewed himself every morning.

"How are my *dim sum* this morning?" he asked cheerily. How are my little hearts, my little dumplings? He had scooped the oatmeal from a small pot on the stove and into his bowl with a flourish. Sprinkled a small handful of raisins on top. Poured in a touch of milk, just the right amount. He snapped open the paper napkin as if it was made of linen and laid it in his lap, then picked up the oatmeal bowl and inhaled deeply.

"Hmmm . . . smell that home-cooked breakfast!" He winked at me.

"Euuuw! Dad! Oatmeal is just so gross!" I wrinkled my nose in utter distaste.

"Want some?" Dad said, offering the bowl to Maura.

"I'll pass," she answered, sipping some orange juice. We always had to buy two kinds of orange juice because Maura did not like the kind with pulp.

"You girls don't know what you're missing!" our father proclaimed, heartily digging a spoon into the bowl. He picked up the paper and scanned the front page.

My mother was not at home. She was somewhere in Germany on an international biochemistry conference. She seldom ate with us, anyway, as she left very early for the university after only drinking tea.

"Come on, Maya, the bus just turned," Maura said, taking

her cereal bowl to the sink. By watching for the distant bus out our kitchen window, we knew we had two minutes to get out the door before it made it to our end of the street.

We ran water into our bowls, hurriedly ran toothbrushes around inside our mouths, and grabbed our bags.

"Bye, Dad." We kissed him quickly. Peck, peck. "Bye, Daddy." My sister and I bolted out the door.

"Bye, girls," my father called after us, not looking up from the paper.

The clinic called our next-door neighbors with the news that our father was dead. When the Baxters came over, I was watching TV in the living room. A *Brady Bunch* rerun, the one when Greg decided he wanted to be hip and started calling his parents by their first names. Maura was in her room, doing her homework; the Baxters made me go get her, then made us sit on the couch.

We're sorry. Something's happened.

Your father is dead.

The words fell on my head like the foam bricks that are used in movies. They look like real bricks, but they do not hurt. *Pupf, pupf-pupf, pupf.* We're sorry. Your father is dead.

Maura was saying something. She was crying.

I stared at the coffee table, the table where the moon cakes had been just two weeks before. One was still in the refrigerator, in the tin box, with its cellophane still intact. It was still whole, uneaten.

The Baxters told us to pack overnight bags. Maura was weeping. I went into my room, looked around. I forgot why I was there, so I just sat on the bed. After a while Maura came in, said something. Then angrily she was getting out my duffel bag from the closet and throwing things into it. She began to yell at me, but for some reason I could not hear her. She took our bags, pulled me roughly by the arm because I would not get up off the bed.

Mrs. Baxter appeared, saying something soft; her words were like water, flowing down my face. She took a tissue from a box on my dresser and wiped my face; and then I realized that it was not her words that were wetting me. Mrs. Baxter took my arm, made me stand, led me down the staircase, one step at a time. I could not seem to remember to take another step after finishing the one I was on.

The Baxters took us home and spent the better part of the night phoning Europe, trying to find my mother, who was not where her itinerary said she'd be. They tried to feed us soup from a can, but we would not eat it. I was mesmerized by the tube of saltine crackers on the table. I kept taking them, pushing the side of the wax-paper wrapping and popping the crackers out, as if I were playing a kind of tiddly winks. I took each cracker and broke it up, folding it in half and then in half again until it was nothing more than crumbs, which I let drop into the bowl of tomato soup. Soon the bowl was a sodden mass of cracker crumbs; it looked like red cement. Maura took the bowl away from me, pulled the tube of crackers from my hands. I looked up at her, surprised.

Later Maura and I sat on the stairs in the dark hallway, holding hands like we had when we were little, listening to Mr. Baxter dial one number after another. There were so many digits; our mother must have been very far away. They finally found her in a small bed-and-breakfast in Salzburg; she had gone there on an unscheduled excursion.

. . .

"I HAD TO come home so quickly I didn't even get to see Mozart's house!" our mother said breathlessly when she got back, as if that was the greater tragedy than having to prepare for my father's funeral. I simply gaped at her.

The next weeks were a slow blue blur of hushed telephone calls and endless, well-meant but horrible macaroni casseroles with cut-up hot dogs in them. The house was filled with guests, plants, and funereal floral arrangements; for months afterward I thought I smelled flowers in the living room and wanted to throw up. My mother made the perfect widow: pale and drawn and lovely, she remained strong for everyone to see.

"Yes, yes," she whispered to everyone. "It's such a shock. The girls . . . I don't know what I'm going to do. . . . But of course I'll return to the university as soon as I can. . . . My responsibilities . . . The work will be good for me."

The night before the funeral I found my mother in the living room drinking a cup of hot tea with honey and rubbing her temples.

"This charade," she said evenly (there was no whispering in the house without guests present), "is exhausting me."

I stood there gripping the edge of a chair; the thick smell of flowers was making me dizzy. Maura pried my hands away and took me into the kitchen, where she made us iron the navy dresses we would wear to the funeral. We did not speak. I turned on the tape player and a woman's voice began wailing a plaintive tune. Tears began running down my face, but I did not wipe them away. I ignored the drops as if this stream was somehow separate from me. The water dripped off my chin and fell onto the blue cotton and the white sailor collar; the iron hissed when it hit the moisture, making a sharp noise like a surprised intake of breath. Finally Maura took a tissue and wiped off my face as if I was unable to do this myself. Then she hit a button on the tape player and the mournful tune stopped in midnote.

The silence was jolting.

I stared at Maura blankly.

She quickly looked away and busied herself with a lint brush. "I don't want to listen to that horrible opera," she said, brushing her sleeves. "I don't know how he could stand it."

I dried a tear that had fallen onto my navy sash, steaming it out with the iron.

"Well," I whispered, "I never minded it."

The funeral itself was a strange, solemn affair. A minister who did not know my father at all led a simple and bland service that consciously avoided making faux pas of any kind, almost to the point of excluding our names lest he mispronounce something. The gleaming metal casket my mother had chosen was closed, so it was as though it really wasn't a funeral for my father at all because nothing about that afternoon resembled or evoked him.

My mother, however, looked ethereal in black.

For all their good intentions our family acquaintances seemed to forget me after the funeral. I made it easy for them. I simply sat in my room with the door shut, sorting and resorting some little treasures I kept in an old moon-cake tin. Then I lay on the bed and stared at the ceiling for hours. I never knew what happened to the moon-cake tin that had been in the refrigerator after my father died. One day I noticed that it wasn't there.

. . .

A FEW WEEKS after the funeral I went out into the garden. The last of that summer's tomatoes were dropping off the vine, so swollen with ripeness that they exploded upon impact with the soil. Flies buzzed around. Bees. The last of the season's squashes and melons had grown obscenely huge; no one had remembered to pick them. There were zucchini more than a foot long and nearly as fat as those tubes of baloney in the deli department. The cantaloupes had caved in or split open and their soft, peach-colored flesh was exposed; ants streamed around the rotting fruit. Suddenly the entire garden seemed to be convulsing. The buzz of insects in the air was deafening, and I swatted the little fruit flies away from my face. The potent, sickly sweetness of decay made my stomach turn. I heaved, wanted to vomit. I ran from the garden, ran from the plants that suddenly had grown huge and prehistoric, their long tendrils seeming to grab at my ankles as I fled.

Later, as autumn turned cold, the garden froze in place, the vegetables becoming like stones. When the next spring came, my mother hired the neighborhood boy to clean out the garden and rototill everything under. She made him plant grass. And every two weeks thereafter a man came in a big truck and sprayed fertilizer all over the yard. Then the neighborhood boy would come back with his dad's lawn-mower and cut it. Everyone told my mother that our lawn looked lovely, but I did not like it.

In the months after the funeral I felt like I was going mad. Didn't anybody but me notice that my father was gone? Didn't they know he was missing? Didn't they even care? What was their problem? It was too neat, the seams too tidy: My mother and sister seemed quiet, but unscathed by death. My mother seemed tired but was more gentle with us than she had been before. She was very polite.

"Thank you for washing the dishes," she would say. "Could you please vacuum the living room?" She stopped asking me about my homework all the time.

My sister turned sixteen, and Mr. Baxter came over to take her out in my father's car so she could practice driving.

We never spoke of my father. It was bizarre, because we all operated as though it always had been just the three of us. I was afraid to say anything; our lives seemed so precarious that I did not want to disturb it.

But one weekend, when my sister and I went to stay overnight with friends "just to get them out and away from everything," my mother cleaned out my father's closets and stripped the house of his presence. His toothbrush and shaving kit—vanished from the bathroom. The Cantonese opera tapes—gone from the kitchen. His coats disappeared from the hall closet. The coaster he kept on the end table by an easy chair was taken away.

It was almost as though he had never lived there. My mother went back to work, business as usual. My sister, four years my senior, was already busy studying college catalogs. I turned twelve. My mother bought me a sweater. My sister made me a Boston cream pie.

The days crawled by.

So I went to my room and counted the trinkets in the moon-cake tin and hid the whole thing under the bed. I sat. I stared at the ceiling. Then I took the box out and counted everything again. I started drawing again in my room, with only a red grease pencil that had a string near its tip; pull the string and a curl of paper could be peeled away, revealing more of the waxy tip. I drew pictures of the globe, with scarlet continents and burning seas. Again and again I drew the world map, with lopsided Europes and Africas that looked like plump, upside-down capital *L*'s. I drew a tree outside, rendered it flaming. In my sister's English literature book, left open on the dining room table, I had read a poem about a scarlet ibis (whatever that was), and then I began to draw birds, another and another with fantastic plumage. Ornate and elaborate birds danced across the pages, dragging their feathers through the scarlet air. But after finishing each picture and signing it carefully, I tore every one of them up, shredded it in the wastepaper basket, hiding the pieces in a paper bag that I kept in there for just this purpose.

Then, after a while, I would get out the moon-cake tin again from under my bed and stare into it. Looked at the things inside, feeling each one.

I counted them, took inventory. This was comforting because the contents were always the same. For hours I would stare into the moon-cake tin, and in doing so could imagine that nothing had changed: My father was not dead; I really was not so alone, so afraid.

So in my room I whispered over and over; I counted out loud, but so that no one could hear but me. I liked the sound of my voice, which soothed and calmed.

One, two, three . . .

A red plastic gumball-machine ring imprinted with "Pistons," a scratched mirror with a plastic lime-green handle, four bottle caps and their peel-off liners that you could save up for valuable prizes in a sweepstakes that expired years ago.

Three, four, five . . .

A copy of daily devotions with a picture of yellow tulips on the cover that had been distributed on a street corner. A plastic shell. A pretty rock. A bottle of gold-sparkle nail polish.

One, two . . .

One, two, buckle my shoe. Three, four, shut the door. Who was the old woman who lived in the shoe?

Four, five . . .

A ring is round, it has no end. Catch the brass ring. What nice tulips on the cover of the daily devotions. March 26. Read: "Joshua 1:1–9. This Book of the Law shall not depart from your mouth, but you shall meditate in it day and night."

Two, three, four . . .

A ring, a mirror, four bottle caps, a book of daily devotions. All work and no play makes Jack a dull boy.

I sorted and resorted. Count two, three, four. Four times four is sixteen; sixteen and sixteen is thirty-two. Inchworm, inchworm, measuring the marigolds . . .

I hid all these things away, hid them in the moon-cake tin under my bed. I did not tell anybody what I had. Those days were filled with a strange darkness. I felt whiny and clingy but dared not ask my mother or sister for sympathy. I felt as though I walked about in a daze, wide-eyed and perpetually stunned. I did not want to sleep at night because I was afraid that if I did, I might never wake up again.

. . .

AND THEN I began to have nightmares.

I had visions of giant, ugly snakes writhing and spitting in our dining room. I saw them opening up the glass doors of the china cabinet, pushing out things that we never had—huge vases as big as fish tanks, one after the other, rolled on the carpet. The snakes, smooth and black and cool, circled the porcelain vases and crushed them in their grips. As the splintered glass pierced the snakes' cool skins and gutted them, they screamed, their mouths gaping open in agony, but no sound came out.

Then all was still.

The room was filled with a dreadful stench, thick like rotting fruit. Shards of the vases were impaled in the snakes' soft underbellies; and their eyes—enormous, bloated, and fearsome—seemed to cast spells in death.

For months I suddenly would wake up in the middle of the night, my eyes wide open. I pinched them shut again, afraid to see if the snakes might be slithering up the stairs and into my room. I squeezed them tighter, but I thought I could hear their smooth bodies gliding across the carpet and around the foot of the bed. I started barricading myself in bed with stuffed animals again, just to be safe. At twelve I thought I was a bit old to be doing that kind of thing, but I couldn't help myself.

I started developing an elaborate routine every night before bed: I checked the closet and all my dresser drawers for anything suspicious. I found a hammer in a kitchen drawer and carried it with me during these inspections in case I had to defend myself against anything that sprang out and attacked me. I would touch my bedroom door once for good luck, then two and three times. I patted a porcelain owl on my dresser, flipped the light switch three times, and waved my flashlight in a counterclockwise circle around the room. Then finally I would hit the light off and bound through the darkness into bed in two leaps. I would lay there, quivering under the sheets, afraid and grateful for sleep. Sometimes the snakes would come. But sometimes not. I could never be sure what caused them.

I do not think my mother and sister knew of my bedtime exorcisms; I would have been horrified if they did. They would have thought it silly and just a lot of nonsense.

One day I put the moon-cake tin under my bed and went outside to play on our new lawn. I don't know why, but I never took out the tin again. And after a while I stopped having dreams.

When you are a child, you never think that your parents will die. They can do anything and everything that you as a child cannot: drive a car, use the stove without supervision, reach the top shelf in the medicine cabinet. They have money in their wallets, can make telephone calls that cost long-distance rates, and see movies accompanied by only each other. At amusement parks they never are too short to go on the rides. They can do anything, fix anything. Parents are invincible. And they will never die.

But the year I turned eleven, I lost the innocence that lets us believe in immortality. My father had been fearless, and still he had died. Who knew what else could happen? I had tried to be good: I had never played near water, and still someone had died. Did that mean I still was to blame? Maybe I should not have read in bed so much. Maybe if I had been a better girl, he would not have been taken away from me. Maybe I should have been more like Maura, who always made her bed neatly and could part her hair in a straight line. Maybe I shouldn't have stolen those cotton balls from his office, stuffed them into my coat pockets so that it felt like I had hamsters in each hand; at home I had glued those cotton balls onto paper and drawn pictures around them so that the fluffy puffs looked like snow falling. I hadn't even felt guilty when I stole those cotton balls. Maybe if I had just felt *guilty* . . .

When my father died, all the warmth in our house seemed to dissipate. The drafts seemed unstoppable, blowing under doors, coming from air vents. My mother turned the heat up, fed my sister and me hot melon soup and cocoa on winter evenings. But even then I seemed to get chilled easily. I still hate winter; I try to hold the cold at bay with all my sweaters and endless balls of yarn. Now that I am older, I often wonder if it is my body that is really cold or merely my spirit that is chilled.

. . .

I WAS ANGRY at my father for a long time, for bailing out early and leaving me to fend for myself. There are still days when I curse his memory and then am sad that I did. For quite some time I was weird about my mother. There was a time when I did not speak to her for an entire year. I don't know how it started. One week I thought about calling her but didn't want to. A few weeks later it was the same way. She called occasionally, leaving messages on my machine, asking me where I was, but I could not bring myself to answer her. I could give no explanation to my sister.

"I just can't talk to her," I said. "No, I don't hate her or anything; I just can't deal with her, that's all." Then one day my mother called, and I was at home. I picked up the phone, and there she was. We talked as if nothing had happened. Chitchat, hi, how are you. Are you coming home for Christmas. That sort of thing.

Suddenly, everything was back to normal, whatever that really means between my mother and me.

· · ·

IN MANY WAYS I understand that my sister and I were blessed with good parents. My mother gave us impeccable taste and an eye for beauty and balance in all forms. She taught us propriety and the art of diplomacy. She gave us restraint, but I was not as apt a pupil as my sister. My mother taught us respect for exactness; in her mathematical world all was precise and orderly. Everything had a reason and was logical.

My father taught us how to laugh, to delight in a bit of mischief and to appreciate the joy of a wink. He showed us how to love the world of growing things, and in this I was a better student than my sister. He taught us patience and endurance of all kinds. He showed us strength in acceptance and that pacifism could be wise.

But we also learned other things.

Our mother taught us coldness. And our father, abandonment; I never have been able to trust quite as fully again.

My family is not a ruined one. We have had to endure an occasional but not endless stream of emotional and financial crises. By all accounts we were a solid family, a realization of the immigrant dream. To any of our relatives in China (had we kept up with them), our pathways were indeed paved with gold. The gods were smiling. We were a family without sons, but two girls were a "small happiness." And happiness, however meager, was better than sadness in America the beautiful. My sister and I were safe: We would not be smothered or drowned as infant girls; we would not be sold as child brides or slaves as our fates might have deemed in the old country. Instead, we would grow up in the promised land of dreams; we would eat our obvious bitterness only in the form of a wrinkled melon that was its namesake.

For a long time I tried to find in other men the love I

thought I lost when my father died. But that love stopped a long time ago. For years I thought it never would be enough.

But now I know that it is.

It has to be; I have no choice.

PUNCTUATING

THE SILENCE

WE AWAKE IN Inner Mongolia, and I cannot believe the land. It is just past dawn and a faint orange glow is seeping into the darkness on the horizon, where low hills lie. It is not long before the light climbs higher, bleaching the night into morning. I can feel the train rumbling beneath my feet, but it is as though we are standing still: I look outside and the landscape does not seem to change with our forward movement. It is almost as if we are standing still, looking at a painting of flatlands in muted light. The grasslands seem to go on forever, interrupted only by low hills in the distance.

The land is breathtakingly harsh.

My God, I think. There is absolutely nothing out there.

. . .

THE TRAIN PULLS into Hohhot, the capital of Inner Mongolia. We get off to find ourselves in a truly colorless, humorless, and ugly town. After the bustle of Beijing, Hohhot feels like the boonies; we think we have been sent to the Chinese equivalent of Siberia. All the buildings are low and, amazingly, possess even less color than those in Beijing. It is hard to imagine that Hohhot actually is a capital because the town does not look like the center of anything. If someone had told us this place was a truck stop on the Silk Road, we would have believed it. We look around blankly. We stare at one another. Clouds of dust rise up from the roads outside the train station, which is a small and dingy building. Finally a van comes to take us away to a hotel.

But our real purpose is not to tour Hohhot extensively; we will set off into the grasslands tomorrow. Today we check into our hotel and take hot showers after being on the train all night. After a good night's sleep in beds that do not move, we set off for the countryside: In essence, we came here to go camping, Mongolian style.

In the morning we drive three hours along a dusty dirt road to a yurt compound, a cluster of movable felt huts like the ones native nomadic Mongolians live in. I gaze out the window all during our trip in utter disbelief: The scenery is simply more of the same—more flat grasslands, more gentle slopes. For all three hours on the road the landscape does not change. It is not like being out in the desert; rather, it is as if we have landed on another planet where there are no trees, no bushes. There are no signs of people anywhere except the occasional truck that passes us coming from the opposite direction, on its way into Hohhot.

. . .

THE YURT COMPOUND turns out to be fake. It's kind of like the Disneyland of Inner Mongolia. As we stagger off the van, sore from our ride, we are welcomed by girls greeting us in colorful costumes trimmed with fur. I feel rather silly; I half expect these red-cheeked girls to present us with flower leis. We all nod politely, then are led to our very own yurts.

As we walk across the dirt paths to a cluster of the movable felt huts, I suddenly sense how incredibly soundless this landscape is. The silence presses into my ears almost painfully.

Joyce must have been thinking this, too. "I can't believe

how quiet it is," she whispers to me, as if she is afraid of disturbing it.

"I know," I whisper back. "It's not exactly New York, is it?"

The yurts have the diameter of a long Cadillac; poles are knotted together cross-hatch style to form its walls, and pieces of felt as thick as the length of your finger are wrapped around that. The whole structure looks rather like a giant saucepan with a lid, minus the handle.

Joyce and I are shown to a yurt, which we will share with Mrs. Petersen, Mrs. Yamamoto, and Mrs. Edward. We bend over and step through the low door. Inside it is dark but cheerful: Bright red comforters encased in red silk are stacked in bundles around the perimeter. There are two low cabinets, also painted red, and a brown table laid out with glasses and a thermos of hot water.

"Oh, this is positively charming," Mrs. Barclay says. "This is absolutely delightful."

The rest of us join her in scampering around the yurt, opening the cabinets and touching the lovely comforters, which are the heaviest things we ever have felt.

"It's so cozy," Joyce says. "But I wonder how cold it gets at night?"

We are kind of afraid to know.

We join the others in the main building, which is modern but round, to make it look like a yurt. Lunch is a rather festive affair, as three men wearing blue go from table to table, singing some sort of zestful tune. They hold strips of pale blue cloth in their hands and sing a certain refrain over and over again to each of us as they pass around a hornful of deadly 63-proof liquor for us to chug. The stuff is nasty, so strong that it burns your lips even as you raise it to your mouth.

· · ·

TOURIST TRAP OR not, we are beginning to like this kind of camping. When one has never been to Inner Mongolia, even simulated life holds a certain authenticity. Our camel ride in particular is terribly amusing. We are standing out in the middle of nowhere (which is very easy to do in Mongolia) when three young men on horseback show up, leading a camel by its bridle.

"Who wants to take a ride?" Mr. Wong asks cheerily. Not surprisingly, Chad volunteers to be the first. Two of the men hold the camel steady while Chad steps onto a small ladder that has been placed near the animal and hauls himself onto its back rather ungracefully. The camel does not seem overly keen on the whole idea; it bares its enormous yellow teeth and glares around menacingly.

"Steady, sweetheart, steady," Chad says, settling himself into the saddle. "Easy, sweetheart."

The camel, however, is not charmed. It dances around on its feet nervously, tossing its head and spitting. I had heard that camels could spit, but having never seen one I did not really believe it. I am now convinced that some camels have a terribly nasty personality. The young men yell something at the animal in what I presume is Mongolian, and the camel stops prancing around, but it seems no less agitated. Nevertheless, one of the men takes hold of the bridle and leads Chad around in a circle on a short ride.

Meanwhile, some other men and two women arrive in a little wagon pulled by a donkey. Mrs. Petersen and Mrs. Barclay are delighted and eagerly climb aboard for a ride. By this time Chad is dismounting from the irritable camel and Robert is climbing aboard. I get a ride, too; it's just like being on a horse, for the most part, except that you are up higher (that hump, you know), the camel's neck seems very long from up above, and its hooves seem to be enormous.

The men who take us around on rides are beautiful; they do not look Chinese at all, but very Central Asian, with their darker complexions and expansive cheekbones. For our benefit they wear festive native costumes, with light blue pants and white tunics that are belted at the waist with a bit of cloth. They move among the animals easily, riding the ponies gallantly. I like how they smile; with such heart.

I will never be a nomad.

The mornings in Inner Mongolia are unbearably cold, and I am miserable. The nights are even worse, when the warmth from sunlight vanishes into vast, open skies filled with stars; there is never a cloud in those nighttime skies to hold in the heat, so by morning the air is frigid. I wake within my immense bundle of bedclothing and know that as soon as I stick my head out, my teeth will start chattering uncontrollably. My morning bathroom routine is a hellish experience as I huddle over the white porcelain sink in a communal bathroom for both men and women, brushing my teeth and dabbing at my face with icy water. There is no warm water this morning; welcome to China, folks. My hands are red and raw and stinging as I dry them on a shredded tissue from my pocket.

God, what I wouldn't give for a hot shower.

. . .

OUR GROUP HAS taken a short drive to another compound so that we can talk to a Mongol family and ask questions about how they live. They, too, live in the middle of nowhere. There is a main Western-style building, long and rectangular, and there are two round yurts.

We go into a yurt that has no furniture or accouterments of any kind and sit on woven mats on the floor in a circle. We are being served milk tea and dry millet from a bowl. I do not know what milk tea is and do not like it; it tastes strange. The milk is probably unpasteurized. The millet is good, but I am not hungry. A woman, who I guess to be middle-aged, gives the millet to us in a small bowl with a spoon. We pour the round, golden little grains into our dirty palms and stare at them. Then we dump the grains into our mouths as if taking aspirin.

I am not really listening to what the woman is saying. She does not seem to have much to comment on, and there are many lulls in our conversation, when we all sit and listen to the wind. After a while I just listen to that; it seems more interesting, more melodic.

I sit across from a handsome young man in this yurt. He wears a thick coat. He does not speak and stares out the open door; he is bored. His face is handsome and smooth, bronzed by the sun, with a restless energy. He isn't brooding, but I can tell he is a rebel. He slouches, takes a big spoonful of millet, tosses it down his throat like a shot, and stares dully outside.

I sense that he fights against his landscape. The flatness of it. The continuity and seamlessness of his life as it has been lived by so many generations. He is trapped in an eerie land that reaches outward in all directions toward the blue seam of sky at the horizon. There is no privacy in this landscape; you can be seen and heard for miles. Take a walk and everyone knows where you are. Scream, and it is as if the gods can hear you.

This man reminds me of an Amish boy I once met in Ohio. He, too, was beautiful and tanned. He rode a horse bareback into green hills to round up horses and cows. I watched him grip the high-strung horse with his knees as they headed into high pastures, the horse fighting the bit and throwing its head into the air with each step. But I think that boy loved the balking of the horse—or rather he loved the fight to make the animal do what he wished. He finally got the horse into step and together they ran into the hills; they were astonishing to watch in movement, fast and dangerous.

The Amish boy and this Mongolian one are alike in spirit—

wilder and more reckless than their patient landscapes. Landscapes can't really be in a hurry or angry.

This is a world that takes your breath away.

The gentle, green-velvety hills are beautiful because they are endless. The quiet beyond the small chatter of our voices is intense, almost weighty. It hurts the ears. There is no silence like this. You feel as if you are in the center of the universe because everywhere you look, there is simply more of the same: grass that barely reaches the ankles, the occasional humble clump of brilliantly blue irises—small and dainty and barely midcalf.

I love the sound of the ponies as they run across the grasslands, punctuating the silence; I love the tiny dots of scrawny sheep as they skitter across the landscape.

But most of all I love the sound of Mongol voices. The people sing with strong voices despite shy hearts—haunting, eerie tunes that carry across the grasslands. The singing begins in the morning as workers saddle the ponies and goes far into the night, long after the time we silly tourists have huddled into our yurts. We have been told that many of these songs were developed centuries ago when the nomadic people rode their ponies through the vast steppes. In the countryside distance was not measured in miles, but in songs. "Oh, it's not far," they would say. "It's only eight songs." These songs are most often about love, which the Mongols say has three aspects: human love, love of one's horse, and love of the land.

And these facets cannot be separated, they say.

This is a world that has no boundaries because the grasslands go on forever, according to the eye. There is nothing beyond the next mountain except another mountain just like it. This is the center of the universe as the gods have deemed it, so let all be. So sing to your lover across the distance, for time is meaningless. There is only hot and cold, day and night, water and earth and sky. This is all as the universe should be, so there are no questions. Just birth unto death and the song in between.

Already a tour van is driving us back to Hohhot to catch the train; we only stayed out here in the grasslands for one night. We fly down the roads, leaving plumes of dust in our wake. I stare out the window, not speaking to anyone; this landscape still mesmerizes me. I stare and stare at the rolling hills, the low scruff of grass, and am continually enchanted. I wonder, If I were to live here, would I tire of this scenery? Probably, but for these few days I cannot seem to get enough of it. I am pulling its seamlessness, its sheer monotony, into my bones. I want to remember the way that nothing looks. This land and I are well suited to each other; it is low and near the ground. It wants to make itself as unnoticeable as possible in the global terrain.

The van suddenly pulls over. I shake myself out of my window meditation.

"You should have gone before we left," Joyce is saying exasperatedly. "Didn't you hear when Mr. Wong asked us before we left?"

"But I didn't need to then," Marcus is saying.

"It's okay, sport," Robert says, thumping the boy on the shoulder as he climbs out of the van. "I need a pit stop myself."

"But where do we go?" asks Mrs. Barclay, horrified. "There's nothing for miles around."

It's true. There is nothing but the rolling flatlands; there are no trees, not even a shrub.

The driver points down the hill, says something in Mandarin.

"The driver says no one will see you if you just go behind the hill," Jim tells us.

"Well, I guess there's no one to see us, anyway," Dr. Theodore notes.

Mrs. Barclay is not convinced. "This is simply obscene," she says. "This is completely outrageous. I cannot believe this."

"Well, it's something you can tell your grandchildren then, right?" Robert points out with a grin. Mrs. Barclay sets her lips in a thin line and snatches up a tissue that Mrs. Yamamoto has handed to her.

We disperse, men and women to different slopes.

"Men have things so much easier," Mrs. Yamamoto says, hiking her skirt up. "It's just so inconvenient for women."

I drift off down the hill since I have no pressing matters to attend to. I come upon a few clusters of those tiny flatland irises, no higher than a horse's hoof. The flowers are brilliant, a deep indigo blue; I have never seen a color so pure. They are so demure, so modest in the rugged landscape. I brush my hand across the stiff leaves; the petals are soft. I dare not pick one.

I turn and see the others gathering around the van and go up to join them. Mrs. Barclay is apparently still miffed. "All I'm saying is that I think other arrangements should have been made." Everyone ignores her and gets back in the van. "Do you understand my point? It's positively indecent." The driver starts up the engine and we set off again.

· · ·

As we travel along, Jim announces that he thinks our driver should sing us a song. The man is from Hohhot, Jim explains. He knows a lot of the area's folk songs.

The man begins. He has a strong voice; we hear him easily over the rumbling of the tires on the dusty roads. Like most of the songs we have heard, it is a haunting melody. It seems to be a sound that would flow easily down these hills, travel great distances. Every now and then he swallows a note, stops it in its tracks, then continues on, giving the melody texture and a sense of dimension. I do not know if it is a song about love or the losing of it, but it could be. I look out the window, and his voice carries me, takes me with him to the place where a heart was wounded.

. . .

I REMEMBER A voice that broke my heart.

It was a long time ago. I was still very young and too eager for love.

I was in college. I had admired this boy from a distance for quite some time, and then one day I heard him sing. It was totally unexpected.

It wasn't much that did it. I remember how shocked I was, this voice that was so different in song than it was in speech. It was a gentler voice, a more vulnerable one. At that moment I wanted to pull him to me, to hold his head near mine.

I can feel my heart quicken.

I am getting unnerved by all this, by all these thoughts that spring up when I least expect them. I would not have thought that Lance would come to mind here of all places, in the northern grasslands. I stare out the window, gaze at the unrelenting landscape, try to make my mind blank again. But it does not work. My mind begins to drift, lose focus.

And as I look out at the grasslands passing in a blur of speed, I begin to think again of the one whose voice haunts me, follows me like a misplaced spirit.

LANCE

I DON'T THINK Lance would have made such an impression on me if I had not been as vulnerable as I was. He simply caught me at the right time, a moment that had been a long time in the making.

. . .

IT WAS THE beginning of my second year at the university; I was unmoored and seemed fated to become a professional student. In my academic life I resembled a herding animal, grazing absently through a pasture of courses that never would culminate in a filling degree. I wasn't crazy about school, but leaving it was unthinkable. My mother and sister were both too absorbed in their own worlds, I thought, to care that I was becoming bohemian. I had given up my color-coordinated clothes and started wearing a lot of wispy flowered skirts; I even bought a pair of fake Birkenstocks and began absorbing much of my social life from the perimeter of coffee shops. I went by myself to student openings of plays and art shows. On Saturday nights I watched reruns of *I Love Lucy* on my roommate's television and ate Lucky Charms for dinner. Yet my purposelessness, cultivated during high school and well honed so far in college, was beginning to irritate me, like a small itch I couldn't quite place. But I couldn't seem to decide to do anything about it. Apparently, growing up had made me shy.

. . .

MORE THAN ANYTHING, I wanted to be discovered.

I wanted someone to come out of the blue and sweep me away—a talent scout, a gallery owner, a tall, dark, and handsome stranger—any knight in shining armor would do. I wanted to be rescued; I wanted to be saved from my own indecision and pale character. If I am discovered, I told myself, my life will change. Like the ugly duckling who blossoms, I will be transformed into a stunning creature with a beautiful neck and the grace of ease.

So I waited.

A girl down the hall from me who was a vegetarian Buddhist taught me how to knit, saying it would teach me patience. "It's best to keep busy while waiting for Nirvana," she told me. "And besides, sweaters make great Christmas gifts."

I knitted. I dreamed.

And then, it seemed, my luck was about to change. I took that Chinese painting class by accident. And then I met Lance.

The moment I first saw Lance is one that stands out so clearly in my mind. It was just like in the movies, when the camera freezes and out in the middle of the crowd you see the hero in the distance. The soundtrack shifts into something momentous. "This is it, you clod," the music seems to say. "This is the leading man. Got it?" It's the same thing in Wagnerian operas. You know, when the Valkyries keep showing up, those trumpets or whatever start blaring; you know you're in for it now. After sitting for hours through that ring cycle, you've got it down pat.

I just never knew that this sort of thing happened in real life.

There I was, sitting at a desk on the first day of spring semester in my sophomore year. It was Western Civilizations II, whatever that was. I already had started what was to be an elaborate ball-point-pen doodle on the cover of my notebook: a patchwork volcano, fashioned out of a hundred little pieces of cloth, all different, was spewing out movie-theater candy and popcorn—Jujubes and Sno Caps, Junior Mints and Milk Duds, all flying through space. I don't remember much about Western Civilizations (except that Prussia and the Austrian-Hungarian empire seemed to have figured prominently), but I still have that volcano somewhere in my stacks of belongings.

I was waiting for a syllabus that Dr. Rubenstein was handing out. A boy walked past, and without lifting my head from my volcano outline I could see the strap of a white bicycle helmet dangling from long, tanned fingers. This boy had beautiful hands, very muscular ones with strong knuckles. As he walked across the room, my eyes went up those fingers to a thin wrist that was encircled by a caramel-colored leather watchband; I saw the flash of a gold-rimmed face on the timepiece. I looked at the arm, long and tanned, with blond hairs. He was wearing a bulky navy sweater with the sleeves pushed up and it had a hole at the left shoulder. He wore black denim jeans.

His face was gently and beautifully sculpted, with a fine nose and very blue eyes. There was a tumble of blondish curls. Boyish and infinitely appealing he was, totally oblivious to his good looks. I listened for his name during roll call: Lance, a name for heroes, cavalier and fearless. The Valkyries. My God!

But I dared not speak to him. He sat in the next row, way in the back and far too distant to pick up a casual conversation with. An innocent "How about those Browns?" simply wouldn't work—especially because I knew nothing about football and even less about Cleveland. Instead, I suddenly became an apt student of Western Civilizations and arrived early to class, just so I could watch him come in the door, the bicycle helmet slung on his fingertips or held in the crook of his arm. As I waited for him, the volcano blossomed on my notebook cover. The patchwork-quilt pattern took on tremendous detail. Each square of fabric had a minute checked or houndstooth pattern or was covered with little sailboats or tiny primroses. Somewhere in the rendering of my fourth or fifth patch of the day, Lance would walk in, or rather would undulate to his desk. I was enchanted by his longness, the incredible distance from his shoulders to his fingertips, his hips to his high-top sneakers. He always wore sneakers in two different colors: one blue, one red, or one each of green and black. I am not a tall person, and his height fascinated me. Anyone who had to duck coming through doors was one to be revered.

I was utterly smitten.

And completely intimidated. There was no way I could speak to someone this tall who moved that silently. I would have felt that I was disturbing a giraffe. So it seemed that I was destined to admire from afar, transforming my passions to volcanic Gummi Bears flying through space.

After the second week of spring classes our professor invited our whole class to his house for dinner. "Very casual," Dr. Rubenstein told us. "Just so we can relax and get to know each other better." We all went, of course. As students we were always famished, and the thought of a home-cooked meal lured us like plump bait. And I, of course, was lured by bait of a certain character.

Dr. Rubenstein's home was magnificent. It was in the woods, up on a small hill that overlooked a forest that was still covered in early February snow. The breeze was brisk and intoxicating. We all leaned over the railing of his expansive back deck and stood in awe of the house and the view. His was the home we all coveted: wooden floors and paneling, cathedral ceilings, rich carpets and tapestries from the Middle East, earthy and beautiful pottery, baskets filled with potpourri and dried flowers. The house had wooden bookshelves stuffed with books everywhere.

Dr. Rubenstein was comfortably dressed in jeans and a loose, ivory cotton sweater with the sleeves pushed up. It was funny seeing him out of his jacket and tie, but he looked good that way. Younger, almost more himself. His wife, Elise, was a warm and casual woman who had an easy beauty about her. The house exuded her personality, and you could imagine her shopping for herb seedlings at farmers' markets. Were the Rubensteins for real? Everything, including the couple themselves, looked as if it had been clipped out of *Metropolitan Home* magazine.

"Man, this is great." We all ogled. "This is, like, so awesome."

"I'm gonna have a house like this when I graduate."

"Yeah, right. You'll be heading for the unemployment line, my friend."

Elise was gracious and soft-spoken. She and Dr. Rubenstein were affectionate with each other, and they served us spinach salads with sun-dried tomatoes, baskets of heavy and wheaty breads with hummus, a giant vat of vegetarian chili, and plates of brownies. We inhaled everything, then collapsed in their living room and spilled out into the sun room. Elise shooed away people offering to clean up in the kitchen. Something operatic was coming from an amazing stereo system; it made the room seem grand and tranquil all at once.

We students made stupid small talk. Although Dr. Rubenstein was relaxed and friendly, we still felt oddly nerdy and nodded a little too eagerly when he pointed out various varieties of trees we could see from the deck. Outside of class most of us didn't even know one another and we felt goofy in this quasi-party setting. I kept my distance from Lance but was always conscious of his presence as he languidly moved through the house as if it were his, stepping around with one blue high-top sneaker, then one red. I watched as he sank into a large, overstuffed leather armchair; he seemed to overtake it, with limbs sprawling everywhere. He looked like a spider with all his long appendages arching out from a slim and compact center.

Some of us chose books from Dr. Rubenstein's shelves and leafed through them, reading his meticulous notations in the margins.

From his vantage point in the leather chair Lance spotted a guitar case propped up in a corner of the room.

"Oh, that's Elise's," Dr. Rubenstein said.

"Does she play a lot?" Lance asked, pulling the instrument out. It was old and a little scruffed and looked ridiculously small in Lance's long arms. He ran his fingers down the strings, which twanged, grotesquely out of tune. He and Dr. Rubenstein laughed. "Guess she doesn't."

Lance tuned the guitar, then began playing a few chords absently. Dr. Rubenstein turned down the stereo. Without warning Lance's voice rose into a tenor that filled the room and seemed to wind itself tightly around my throat.

Everyone stopped what they were doing and looked up.

Lance's singing voice, so rich and incredibly different from his speaking one, drifted through the wooden and airy room. If a sound could be a color, then his voice was like a shade of amber, languorous like honey. It was a voice that could break hearts. He sang absently to himself, as if no one else was listening. He played two songs I didn't know; someone later said they were Bob Dylan's.

I watched him. I watched his mouth. I stared at his hands moving across the strings. I was transfixed as he held the instrument gently in his arms and made sound come out of it.

I remember neither the words nor the melodies. I simply

remember the sight of him singing and the realization that here it was: This was the man who could save my life.

And in that instant he happened to look up and caught me staring at him. I turned my eyes quickly, mortified that I'd been spotted, and concentrated on the red triangles in the kilim carpet under my feet. But then I looked at him again, sneaking a look out of the corners of my eyes. He grinned slowly, without parting his lips. He was done singing, and the last notes of the guitar were suspended in that house of wood.

The next day, after class, Lance asked me to go for a walk.

I do not remember anything clearly about those first weeks I spent with Lance. All that comes to mind is that my body felt different, all loose and warm. My head did not seem fitted securely on my neck but would droop dreamily to the side as I gazed tenderly at chalkboards and traffic lights. On our first walk Lance took me out on the roof of the science building (I do not know how he knew to do this) and showed me constellations. And then he brought me downstairs and found a key that was hidden underneath a jar of boric acid.

"Come on," he said, opening a steel door. "Come on in."

"Is this okay?" I peered around behind us.

"Never mind," Lance said, taking my hand. "I want to show you something."

I stepped into what was the biology greenhouse and, in spite of myself, gasped. Lush plants hung from the ceiling in pots and lined the metal tables. Whole flats of blooming geraniums and pansies and other flowers I could not even name were lined up on another bench.

"Oh, Lance, it's beautiful!" I told him. "I never knew this was here."

"Most people don't. Look, come on in here." He pushed open another metal door that made a rasping sound. Immediately we were hit in the face with hot and thick air, heavy with moisture. In the dim security light I suddenly found us surrounded by orchids. They were unbelievably beautiful, like delicate birds standing on slim, insubstantial legs. Their petals were purplish and white, and they stood everywhere, like a roomful of modest girls with their heads slightly bowed.

"How did you find this?" I asked breathlessly.

"Oh, I just knew," Lance said absently, walking around the small room. "But pretty cool, huh?"

I was getting really warm in my winter coat. "What are you doing?" I watched in mild horror as he plucked a white orchid shaped like a bow from its stem.

"Here," he said as I watched him stupidly. "Go on, take it."

"Oh, I don't think I should," I said nervously. I was starting to sweat.

"Don't worry about it," he said. "Just take it."

I took the amazing flower and smelled it; there was hardly any scent. Then Lance pushed the door of the orchid room open, and we stepped out into the main room, where it was a little bit cooler. I followed him as he drifted up and down the aisles, looking at all the plants.

Then, in a burst, he leaped up onto the metal tables and began walking down through the middle, where there was a slender path with no pots. He held his arms out for balance and began whistling "Tiptoe Through the Tulips."

"What are you doing?" I laughed.

"Oh, won't you tiptoe through the tulips with me," he sang. "Come on, Maya, come on up." He held his hand out for me, but I refused to climb up. So he just stepped around on the tables by himself, whistling. After a bit he bent down to pull up a few handfuls of impatiens and pansies from the seedling flats.

"For you, my daahling," he said as he presented the bouquet to me with a flourish. "For you, only the best." He smiled rakishly at me. Winked. Then jumped down. I grinned up at him adoringly as he took my hand and led me outside.

. . .

Lance and I spent a great deal of time together. I loved being at close range so I could marvel at those bones; he seemed so dramatically different from me. I thought I seemed so small by comparison, so puny. I had never imagined anyone's legs could be so long. Once, when standing next to his bicycle, I realized that the seat nearly came up to my chest.

. . .

"SO WHO'S YOUR honey?" one of the girls in the dorm asked me one day as we brushed our teeth at the communal bathroom sinks.

I spat out my toothpaste. "Lance. But he's not my boyfriend or anything. We're just friends."

"You expect me to believe that, girl?" Charlene threw her toothbrush in her toiletries bucket and said, "You're going out with something like that, and you're gonna tell me you just sit around and talk about the weather? Give me a break." She pushed open the door and turned to me.

"If you're doing that, girlfriend, then you're stupider than I thought." She started going through the door, then popped her head back for a second and added, "No offense."

She swung the bathroom door shut.

I looked at my reflection in the mirror and wiped some toothpaste from my chin. I liked him a lot, but Lance and I weren't really dating, were we? I thought about this. We never did things that normal people did on dates. We didn't go to movies or hang out, drinking beer. He never came on to me; he was affectionate but in a big-brother sort of way. And even that was inconsistent. I was beginning to find out that Lance could be moody, turning like a sudden change of weather. I was drawn to his beauty, surely; but I suppose there also was something alluring about his mercurial temperament, something amusing about his quirkiness.

. . .

SOMETIMES I VISITED Lance late at night. His room was large and mostly empty, except for his bed, a minirefrigerator, an ancient stereo, a cardboard box with clothes spilling out of it, and books scattered randomly about. He also had a clay pot sitting in one corner with a dead plant still in it.

"Throw it away?" he asked me incredulously when I questioned the presence of this deceased vine. "Why would I want to throw it out? There's nothing wrong with it."

I found Lance's quarters spartan and a little disturbing, as if he wanted to be ready to make a fast getaway. But still I liked being there, away from my dorm and all its institutional, standard-issue furniture. His room was spare and unconventional, like him, and this pleased me. Lance always made me feel as if I was being daring, living on the edge. But on the edge of what I still don't know.

He and I had this bizarre ritual where, in the dark, we would lie opposite each other on his big, rumpled bed with the tops of our heads touching, talking long into the night or singing jingles from commercials we remembered from when we were kids. Then we would get up, turn on the light, and Lance would boil hot dogs on an electric hot plate plugged in next to the stereo.

"For you, my sweet," he would say, handing me a paper plate and leaning close into my face. "For you, my love, only the best." He would linger there for an excruciating moment; I could feel his breath on my cheeks. Then he would pull away suddenly. Sometimes he broke into songs from Broadway musicals or even Christmas carols.

"I have often walked down this street before, but the pavement always stayed beneath my feet before," he would croon in that lovely tenor, holding a paper plate tenderly at his heart. "Are there lilac trees in the heart of town? Can you hear a lark in any other part of town?"

I would giggle, burrowing into his rumpled bed as he broke into bizarre tunes, segueing from one unexpected melody to another with much bravado.

"I'm gonna wash that man right outta my hair, I'm gonna wash that man right outta my hair!" Lance sang, brandishing a plastic knife.

Then holding the mustard jar heroically in the air:

"Bring a torch, Jeanette, Isabella! Bring a torch to the manger now!"

I screamed with delight.

Finally Lance poured cheap red wine into paper cups and we would sit down to our midnight feast. He would read to me from the books strewn about his apartment. In particular, Lance had a fascination with the dictionary and haphazardly would open to a page and begin reading out loud.

" 'Hill myna,' " he would announce, eating half a hot dog in a bite. " 'An Asiatic bird resembling a starling; it has the ability to mimic human speech and is often kept as a pet.'

"Amazing, positively amazing, don't you think, Maya?" he would ask me, chewing energetically. "There are millions of birds out there we don't even know about. All we have around here are goddamned robins and crows. I wonder if anyone in Ohio has ever seen a hill myna." He swallowed the other half of his hot dog and flipped through a couple more pages in the dictionary.

" 'Holy Innocents' Day. December 28, the day commemorating the slaughter of the children by Herod.' Good God, people are mad. Mad out of their minds. Slaughtering children; people are so completely fucked up, it blows my mind."

Then he would jump up suddenly and turn to the hot plate. "Do you want another hot dog?"

Lance was able to eat an amazing number of hot dogs in

one sitting. I would down one or two; he usually would polish off the rest of the package over the course of a couple of hours. I was amazed that he could eat that much and still be a stick; then I realized that his eating habits were as erratic as the rest of him. Lance could go almost two days before remembering that he had not eaten.

After one of these spells Lance took me down the twenty-four-hour grocery store aisles at three in the morning looking for coffee and lime Jell-O. (Lance already had hot dogs in his tiny, ice-encrusted freezer.)

"I just have this craving for Jell-O all of a sudden," Lance said, scrutinizing the perplexing array of little boxes. "Or maybe I should get pistachio pudding." He picked up the box and began reading the instructions. " 'Milk,' " he read. "Do we have milk?"

"Well, if you're going to get pudding, at least get chocolate," I said. I am very particular about pudding.

"Or what about tapioca? I used to really like tapioca when I was a kid. Oh, wait." His face fell. "You have to let this refrigerate forever."

"But you have to let Jell-O sit, too," I told him. I was getting impatient. We had an all-nighter to pull, and I wasn't exactly in the mood to deliberate about the merits of one box dessert over another.

I finally helped him decide on a package of chocolate cake mix that could be microwaved. We could stop off at my dorm and fix it in the kitchen, I said.

"And look," I pointed out, utterly charmed. "It even comes with its own little baking pan."

. . .

NO ONE WOULD have understood those late-night visits. There was no way to explain that a man and a woman had been in bed with the lights out, had given each other back massages while jazz played on the university's classical music station, then had done nothing more than get up and eat hot dogs with gourmet mustard and Fritos while singing P.D.Q. Bach and reading the dictionary. So we never told anyone.

. . .

USUALLY, AROUND 4:30 in the morning, Lance would take me home on his bicycle, which he called Ralph. I rode on the back, sidesaddle, with my arms wrapped around his slender waist, cheek pressed into his warm shoulder and eyes closed to the rush of cold as we sped through the night. It was so exhilarating, so deliriously romantic to be taken home at that early hour, when everyone else was asleep. It felt furtive and on the brink of dangerous.

"Let's ride around some more," I would tell Lance. "I don't want to go home yet; take me for a ride."

And he would pedal down to the railroad tracks at the outskirts of town or to the water tower up on a hill. He always raced downhill, speeding downward, and I was so terrified I could not even scream as we hurtled through the darkness. I clung to his waist. I stared at the stop sign at the bottom of the hill, illuminated by a streetlight. We raced toward the intersection, and I thought we would surely die.

But something in me loved it. I was with Lance, and for whatever reason I trusted him. We sped through the intersection, whizzing past the stop sign. He would coast for a while, then pedal down the residential streets with their modest houses and small front yards. Porch swings hung still. Finally he would drop me off, and I would stand there, next to the bike, reluctant to go inside my dorm.

"Hey, I'll see you," Lance would say, punching me in the arm. "I'll give you a call." When I wouldn't move, he sometimes would shove off and leave me there on the sidewalk. "Go inside," he would call over his shoulder. "It's cold out here."

I would watch him disappear around the corner, and then, finally, I would go inside.

When I woke up around noon after these visits, I turned around instinctively in my bed to reach for Lance and was surprised not to find him there. Yet in that delicious, hazy lull before consciousness, I almost could feel him beside me. I almost could open my eyes and see the curve of his lovely back, move closer and press my nose into his spine. This, I imagined, would wake him. And he would turn, pivot on a hip and wrap me up in his long arms, not even quite aware that he had moved at all. In the reality of those late spring mornings, I instead would reach for the pillow, draw it close to me as I curled into the shape that infants take when still in their mothers' wombs. The pillow was a sad substitute.

. . .

WE NEVER SLEPT together, Lance and I. He thought it best not to, as if it would jinx our friendship. I obsessed about this, wondered if there was something wrong about me. Did he think I was fat? Was it because I was Chinese? Sometimes, when my roommate wasn't at home, I would spend an inordinate amount of time at a small desk mirror, sucking in my cheeks to see what I would look like with cheekbones. I played around with eyeliner, trying to give my eyes some depth. But in the end I gave up. My face, I decided, was like a plate: round and completely two-dimensional. If Lance wanted a girl with cheekbones, it probably wasn't going to be me. I decided I had just better accept our chaste and weirdly erratic relationship.

We took long walks around the campus at dusk. He never took my hand but walked so close that our arms touched.

The first time we walked, he kept inching over until I nearly fell off the edge of the sidewalk. Finally it occurred to me that he just wanted to be close, so I let him touch me. I tried to hold his hand once, but he snatched it away.

"I don't want to get involved," he said, jamming his fists into his jeans.

"This doesn't have to be complicated or anything," I said hopefully. I was so young then, so fresh. I was nineteen.

"It always gets complicated," he told me. "Look, let's just not talk about it, okay?" I could tell Lance was getting uncomfortable because he started walking faster, and I had to skip-walk to keep up with him.

"But it doesn't have to get complicated," I pressed on. His pace was picking up. I felt as if I were a small dog, dodging about at his heels, trying to test its master's patience. "I could be really cool about it, Lance. Nothing intense, you know? I mean, I think it could just be like it is now. Like friends, right? But more, well, you know . . . ?" I nervously tore at a ragged cuticle with my thumb as I hop-skipped sideways, struggling to keep up with this incredibly long and quick enigma.

Lance was lighting a cigarette.

"Since when did you smoke?" I demanded.

"Since I started getting stressed. Look, Maya, drop it. Just drop it." He jammed a crumpled pack of unfiltered Camels and a cheap yellow lighter into his denim jacket, then inhaled violently.

"Okay, fine. Fine," I said, throwing up my arms theatrically.

"Good." He strode on, sucking down smoke. His pace was insane.

"Lance. Lance, will you *slow down*? My God, it's like you're in a marathon or something."

He tempered his stride. "Sorry," he mumbled sullenly. He took one last drag on the cigarette, then threw it on the sidewalk and stepped on it. Then he bent over and picked up the butt and put it in his pocket; Lance did not believe in littering.

We walked on, not speaking, but it was not an uncomfortable silence. We drifted through the campus, which was gray in the early spring light. The grass had not revived from the winter, and it lay wet and dreary, like the sky.

"Did you ever believe in the Easter bunny?" Lance said suddenly.

This question had no preface, gave no clue as to where Lance's mind had been. I was slowly getting used to his migrant thought process, which traveled in its own odd cycles.

"Not really," I answered. I thought a bit. "I mean, why would a rabbit come around bringing candy you could get at Woolworth's? It just didn't compute, you know?"

Lance seemed to consider this. He pulled at his hair, grabbing a fistful in his right hand as if his next thought could be yanked out that way.

"Adults treat children like shit," he erupted suddenly. Where had all this come from? What did this have to do with the Easter bunny? "Why do they tell them that watermelons will grow out the tops of their heads if they swallow the seeds? Why do they make these innocent kids put teeth—*teeth*, for Christ's sake!—under their pillows so some goddamned fairy can come around and give them money in exchange for it? *Money*. Can you believe it? And those poor little bastards buy it. What a sense of values."

He flung his arms out and looked up at the sky, which was darkening. I suddenly realized how cold it was getting.

"Childhood should be outlawed," Lance announced, staggering around as he looked up with his arms outstretched. I looked up, too, but I didn't see anything. What on earth was he doing?

"What about modern science?" Lance went on ranting. "There's got to be a way to simply bypass the maturation process altogether. We can put a fucking man on the fucking moon, yet we still tell small children that some dumb rabbit comes around at Easter and gives them enough sugar to make them hypertensive for life. I swear to God, life makes no sense."

In this pause I thought it prudent to point out, "Neither do you."

He dropped his arms and looked at me quizzically.

"Guess not, huh?" He jammed his fists in his jeans again and started walking, kicking the pavement deliberately with each step of his green high-top, then his black.

"Lance?" I said tentatively. "Do you like me?"

He stared at me. "Of course I like you. Why do you think I spend so much time with you?"

"Well, I don't know, sometimes it seems like you don't."

The silence filled up the darkness between us.

"Lance?"

"Yeah, what?"

"I was wondering if, like, you were seeing any other girls?" I started babbling. "I mean, I know we don't have any agreement or anything, and it's not like you can't, I know, but I was just wondering if you were, you know. Does that make sense?"

"You don't have anything to worry about." He pulled out the crumpled pack of cigarettes and the yellow lighter again.

"But I do, you know? It just seems strange, that's all. I mean, I know we're just buddies and everything, but . . ."

"But what?" He lit a cigarette, cupping the flame with his long fingers.

"I don't know, it just seems weird sometimes, that's all."

"Weird like how? Maya, what do you expect? You hang out with me, you've got to expect a relatively high weird-ness density."

"Yeah, I guess."

Finally I just blurted out, "Do you think I'm pretty?"

"Honey child!" He clasped his hands to his heart and drawled dramatically, "I just think you're the prettiest thing this side of the Great Divide! So don't you go and worry that pretty little head of yours!"

He smiled so charmingly at me, so wonderfully. Lance had snapped back into what I thought was himself, at least for the time being, and I beamed. I threw my arms around his neck. He picked me up and whirled me around a few times, then set me down and waltzed a few steps rather expertly, dragging me along. He took one last drag on his cigarette, threw it on the ground, and stepped on it. Then he picked up the butt and put it in his pocket.

"Come on, my sweet," he said. He hooked my arm into his and went to buy me coffee.

We drank a lot of coffee at the Macadamia Nut Café; I think that entire semester was spent under the influence of caffeine and utter infatuation. The café was at the back of a bookstore that sold volumes of poetry and blank greeting cards with pictures of unicorns on them. I liked the Macadamia Nut. There, I could pretend I was somewhere that seemed chic, like in Carmel or Monterey, which Lance had visited once and loved instantly. There, he said, you could walk to the sea and feel cold mist wetting your face.

I liked to pretend that I was one of the Beautiful People, sitting in a coffee shop dressed in the kind of shabbiness that one had to pay a great deal for—droopy clothes made of natural fibers in depressing colors. I instead settled for fifty-percent cotton mixed with something synthetic. But I always took care to tie my hair back in a floral, crinkled scarf that looked as if it was going to slip out at any moment. This was a very studied casual appearance. I think it had something to do with seeing too many ads in glossy magazines, where women look great reading the newspaper and drinking flavored coffee that you spoon out of a tin. This, I suppose, was shabby bohemian chic.

Lance and I would go through the bookstore, picking up books with interesting spines or with indecipherable titles. I used to stand for a long time looking at the selection of journals with blank pages—the ones that had pretty, soft, padded covers and creamy, lined pages. They always started out with a title page in good stock with "This Book Belongs to————." I would touch the heavy paper with my fingers, inspect the satin ribbon that sometimes was attached for marking pages. Lance bought one of those books for my birthday, but I never used it. In fact, I was terrified of it. It was impossible to write in this journal because it was an already published and bound book, inhibiting and glorious in its emptiness. So I just thanked Lance and put the book on a shelf next to a copy of the Bible, which also was never opened.

After browsing in the bookstore Lance and I would take a table at the café so that he could sit with his back against a wall. He once had a friend from Queens who did this, so he could see if someone was going to knife him. Lance thought this was a good idea. So we would sit in the Macadamia Nut, with Lance against the wall and our hands wrapped around mugs of steaming coffee or hot almond milk.

Lance fit in well at the Macadamia Nut, with his beautiful face and long eyelashes, his limbs tanned from cycling. His blond, curly hair hung pleasingly in his face. He looked like someone in GQ, like those men in linen suits the colors of spices—sage and nutmeg, basil and cardamom. Men with wonderful, chiseled faces who seemed as if they'd been sculpted by particularly vain mothers while their babies still lay in vitro.

In a way it was rather thrilling for me to be there with

Lance. I believed his company made me look more interesting than I really was. Who was I really but a misplaced midwestern Chinese kid whose Spanish was almost better than my Cantonese? My only claim to fame at that time was that I had seventeen pairs of sunglasses, three fat goldfish, and an irrational fear that things would fall off the backs of trucks and hit my car while I was driving on the freeway.

I had never been one of those types to worry about the see-and-be-seen scene. But there at the Macadamia Nut with Lance I could imagine that I was naturally witty, charming, and thin. I felt coy, and sat with my hand artfully placed at my chin. Lance had heard of all the poets whose collections were on the bookshelves. He smiled at all the girls behind the counter and asked them their names. By late spring the girls made us iced cappuccinos with extra whipped cream without being asked. Much later, after Lance was gone, I tried to avoid the Macadamia Nut because the girls there still asked about him.

I did love Lance.

I was very fond of him; he took me to places I had never known before, like the planetarium and the map archives on campus. I learned a sense of daring and acquired an interesting collection of new vocabulary words. And without knowing it he gave me thoughts that I didn't know existed. At the time I thought he was the kind of man I wanted to marry: adventurous, dashing, and handsome, with skin the color of honey. He did outrageous things on the spur of the moment. One time, in the middle of the semester, he cycled to the Atlantic Ocean, spent an afternoon at the beach, then turned around and came back. He was gone for weeks.

"I'm going on a ride," he had told me. "I'll be back in a while." I saw that he wore his backpack and had a sleeping bag strapped to the bike.

"Where are you going?" I had asked. I was standing outside the lobby of the dorm, a few pieces of junk mail in my hand. I remember that I was wearing an indigo Indian-print skirt and strands of beads I had strung myself. The vegetarian Buddhist girl who was teaching me to knit was having an odd influence on me.

"I'm not sure yet, but I have to get out of here for a while."

"But what about classes? What about that paper for Civ?" I couldn't believe he was just up and leaving. I could barely stay home sick without feeling pangs of remorse. I was not a stellar student, but guilt was a driving factor for good behavior throughout my educational career.

"I'll deal with it later," Lance said, shrugging it off. "Look. I have to go. I'll call you when I get back." He mounted the bike and got it going down the street in one swift motion. He seemed distracted. He didn't even look back, and he hadn't even given me a hug. I stood outside the dorm, feeling cheated, and watched him pedal away. He was gone in an instant.

Lance was like that.

Beneath his golden calm there was always an undercurrent of vague sadness. Then suddenly he would explode in a rush of energy or rage; he would just want the world to stop spinning, and sometimes he would disappear for days. Sometimes he left town; other times he just wouldn't call. He needed to be by himself.

His classwork never seemed to suffer from his unexpected excursions. He was very bright; he read a lot on his own—public policy in the Soviet Union, astronomy, Goethe, Carl Jung, everything. Somehow he always managed to show up for exams and take them as offhandedly as if they were Sunday crossword puzzles. And he did fine, sometimes better than me, which was really irritating.

But one time he took me with him when he left. He took me to see the ice melt.

It was late March; I thought Lance was being ridiculous. But he insisted. So he borrowed a friend's beat-up, mustard-colored Fiat, and we drove six hours across Pennsylvania to the Delaware River.

"Can't we just go up to Lake Erie?" I asked dubiously. "Don't they have ice there?"

"No," he insisted. "We have to go to Narrowsburg."

I didn't even know there was a real place called Narrowsburg; it sounded made-up, like something in a children's book. All the way there I tried to imagine what a place named Narrowsburg, New York, would be like. I imagined a Hollywood set, where all the buildings were really just fake storefronts. And when you saw the buildings from the side they almost disappeared altogether because they were so thin. Like those fish in tropical tanks: Look at them in the face and you can see right past them.

I sat with my feet up on the grimy dashboard and ate potato chips while Lance drove. My fingers got all greasy and salty and I had to wipe them off on my jeans. We listened to the radio for a while, but all the tunes were bad. It was a cheap radio to begin with, an ancient one with those black buttons to punch. And the reception was terrible because we kept driving for miles and miles down the Pennsylvania turnpike, which seemed to pass no towns at all. Or at least towns big enough to have radio stations.

Hanging from the rearview mirror was a smiling stuffed zucchini made of cloth with droopy arms and legs. It wore a little baseball cap with an orange letter *W* on it, but Lance didn't know what this vegetable mascot stood for. I played with its little hands and feet for a while but got bored. It's very easy to get bored when driving through Pennsylvania with no radio. And I couldn't take the wheel because the Fiat was a stick shift, and a temperamental one at that.

So I amused myself by trying to peel off the pennies that were corroded and fused to the dashboard. Someone had spilled coffee all over the coins and now they were all but permanently stuck there. I got about half of them off, but by then my fingertips were numb, so I gave up. I just stared out the window at the endless miles of highway and naked trees by the roadside.

. . .

I SUPPOSE THERE is something to be said about going to the places of your childhood. To Lance, the flat fields of northern Ohio seemed to be either a giant suburban shopping center or a big field, vast and overtended, mechanized into submission to grow crops for ultimate human consumption. He grew up in the low, scruffy mountains of southern New York State, where he would sit and watch the Delaware River for hours. During the summer the water was crowded with canoeing tourists, but the rest of the year he had the river to himself. Like everyone who lived along the river, he felt the water belonged to him alone; it was his own private altar, movie theater, and book.

Narrowsburg lies in the folds of the mountains north of the Pocono honeymoon resorts. It's practically a single street in the valley, hugging the river like a water plant. Along the street are a tiny cluster of shallow, dim summer houses. We saw the buildings from a distance as we descended the mountain, and they looked like a litter of pale and slightly ugly stray puppies.

In one of the flat white clapboard houses lived Lance's grandmother, an enormous pink woman with a halo of grayish hair and a worn cotton apron imprinted with giant green daisies. She seemed to have pounds of excess skin on her body, and it drooped with age from her chin and arms, jiggling when she spoke or moved her hands. Her bosom was huge, and even through her peach housedress I could see her thick bra straps digging painfully into her fleshy shoulders.

Everything about her was enormous: her size, her voice, and her eager affection.

"Hello, welcome to Narrowsburg!" she greeted me, swallowing me up in a huge embrace. I felt like I was being crushed by a huge, pink, and warm pillow. In her arms I felt bony.

"Hello." I smiled wanly when she released me. I felt disoriented. "How are you? It's really nice of you to let us stay," I said mechanically, feeling the blood rise back to the surface of my skin after it had been squeezed away.

"Oh, it's nothing!" she pooh-poohed, waving me away with her hand and her wattles of excess flesh. "Now just look at you! Aren't you just the cutest thing?" She held me at arm's length to look at me more carefully and winked at Lance. "I love it when all my grandkids bring their friends." She scrutinized me for a moment longer. "Now, wasn't your cousin Brad dating an Oriental girl?" she asked Lance.

"Grandma, I really don't know," Lance said. "I haven't seen Brad since I was nine."

"I think she was Korean. Are you Korean?" She looked at me earnestly.

"Grandma, please," Lance said, extracting me from his grandmother's grasp and guiding me toward the living room window. "Can we spare Maya the twenty questions?"

"Oh, all right!" His grandmother laughed, waving him away with her hands. The pouches of flesh on her upper arms waved a second longer. "But I do remember her saying she was Korean, now that I think about it." She paused. "That girl had the most beautiful hair. It's just like yours, honey," she marveled.

I laughed nervously.

"Grandma, come on." Lance sighed. "Let's show Maya the water."

. . .

THE RIVER WAS silent—a smooth stretch of white glass poured between a valley of naked trees.

It was beautiful.

The snow had melted some. Outside, Lance and I walked through the snowy slush, not talking very much. It was only two months into our friendship, and we already seldom talked very much—at least about anything substantial. We still sang silly songs, and Lance would read to me out of the dictionary, but that was it. The silences were unnoticeable at first, then grew longer and more frequent. For a long time I told myself not to worry, that we were lucky that we could be together and not have to say anything. It didn't occur to me until much later that it was not that we didn't have to speak, but that we didn't want to.

That evening we ate at the small diner in town, where they served meatloaf and gravy with instant mashed potatoes and coleslaw. To my surprise, it was very good.

We stayed two nights. On Saturday morning Lance helped his grandmother clean the old leaves from the gutters. The down spouts had been clogged since fall.

"Now you didn't have to do that," his grandmother admonished him. "You don't need to be doing chores when you come to visit. So you just sit yourself right down and talk to your grandma." He left the gutters unfinished and followed her inside, where she pulled out the kitchen chair for him and patted the seatback.

Lance had a scattering of aunts and uncles who still lived in the valley around Narrowsburg. He and his own parents had moved away to Cleveland when he was in junior high school.

"Did you know your Aunt Sylvia broke her hip?" his grandmother began, leaning forward confidentially. "She was trying to sweep the snow off her back porch. At her age!" That was the beginning of a long discourse on the ailments of Lance's family. After a while I excused myself and went to read in the living room, bundled up under a mound of pink and brown crocheted quilts made of drugstore yarn, the kind I detest. I picked up a *Reader's Digest* from the end table and tried to read a story about a family trapped in their car during a blizzard but could not. So I just looked out the window at the river, silent and still.

Soon, I slept.

. . .

"I CAN COME back to do them." Lance's voice broke through my sleep-clouded stupor.

"Now, aren't you the sweetest thing," his grandmother said. "George Phillips—he lives next door, you know—he used to do the leaves, but he's not supposed to do anything like that since his triple bypass. And I'm not about to have him keel over in *my* backyard." There was the screech of a chair pushed back. "Well, I'd better wash up and get supper started." I saw her walk slowly and painfully to the bathroom, her swollen ankles unable to bend.

Sunday morning the ice broke. The sound was incredible; there was a sense that the Earth was splitting. Lance and I grabbed our coats and stuffed our feet into shoes. We ran to the old metal bridge, where the townspeople already had gathered. They clung to the railings, looking at the river. There was a dull rushing sound, like a waterfall from far away. The center of the river seemed to split slowly and melt away as the current rushed through and under the narrow passageway. We went and got coffee and eggs at the diner. When we came back, huge chunks of the river had broken and the river was running as if trying to break free from a long and unjust imprisonment.

Huge, prehistoric glaciers flowed downstream like massive, flat ships. The ice piled up in the eddies, pushed up on the riverbanks by oncoming ice.

"Look at that," the people said, pointing downstream. "The water's rising fast."

"The Jamerson house is gonna have ice pushed right up onto their porch," someone predicted. "I told him they was building too close to the water. Who ever heard of putting a house there?"

Later Lance and I walked down to the Jamerson cabin; the mounds of ice had stopped four inches short of their house.

By Sunday night the water was running freely, but darkness fell quickly and we couldn't see much. The river was illuminated by the thin strip of light from a backyard lamp; our whole view of the Delaware was reduced to a two-foot slice of water that cut diagonally toward the opposite shore.

· · ·

"I DON'T KNOW why you have to leave in the dark," Lance's grandmother said. "This is silly. Why don't you wait until morning? What's you kids' hurry?"

"We have to go back to school," Lance told her, bringing our knapsacks into the kitchen.

"Well, I don't know what your rush is." His grandmother sighed. It was nine o'clock and darkness had fallen four hours ago. Lance sat down at the kitchen table and picked up the pepper shaker, then set it down in the exact center of one of the flowers on the plastic tablecloth, then another. I leaned against the doorway.

Lance's grandmother made us liverwurst sandwiches and gave us a thermos of hot coffee. I helped tie the little twist ties on the bags.

"Now, you come back with Lance in November when he comes to do the gutters," his grandmother told me. "You come back and visit."

I told her I would, even though I suspected I would not. We kissed her good-bye and set off. It was 9:40, and even I wasn't sure why we had to leave that late for a six-hour drive back to Ohio.

"It's better to leave the river in the dark," Lance told me as he cranked the engine of the Fiat. "That way you can hear it running, but you can't see it; it's great."

As we drove out of Narrowsburg, we left the windows open even though it was very cold and we listened for the low rush of water. A sliver of the moon was out, and as we climbed higher and higher out of the valley, we could see the inky blackness that was the Delaware. An occasional light shone across the satin river and we could just barely see the ripples, the hurrying little waves as the water ran and ran toward morning.

. . .

LANCE NEVER DID go back to Narrowsburg.

I often think back to that night when we drove out of the valley in the darkness and listened to the river run. I don't know if Lance knew then that he was leaving for good— away from Narrowsburg and away from his life in Ohio. All I knew was that I was in this strange mustard-colored Fiat with the stuffed zucchini hanging from the rearview mirror and that I was freezing to death with the windows down. I didn't question Lance's silence or mine; I didn't question much of anything in those days, and I've learned since then that that is a mistake.

The semester came to an end.

The last months with Lance were strained. He had more of his dark moods, and when we did spend time together, he was distant. We still did our hot dog ritual but were quiet through most of it. We lay on his bed and stared at the ceiling, listening to the radio. Afterward, Lance would go to the hot plate and watch the roiling water a long time before he put the hot dogs in. He didn't sing anymore or read me anything, even out of the dictionary. In general, Lance became oddly silent and still, less prone to his spasms of raging philosophical thought. When I questioned him, he would just shake his head and not say anything. He let me put my arms around him, but I do not know if I was of any comfort, because he simply sat there like a statue, his mind elsewhere. I felt I was embracing a block of limestone. Sometimes I even cried a little when I held him, without him knowing it. I felt terrible, not knowing what to do. In a strange way it was as if I had a sick pet; the poor thing just would look out into space and I had no way of knowing what was wrong.

At the end of the term Lance failed Western Civ because he did not show up for the final. I was jumpy throughout the exam period, expecting and hoping that he would come through the door at any moment, his bicycle helmet hanging from his fingers. But somehow, even as Dr. Rubenstein handed out the pale blue exam books and Lance's seat remained empty, I knew that it was not going to happen.

After the exam I ran over to Lance's place, but no one was home. I asked for him at the Macadamia Nut, but no one had seen him. The next day I stopped by again at his house and found him outside on the porch, cleaning his bicycle. The air was vaporous with kerosene. Ralph looked gutted; the derailleur was a disembodied heap on the wooden floor, pedals and chains and screws heaped about. Lance calmly was swirling ball bearings in a tin can with kerosene. He did not look up when I appeared. The sound of the ball bearings running around and around in the can was hypnotic and almost religious; it sounded as if Lance was performing some sort of technological Buddhist rite.

"What happened?" I asked him. "Where were you for the final?"

"I couldn't make it." He set the can aside and picked up

some other metal part. I think I had heard him say before that it was a sprocket.

"Did you go somewhere?" I pressed him. "Did you ride somewhere?"

"No," he told me blankly, beginning to scrub the sprocket wheel with an old blue toothbrush dipped in kerosene. "I was at home."

The kerosene was starting to go to my head.

"At home? You were at home? Did you oversleep or something?"

"No, I was up," he said, putting the sprocket wheel down on a piece of newspaper. Lance got up, wiped his hands on his jeans, and took out a cigarette. He walked to the edge of the porch, away from the bicycle, and leaned on the low railing. He had started smoking regularly by then, which worried me. I also didn't think it was such a good idea to smoke around the kerosene ("Keep away from open flame" was what gas cans always had on them, right?), but I didn't say anything. He inhaled slowly, then held the smoke a long time in his open mouth, watching the wisps drift out.

"I didn't want to go," he said finally.

"I see." I had nothing more to say, I suppose. By then I had stopped asking him too many logical questions, had stopped trying to get him to an even keel. It seemed he didn't want to be on one.

"Are you going home soon?" I asked, picking at some peeling paint on the railing.

"Yeah, I guess. Pretty soon." He threw his cigarette down on the porch and stepped on it. He left the butt where it was and turned back to the bike. He wiped his hands on his jeans, picked up the blue toothbrush, and began working on another sprocket.

I started down the porch steps. "I'll call you, okay?"

He appeared mesmerized by the movement of the brush

against the metal. "Okay," he said absently. He dipped the toothbrush in the tin of kerosene.

I left him there, not knowing what else to do.

. . .

THE CAMPUS HAD cleared out, leaving it strangely desolate in the budding summer. Something in me ached, seeing the grounds empty and alone. The dorm was nearly empty; all the doors stood open and you could see the gaping hollow rooms. My sister picked me up in her car on her way home from Yale. Later Lance said he had hitched a ride home to Cleveland with the friend with the mustard-colored Fiat.

During the summer we phoned each other a few times, but the conversations seemed awkward and strange. We hung up quickly. Perhaps we needed the night, with the tops of our heads touching, for any remaining sense of ease; the darkness had hidden all kinds of truths. When I went back to school in the fall, Lance wasn't there like he said he'd be and I wept uncontrollably for days.

I never saw him again.

I didn't even try to call his parents' house; I knew that he had gone without a word or a reason, and that I probably would never know what his motives were. His leave-taking left a hollowness that I cannot even begin to describe. He simply was no longer there: I had no pictures, no letters or even a forwarding address. Nothing except the cloth-covered journal that he'd given me for my birthday. I opened the book, and it made me feel sick. For there it was: pages and pages of utterly blank paper, a book with neither secrets nor clues. I pressed the open volume to my face and smelled the glue of the binding, feeling the creamy white pages against my skin.

Once or twice during the following year I walked past the

dumpy little house where Lance had rented his room. I looked up at what used to be his window and wanted to weep at the sight of a plant hanging in a macramé holder. Lance had never had any plants, at least any live ones. There only was that dried-up plant around, with that shriveled stem that once had been a philodendron. It's very hard to kill a philodendron.

. . .

I THOUGHT I had a broken heart.

Like my father, Lance had left without notice, and perhaps that was what made everything worse. I thought I could not bear it. At first Lance became a myth in my mind, greater in memory than he ever had been in reality. I thought he was the funniest person I had ever known, the most intelligent, the most beautiful. I realize now that he never had been a terribly good friend; if I met him today I am not even sure that I would like him very much. He had been moody, erratically playing with my affections. I don't know that he toyed with me on purpose, but the result was the same: I never knew where I stood except that it was too close. He had come into my life at a time when I thought I wanted to be saved by a knight in shining armor. Lance had been a name for heroes, and I had thought he would be the one to sweep me away from myself. He had the spirit of a hero, but he did not have the single-mindedness of one. Nor, I suppose, did he have the courage.

Over time he receded in my memory. Other men occupied my fancy, and Lance no longer was so much the golden boy. I heard through the grapevine that he had moved to California, and I thought this suited him. I imagined him in the sun, riding his bicycle through the mountains. I imagined him silent, looking into the hills.

And then I hardly thought of him at all.

•

But two years ago, out of the blue, a college alumni newsletter was forwarded to me from my old address. I was about to pitch it into the wastebasket but then decided not to be so heartless and leafed through it quickly. It was mostly stuff about fund-raisers, homecoming, a new dean.

And then, there it was.

Just a paragraph in the "In Memorium" column.

Lance, who "had attended" our university, was dead. Contributions could be sent in his name to an AIDS hospice center.

I blinked.

I read it again.

My mind ran, taking quick inventory. Was there something I should have known? Things I should have seen that might have helped in the end? It was silly, of course. I couldn't have prevented anything; it wasn't as if he threw himself off a building or gassed himself in a garage. I have known people who have done these things, or at least known their survivors. Lance did not die by choice.

Oddly, I did not cry.

I went to my bookshelf and took out the padded notebook he had given me years ago; the cover bloomed with orchids. I opened it, fingered the satin ribbon, which was two shades of the purple now; the part between the pages had not faded. The pages themselves were still blank, filled with their crisp nothingness. Now it seemed somehow even more appropriate that Lance had left no trace.

. . .

IN DEATH, LANCE has loomed large again in my mind, has become mythic. He takes a place beside my father as one who was taken too soon from this world. It's strange, but if I had not learned of Lance's death, I believe he would have receded further and further into indistinct memory; he would have remained merely another failed love affair, a boy on whom I had a girlish crush. But now that he is dead, it is as if his ghost keeps his memory alive.

He comes to me in quiet moments. It's as though he steps quietly into the room, his footfalls whispering around the corners. There usually is piano music playing, or saxophone. I used to think Lance would have been very good at the piano with those long fingers of his. He would have been able to make those long reaches across the black and white keys.

But then he had gone to Monterey, to listen to the sea.

So that ended everything. Everything, that is, except for the fact that his soul lingers at the periphery of my sensibilities, as if waiting for some kind of absolution.

A TEMPLE
IN THE MIST

WE ARE ON the train, rumbling through China, and the man in Dr. Theodore's compartment coughed all night. His son breathed loud and raspy, occasionally letting out a yelp or a scream. This morning men got up and cleared their throats from their guts, as if cleansing their inner organs by way of their mouths. Now the muddy Yellow River wends past our windows; a pile of sunflower-seed hulls left from a previous tenant sits on our tiny, dusty table. The window is cracked, letting in crisp but clean air. The curtains look like remnants from a 1949 Woolworth's closet sale.

By some typical fluke of Chinese travel-industry bureaucracy, we find ourselves exiled in the second-class hard-sleeper compartments, lost city kids in the Chinese countryside of the Everyman. It is rather an adventure, and small solace to think that the third-class hard seats are an even rougher way to travel. We sleep six to a compartment with an ancient, nonfunctioning fan, no door or curtain (or, therefore, privacy), a wheezing, cataract-ridden man with a nonstop cough, continual wafts of cheap Chinese cigarettes, and ugly scenery rolling past.

Still, for me there is a sense that this is part of the real China that tourists are so often protected from. We can be such wimps, turning up our noses at the slightest inconvenience that the Third World may present. I would cringe if anyone termed it quaint, because it isn't. It is not a pleasant experience to be surrounded by such rudeness, to have a filthy mop swished by our feet, to see the suspicious-looking thermoses filled with the even more suspicious-looking boiled water. It would be tempting to call it camping out in the Third World, but then you remember that people really live this way.

Gradually, I can see the countryside turn a little bit more lush outside the window. The green passes, more green. Young blades of rice stand in the flooded paddies. Taut bodies are in the fields, brown and sinewy, with broad-rimmed bamboo hats on their heads. Now hills and trees go by, more and more. Dirty children stand by the tracks and watch us pass. Some wave. They wear blue or gray or faded but exuberant reds; their clothes are thin, their feet are bare. A few chickens are in backyards; a scrawny goat is tied to a pole. Smoke rises from outdoor kitchens, billowing out from battered woks. Houses made of stone and thatch are leaning, with missing bricks.

"Oh, look at all that." Mrs. Petersen sighs. "I can't believe they're so poor. I can't believe this poverty. How can they live like that? It's so dirty."

I find myself resenting this statement.

The China that passes outside these windows is real, so real, yet not within my perceptions of reality. It is as if I look at China through a kaleidoscope, with mirrored shapes and twisted colors. A prism of what is real and what is not. Regardless of what I see, I do not think it is my place to say what is good or what is bad, what is clean and what is filth. My sister would hate this experience, I think. To this day she can't even stand pulp in her orange juice; she would have little tolerance for the earthiness that is China.

· · ·

VOICES ARE IN the hallway. Yelling, not in anger, but loud. Chinese are so often loud, no Western manners or sensitivities of what is too loud or not in public places. But then they can be so quiet. Hundreds of them, not a peep.

I turn, look over my shoulder to the open passageway. A woman in a simple, short-sleeved white shirt carries a baby on her left hip down the corridor. She yells something into one of the open compartments down the hall. She vanishes from my sight.

Small ledges and seats unfold from hinges beneath the windows in the passageway. The Chinese men pull them down, play cards, smoke. I see the outlines of their undershirts beneath their shirts, worn and washed thin. They are all lean, their faces carved with little valleys, their eyes narrowed, looking into the sun. They crack sunflower seeds between their teeth and spit out the hulls onto the small tables. They clear their throats and spit out the dry, harsh cigarette smoke and the dust of China. Gusts of wind from the open windows blow the hulls all over the floor; they crunch like broken glass when walked upon.

I have to go to the bathroom. I climb down from the second bunk, down the metal ladder. I feel unsteady on the floor, as if I have no sea legs. I walk down the corridor to the bathroom, trying to peer into the other compartments without being too noticeable. Women and babies are clustered around the small tables. Piles of orange peels lie on the grimy tabletops, along with peanut shells, plastic bags filled with more provisions, thermos bottles of hot water, and tin mugs of tea. Everyone blends together; we look alike, all of us, like passengers to hell.

The bathroom is locked. Someone is in it.

I stare out a window and wait. I stare at the character for woman on the bathroom door sign. It looks like the capital letter *L* that you can make with your thumb and forefinger on your left hand. Make two, one on each hand; the right hand will make a backward *L*. Now bring your hands together, cross the two *L*'s, one on top of the other. That looks like the Chinese word for woman. I stare at this sign some more, look at the picture that means woman as if I have never seen it before. Some people say this word is supposed to look like a picture of a woman kneeling, but I can't see what they see.

The latch clicks open, a woman adjusts her black skirt, looks at me curiously, unsmiling, disappears down the corridor. I go in, lock the door. I find an old tissue in my pocket, drop my shorts, and squat over the porcelain oval on the floor. It's hard to aim when you have to keep your balance and pee all at the same time on a moving train. I toss the tissue into the wire basket next to the toilet; fortunately, the windows are open, so the bathroom doesn't smell.

We're not supposed to go to the bathroom when the train pulls into stations and stops; all the piss and shit drain directly on the tracks and would stink up the stations if everyone did their business then. I rinse my hands in the tiny sink, wipe them dry on my shorts, and go back to our compartment. The men are still playing cards, smoking, and eating sunflower seeds. Chad is playing Chinese chess with one of the men. They sit on the little fold-out stools and do not talk. Each has a hand pressed up against his forehead as he stares intensely at the chessboard, furrowing his brow. They are mirror images of each other from opposite ends of the Earth. I climb up the ladder to my bunk and lie down.

It saddens me to have left the grasslands. I was beginning to think that the Mongolian landscape suited me: all that nothingness, going on for miles. I rather liked that desolation, that reduction of Earth to its most simple elements. Nothing is too outlandish. The curves of the Earth were demure and steady. The sky was huge. The plants were low and near the ground; that was the perfect landscape for those of us with the temperaments of mushrooms. But who am I kidding? If I were to live there, I surely would go mad. The cold alone would make me crazy before the monotony of the landscape seized me. And even now I miss my cats, my knitted afghans. I want a cappuccino with extra milk; New York, even with its myriad ills, has its advantages, most of them related to calories or caffeine.

Our train moves westward, into the depths of China. It is so isolated; it's hard to imagine what cities are like, with throngs of people. Already Beijing exists only in the state of dreams, and Hong Kong, which is the end of our journey, is mere illusion. I am anxious to move on, anxious to continue rushing through this Chinese landscape—to what, I do not know. Perhaps it is the opposite. Perhaps I am rushing through China away from all my guilts.

I am tired and slip into a daytime sleep like a drunkard.

The train expels us into Yinchuan, in the Ningxia Autonomous Region, in the west of China. This is one of the poorest provinces, with biting winters and hot summers. If you were to go much farther west, you would hit Qinghai Province and Tibet, with mountains, deserts, and places where people cannot live. So Yinchuan is like a strange kind of oasis, a huge capital on the brink of nowhere. You can sense its isolation despite all the people; it is not like Inner Mongolia, which simply was like being on the moon or another planet in a way. Here it is as if you have stepped back in time to the late 1940s. There seems to be a kind of innocence here, like the demeanor of a toddler who has not quite grasped the concept of sin or been tempted by its intoxicating lures.

. . .

THAT EVENING I write postcards. I send one of the Summer Palace to my sister, another one of the Forbidden City to my mother. I write on cards that I bought in Beijing. They both pretty much say the same thing:

> Dear Mother/Maura: Hi. Am still in China (in case you couldn't guess). Beijing duck was good. Saw usual suspects (Great Wall, etc., etc.), which were as big as I imagined but more dusty. Rode camel in Inner Mongolia; both were bigger and dustier than I thought. Ha. More later. Love, Maya.

To Renee, I send a postcard of the Great Wall:

> Hi. I was here. Have the cats eaten the plants yet? Bye, Maya.

And then, I don't know why, I begin a letter to Alex. I start in on fine, pink air-letter paper that I also had picked up in Beijing, along with a packet of pale blue air-mail envelopes. These colors are absurd; my letters will look like birth announcements. Without really thinking I start:

Dear Alex,
　　I'm not sure if this letter will get to you in time, but I wanted to say that I will be in Hong Kong at the end of the month. If you're not busy. . .

I tear that up and start again:

Alex,
　　I'm touring China, as you can see. Our trip ends in Hong Kong at the end of the month. I just wanted to let you know that I would like to get in touch with your father in hopes of contacting you. If it's not a good time for you, just tell him. Hope everything is okay.

　　　　　　　　　　　　　　　　　　　　　　　　Maya

I stare at this letter for a while, agonizing over it. Then I fold it quickly and put it in a blue envelope, addressing it to Alex, care of his father. I leave no return address. I stare at the envelope for a while, looking at the letters that form Alex's name, and then on the next line his father's name.

Suddenly, inexplicably, I miss my own father. The sensation wells up from nowhere, a longing for something I cannot even articulate. I lean back in the straight-back chair, which wobbles a little with my movement. I touch the desktop absently, tracing the uneven glaze of varnish with my fingertips. I suddenly feel very far from home. But not the home I have in New York, which after all these years still seems ephemeral. No, instead I feel very far from the home of my childhood, which lay beneath the expanse of a midwestern sky. I feel far from the house surrounded by big trees, far from my father's garden filled with melons and beans and leafy things. I remember so well the sight of his hands moving through the earth, kneading it like dough, breaking up the clods; I remember him cupping a seedling in his palms and gently lowering the modest root ball into the moist soil, letting it go like the end of a prayer. Again I stare at the desk, watching my hand move across the wood. My hands look a little like his, a little bony. Maura has my mother's hands, which are longer, more tapered.

Again I miss him. The feeling rises beneath my ribs, welling like a vapor that grips my flesh a little. I look back at the envelope on the desk, at the letters in Alex's name, his father's name. I read the address. Quietly, Lance enters my mind, too. I do not think of anything specific; his name simply comes to me like an unexpected echo, accompanied by slow sadness. All of these thoughts are a natural progression, as though they were a sequence of numbers that comes up again and again no matter how the data is manipulated. Pi. The speed of light. The force of gravity per second. The men who are no longer in my life. They always come up the same, no matter what I do.

Our stay in Yinchuan turns out to be one of the more pleasant to date, kind of like being in a big small town where the folks are nice and the price is right. We visit the requisite temples, one after the other. The lama temple is an incredible feat of paint-by-numbers gone crazy, with every beam and wall and bit of ceiling covered with intricate patterns and colors. It is quiet in the small compound, and we hear the sound of our feet distinctly on the dusty ground. We are tired, and the afternoon has turned hot. Our van wends its way back through the maze of tiny streets, and our guide happens to mention that we are passing the free market, which the government does not control.

"Can we stop there?" Robert pipes up. "Could we just spend some time there on our own?"

The rest of us agree; we are tired of being herded around. Jim holds a conference with the driver, then lets us off.

"Hello, hello! Forty-five minutes, please. Then we meet here at the bus, okay? Forty-five minutes only. Please do not be late," Jim says as we clamber eagerly off the van like so many eager schoolchildren given an unexpected recess.

We buy bottles of water from a woman pushing an ice cart. Other vendors are selling piles of leather belts, frilly blouses, dwarf cabbages, and poorly made shoes. Other pushcart vendors wander past us, yelling something I don't understand; but then I see little children buying Popsicle-type things. Chad buys one, too, and says it tastes like frozen tasteless Gatorade.

It's nice to have these few moments to ourselves as we drift around, happily unsupervised. Mrs. Barclay wants to buy a woven straw hat; Robert helps interpret and dickers the price down.

"She's saying it's a very good hat to keep the sun out," Robert translates.

"HOW MUCH?" Mrs. Barclay says in English, very slowly and loudly to the woman, as if she might be deaf. "HOW MUCH IS THIS?"

The woman and Robert engage in an animated conversation. The woman is wearing a navy cotton shirt and seems fairly young, perhaps in her thirties, but her teeth are bad, making her look much older. Robert is telling the woman about our tour group and where we have visited so far. Meanwhile Mrs. Barclay tries on different hats for size, looking at herself in a small hand mirror. Finally the woman giggles at Robert and points at Mrs. Barclay.

"What's she saying?" Mrs. Barclay demands, looking up from the mirror. "What is she saying?"

I smile. Because if I understood correctly in my mediocre Mandarin, I think the woman just said that Mrs. Barclay looks like a white chicken with a hat on.

Instead Robert says, "She says it's twenty-five *kuai*."

"Is that a good price?"

"Well, it's only five bucks, but you have to consider this is China. I'll try to get it down." Robert and the woman continue chattering.

"Here, just give her fifteen," Robert says. Mrs. Barclay hands over some battered bills, then checks herself in her hand mirror again as the woman titters to her friends, who have clustered around her to witness the transaction. We have seen no foreigners in Yinchuan since we've been here, so we probably are quite a spectacle. Mrs. Barclay is pleased with her purchase, however, and turns to the women. "Shay shay, shay shay," she thanks them in attempted Chinese. The woman nods and thanks Mrs. Barclay profusely in return.

. . .

OUR FORTY-FIVE minutes is up already, and we all reluctantly get back in the van, laden with bottles of water and bags of peanuts.

From the market we embark on a longer trek, taking a one-and-a-half-hour ride to the Qingtong Gorge, where the Yellow River has been stopped up to use it for hydroelectric power. Our guide calls this a scenic spot, but it's not much of one. The landscape here is in varying shades of brown dirt; the roads, the mountains, almost everything, seem to be yet another earth tone. Then without warning the fields suddenly burst into green rice paddies. It is an unbelievable green, a color that cannot seem to exist naturally in this world of brown. Ningxia Province is known for its elaborate irrigation systems, and this is its fruitful evidence. This is supposed to be one of the most fertile spots in all of China, and it boasts that it produces the best rice in the whole country. The emperor was served rice from only this region, Jim tells us. So if it's food for the emperors, then it's food for the gods.

. . .

BACK IN YINCHUAN in the late afternoon Robert, Joyce, Chad, and I go for a walk through the streets during our break before dinner. The shops are open, and we browse in bookstores, look at expensive suits. It is pleasant in this town. Oddly, we feel at home. People smile at us curiously, as if we are a group of eccentric but harmless neighbors. We find a post office and I buy stamps from a bored clerk. The building is incredibly gray and dingy, with dim fluorescent lighting. I realize the stamps are not gummed; the clerk waves her hand toward a table in the middle of the room, where there are wooden sticks protruding out of jars filled with suspicious, yellowish goo. I smear some of this stuff, which I presume to be paste, on the backs of the stamps and to seal Alex's letter. I walk over to give the cards back to the postal worker. She is reading a magazine and waves her hand toward the outside. We step out and find a metal box nailed to a post. The white paint is peeling off.

"Do you really think they'll pick this up?" I ask as we deposit our postcards. "This thing doesn't look like it's been used for years." We peer inside, but there's nothing in the dark space.

"Oh, well," Joyce says, tapping on the box. "Just knock on wood."

"Oh, that will do a lot of good," Chad points out.

"You're quite right," Joyce says, and raps him above the ear with her knuckles. "That should do the trick." She grins engagingly at Chad, who sneers at her.

The others set off down the street, but I falter there for a moment, staring at the pale blue envelope with Alex's name on it.

"Are you coming?" Robert calls.

"Yeah, in a second." I open the little door of the mailbox again, then look back at the envelope. Finally I let the door fall shut, stuffing the envelope in my bag instead.

We traveled by overnight train from Yinchuan to Lanzhou, which turns out to be a bona fide coal pit. It is truly a dreadful place. We step out from the station and the caustic air rakes our sleepy lungs. Poor Marcus begins coughing instantly and has to eat a throat lozenge. We are taken for a drive up one of the surrounding mountains, and an incredible pall of smog just hangs over the city, so it is impossible to see what the place looks like. The whole atmosphere is stifling and makes me feel irritable and anxious. I can't imagine how people can stand living here. Our purpose was to see what a central Chinese industrial town is like, and a glimpse has been enough. Huge, grotesque smokestacks belch black and gray smoke into the sky. The air is like acid; and we had thought Beijing bad.

"I really do not see the need for us to remain in this hideous city for two days," Mrs. Barclay tersely informs Jim. "These conditions are appalling."

"What about the others?" Jim asks, looking at the rest of us. "What do you want to do?" We nod wanly; we all want to leave.

"Okay, okay, this is against the schedule, but I will call the director in Beijing." We head back to the hotel, and Jim goes to phone his boss. We mill around in the lobby, listlessly reading paperbacks or writing a few postcards. I stare into the glass cases in the gift shop, looking at the cheap souvenirs on display. One section has rather nice jade carvings and porcelain vases, but these things are expensive. Jim returns in a half hour. Amazingly, the Chinese bureaucracy has made an error in our favor: Due to scheduling problems, we were scheduled to leave a day early, anyway.

We take off the next day at the obscene hour of 5 A.M., when admittedly even Lanzhou looks picturesque in the dawn. We see the sun rise over the airport, which we reach in record time because our driver has sped down the dirt road like a maniac, no doubt with the philosophy that if you fly over the bumps, you will feel fewer of them. At the airport we are fed a massive breakfast of scrambled eggs, Chinese sausage, and tureens of rice porridge. For some reason we are ravenous after our early morning journey and eat greedily. After our meal we find out we have a whole hour more to wait before boarding.

"Why did they make us get up so early?" Marcus whines. "We could have slept a whole 'nother hour." The boy wraps his arms together on the table and puts his head down petulantly. Dr. Theodore doesn't say anything but absently strokes his son's back.

The rest of us nod grimly, in a half stupor from lack of sleep and a big breakfast.

. . .

I HOLD MY chipped mug of bad coffee and stare out the window. The light is orange and brilliant. All at once I am exhausted from traveling. It seems we have been on the road for months, but in actuality it only has been a few weeks. I am getting tired of it, of this being constantly on the go with different hotel rooms every night and all my meals in restaurants with Chad and Mrs. Barclay and all the others. I am cranky. I want to drink water straight from the tap. I want a cheeseburger with a large order of fries. I want to knit something. (I didn't bring my knitting because I was afraid people would think I was weird; now I miss it.)

Am I having a good time? I wonder. Am I glad I came?

I'm not sure I can say.

I'm just here, and this morning it's all I can do to hold my head up. I want to crawl into my own bed and sleep. I miss my bed, the broken-in feeling of my thin sheets. I miss my pillow. I miss the favorite, thin pillow of the one I love, but I haven't had access to that pillow for quite some time. I know it is foolish of me to miss it, but I do, anyway.

We fly to Xian in a big plane. It is a wonderful flight (maybe especially so because we are flying away from Lanzhou). It is a journey complete with a proper, expressionless cabin steward who systematically distributes not little packets of airline peanuts but a rather bizarre assortment of taste treats: awful mystery-fruit drink in little boxes ("that not only effects [sic] and strengthens the health but also revitalizes and restores the action of the sinews"), bags of candy that taste like mentholyptus cough drops, and entire boxes of 48-count orange-creme cookies.

"You mean we get the *whole* box for ourselves?" marvels Marcus, who is thoroughly delighted at this prospect. He is even more delighted when Mrs. Yamamoto and Mrs. Barclay give him their boxes.

"Wow, this is so awesome!"

His glee is dampened, however, when his father insists on

counting out four cookies for him and packing the rest in his carry-on bag.

"Being a kid is pretty shitty, isn't it?" decides Chad, who has consumed an entire row of orange-creme cookies and is starting on the second in earnest.

Joyce rolls her eyes and hands her cookies to him. "Here"—she sighs—"take these. They're probably made with animal lard."

As we start to land, huge plumes of cold white steam begin billowing through the air vents. A group of Taiwanese tourists in the front of the plane have completely disappeared in the clouds and swat at the steam with handkerchiefs. Jim keeps assuring us that everything is all right, that it is only the oxygen condensing as we decrease altitude. We begin laughing hysterically. We would have felt as though we were being gassed to death over Shaanxi Province if only we weren't laughing so insanely.

The rest of the plane is full of Japanese tourists who have just made a pilgrimage to the Dunhuang caves in northwest China to see the Buddhist carvings. In their company is a little, stooped, bald nun whom I find utterly enchanting. She is so tiny that she barely is taller than the seatbacks. I want to touch her hands; I want to ask her how her trip was. Those caves are on the Silk Road; the carvings were meant to tell the stories of Buddhism to those who traveled through the area. The nun's face is shriveled, like a blanched raisin. Her mouth folds into her head, as if she is trying to swallow her lips. But her eyes are bright and she looks so happy. I want to talk to her but can't seem to say anything as she passes; I simply look at her and am delighted. I wish I could ask her what her pilgrimage was like. I wish I could ask her if Dunhuang is someplace I should go; if by going there I'll know why I'm here.

. . .

OUR DAYS IN Xian are full. First we take a drive to see the terra-cotta soldiers, which were discovered by a surprised farmer digging a well. I have seen pictures of these figures in *National Geographic*; I have even seen a few of the statues themselves in museums—one or two imposing men in full uniform, standing at attention on a well-lit platform. It is strange to see them here in China, dusted off slightly and standing in the pit where they were buried: whole battalions of soldiers and horses with the earth excavated around them. Huge, cavernous buildings have been constructed around the historic sites; it is as if we are touring airport hangars. The light is bad; we feel as if we are peering into graves, which, really, we are. Our tour guide explains that each of the hundreds of figures is different. The faces, the way each holds his hands or his weapon, and the battle dress of various ranks distinguishes each statue from his mate. We nod in amazement. All this work was commissioned by a single emperor who wanted to exist splendidly in death.

. . .

ON ANOTHER JOURNEY we venture to the Huaqing Hot Springs Palace, a tranquil place at the foot of the mountains. The most beautiful courtesan in China is supposed to have come here to bathe in these waters; the deliciously plump Yang Guifei is legendary and notorious. One of the Tang Dynasty emperors, at the age of sixty, was utterly besotted with this woman, who was one of his son's concubines. Soon her family began to monopolize one of the government ministries, and the whole thing became incredibly sordid and political, with the ensuing eventual decline of the Tang Dynasty. Despite this turbulent history, the palace here is pleasant now. The ponds have a greenish film on top because the water is so still, but the surface is clotted with the thick clusters of lilies in bloom.

. . .

IT IS THE next day, and we climb a hill in a van to the tombs of Empress Wu and Emperor Li; we are told who these people were, but we instantly forget. China's history is long and involved. We stare at these blocks of stone in the sky. A row of horses carved out of rock lines the road, grand monuments to the dead. Hawkers selling local souvenirs rush up to Dr. Theodore. I manage to slip away because I do not look so outrageously foreign. Mrs. Edward and Mrs. Petersen are surrounded by women and children, waving colorful little sewn tiger and dragon ornaments on sticks.

"No, no, thank you," Mrs. Edward tries to say, waving her hands. "Thank you, no." The hawkers desert her and flock to Mrs. Barclay, waving their bunches of sticks in the air at her.

"Hello, hello!" they say in English, trying to catch her attention. "Hello, yes, yes!"

. . .

I EXTRACT MYSELF from the crowd and walk up the dusty road a little way.

When I die, I think, there will be no stone steeds leading my way to heaven; there will not be mythical lions guarding my grave against evil spirits. Instead, there will be nothing at all that has marked my presence on Earth. When the memory of me dies with those who did remember, then, I, too, will have vanished from the land of mortals. I know this because I know virtually nothing of my grandparents and great-grandparents. Their bones seep into the earth and there is nothing left. Their souls—if there really are such things—exist in a way that is unreachable to me.

And when I die, just think: The memories of my father and Lance will be gone, too. Even my guilts will have followed me to the grave. So there will be nothing. It is like a stone that is dropped into the water: the waves pulse out for a while, then all is still. The stone has disappeared, and the water is like glass: smooth and endless, undisturbed. The place where the stone went down cannot be made out. The water keeps all its secrets.

On our third evening in Xian we all go out shopping. The sidewalks around our hotel are thronged with vendors selling hanging hand-scroll paintings. Little shops sell hundreds of "chops," those rectangular blocks of stone that are carved with names in Chinese, a kind of durable rubber stamp.

"Hello, hello, change money?" men ask us on the street. No, we say, shaking our heads. No thank you.

I'm getting tired of standing out all the time, of appearing so obviously Western with my camera and my neon nylon waist pack. I'm tired of people trying to sell me things and of students—however earnest—who stop us on the street and want to practice their English with us.

I want to break away from the crowd; I don't want to wait for Mrs. Barclay, who I know will take too long exclaiming how utterly precious everything is. If I stay with her, she might grab me suddenly and say, "Tell him I want three of those carvings. How much does he want? Forty *yuan*? What is he saying?"

I drift away, saying I want to walk on. Mrs. Barclay looks at me suspiciously.

The sun has disappeared, but it is still very bright outside. I walk up the main avenue, past the vendors with their hand scrolls hung up on sidewalks for blocks.

"Xiao jie, xiao jie!" they call at me, wanting me to stop and buy. "Miss, miss, hello!"

I wave my hand blandly at them. I want to blend in, get lost in the slow, steady flurry of the streets. At intersections I melt in with the crowd, cross these streets as if I have been walking them forever. Bicycles cross in front of us; no one pauses, no one gets run over.

I walk past a group of young men sitting rakishly on benches and leaning up against a brick divider that is the color of sand. They are drinking bottles of orange soda and mugs of tea; they smoke cigarettes. Clouds of smoke billow around them. They are so cool, too cool, these city boys. I suddenly feel self-conscious as I walk past. I know they are watching me, this Chinese woman who is so obviously not Chinese. My cheeks flush in embarrassment.

"Hello! Hello!" they call. These are not the voices of street vendors; even in China I can tell the difference. I keep walking past, not looking at them.

I walk and walk. Why does it take so long to pass these men? Why so many steps before I am safely out of view? I look straight ahead, keep my feet moving.

Finally I am nearly past them all. Two more men. One more.

"Hey, gorgeous!"

There is laughter.

Wait. Did one say what I thought he said? No, impossible. You're thinking too highly of yourself, I say in my head. My face flushes deeper. I keep walking down the sidewalk; my back prickles from their stares. I try to quicken my pace; I don't want to hear what else they might have to say.

I want to be invisible.

. . .

SUDDENLY, I DECIDE to try an experiment. A daring one, at least for me.

I dart into the Chinese department store. I climb the stairs to the third floor, where there is women's clothing. There are four long aisles with glass cases at waist height. Behind the saleswomen rises a wall on which blouses, skirts, and dresses are hung. The aisles themselves are clogged with women struggling to pull clothing over the outfits they already are wearing; there are no dressing rooms. I hate most of the clothes. Too frilly, in stripes and cheap prints. I drift up and down, staring at the clothes.

Finally I choose.

A navy skirt, made of polyester that does not wrinkle or breathe, a light blue poly-cotton blouse with long sleeves, and a simple Peter Pan–type collar edged in lace. Around the corner I find cheap black Chinese shoes, flat with a cloth strap, and a pair of thin cotton socks.

I sneak back to the hotel, clutching my packages as if they are illegal. I pull on the skirt; the elastic waistband creaks as it squeezes past my hips. I button the blouse, put on my new socks and shoes. I take off my watch, snap off my barrette, wipe off my lipstick.

I stare at myself in the mirror, my body clad in these poorly made and slightly scratchy clothes. Do I look Chinese? It's the same me. I wish I were paler, thinner.

Peeking out the door, I dart down the hallway, slip into the elevator and through the marble lobby. I feel the bellhops looking at me. What must they be thinking?

Out on the street I breathe a little easier. I slow down my pace, try to appear impassive. My feet already hurt; the cement sidewalk is hard through the thin soles. But I was not about to wear high heels as so many fashionable young Chinese women do.

I fall into the flow of street traffic. I squint without my sunglasses. Do I look the part? Do I look like I belong here? I hope no one asks me a question or talks to me. I am terrified that someone will make me speak.

I see a bookstore, go in. Inside it is quiet; people stand silently, looking at magazines and books bound with paper covers. I cannot read a thing except a few sporadic and unenlightening words: *mountain, seven, year, water.* I pick up a magazine with a picture of a girl smiling on the cover. Inside are black and white photos of young Chinese men and women, advertisements for bottles of something. Thousands of characters I do not know. I pretend to flip through it. I inspect stationery, feel air-letter paper. Look at a Chinese-English dictionary.

A woman bumps into me.

"Duibuchi, jie jie," she says to me. Excuse me, older sister, she is saying.

"Meiguanshi," I whisper. Don't worry about it, I reply in Mandarin, barely audible. I keep staring into the dictionary, transfixed. Out of the corner of my eye I see the woman paying for a book and leaving.

I hold my breath.

She exits, and I slowly follow her out. She is almost out of sight already, but I see her, up ahead in the crowds: a slender woman in a neat lavender dress, her feet in sandals. She is carrying a canvas bag over her left shoulder; her hair is in a ponytail. She turns suddenly down an alley. By the time I reach that spot, she has disappeared down the narrow, dark passageway, which no doubt leads to a whole catacomb of apartments.

I walk on a bit more, not really looking at anything. A small, pleased smile creeps onto my lips and I look down at the pavement so no one will see my face.

We are leaving Xian, moving on into the south.

I feel a little sad to be departing from this city because we have spent more than just a day or so here and more than a day anywhere almost means home. There have been more Caucasians here than we have seen for nearly two weeks since we left Beijing. We could be mistaken for Europeans because I have seen no other Americans. But then again maybe not, because even the Europeans look different from us. The Italians and British we saw wore extremely well-cut clothes and carried themselves differently. With our shorts and T-shirts and loose limbs, we looked very American, I think, very casual and a bit unsophisticated.

I think I am sad to be leaving Xian because it has such a sense of place, of time past. It is not like Beijing, which teems with bureaucracy and stiff upper lips. Nearly twelve hundred years ago during the Tang Dynasty, Xian was the capital of China. Formerly it was called Changan, the capital of "everlasting peace." China was fearless then, strong and wealthy and a place of excitement; it was the period when poetry and figure painting flourished, when there was grand feudalism. Its contemporaries were Rome and later Constantinople, and they all vied for the title of the greatest city in the world. Today it is one of the few cities on Earth that still has its ancient wall; at night it is lit up with strings of white lights and you can see people strolling around on its wide top. It all looks very festive and romantic.

By now, though, Xian is a city that truly has lost the grandeur of its days as the shining jewel of the Middle Kingdom. Its opulence has tarnished; all of its rich funerary objects have been darkened by years entombed with the spirits of dead emperors and embittered eunuchs, ignored concubines and abused handmaidens. Like the Rome and Constantinople of old, Xian has had to become a new city, with cars and televisions and satellite dishes. There are karaoke machines and cellular phones.

But Xian is a city full of everyday life. The things here hold a kind of beauty that sounds absurd for me to describe: cabbages in a cart lashed with twigs; a small child on his haunches, peeing in the street; the ramshackle houses worn around the corners by the wind; the meticulously neat fields of tomatoes and beans climbing up on their tripod trellises; a woman with her arms around the waist of a man while perched on the back of his bicycle, sidesaddle—all of these things struck me as somehow lovely and wonderful. So I am sad to be leaving Xian, this place that is so grand and so ordinary all at once.

We arrive in Chengdu by plane late in the evening, nearly 10:30. But still, the city seems quite alive. Chengdu seems happily far from the constraints of Beijing, a town raised on the fire of its spicy Sichuan cooking, where clothes seem a little brighter and people bustle with self-made activity.

Men and women are frying meat on the streets at half-past ten at night, the streets aglow in the lights from the stalls. In the cool evening, when everyone is out on the streets milling about, the street vendors cook. Tables and chairs are set up in makeshift restaurants on the sidewalks, the wobbly tables covered with oilcloths; a soy-sauce tin of chopsticks is in the center of each. People eat ravenously, as if they haven't eaten for weeks. They wolf down giant bowls of food, heaps of vegetables and mountains of rice. They talk with their mouths full. Some wave their chopsticks around in the air wildly, making various and imperative points in some unknown but vigorous debate. All the stores are open, the harsh and glaring fluorescent light pouring out of the doors. Music blares from tinny radios, rather ghastly Chinese music that intimates lovers gone astray and lives no longer worth living. A heavy bass beat pulsates from a disco, a marquee flashes in a race of chasing yellow light bulbs. A woman sells bananas on the sidewalk, spread out on sheets of newspaper. She throws the fruit on a scale she holds in her hand and spits out the price, *"Si mao!"* Forty cents! She says this like a curse, like a wicked wish cast upon her enemy's child.

The sounds, the night, reach into the wee hours, reach past nightfall, which comes at 10:45. Then the streets are dark. China has no streetlights, and cyclists speed home in the dark without ever crashing. Like bats, they are drawn to their destinations as if by smell or sonar.

In the side streets women toss out basins of dishwater.

Children play and are called in. A man tries to sell paintings to a Taiwanese tourist. The evening is loud and boisterous. People shop and barter with abandon. A woman sits in her vendor cart, reading a book in the glow of her lamp. Soft drinks and juices in cartons are lined up on the top of the cart. She has no bottled water. Another vendor down the street does; it's three Chinese dollars, which is more expensive than it should be. The stars are bright in the sky now; the half moon hangs in the sky like an ornament.

The next day we visit the bamboo and embroidery factories, where women sit all day making incredibly, ridiculously tiny things with their hands—baskets woven from the threadlike fibers of bamboo or wall hangings with the most delicate feather stitches of silk thread.

In the embroidery factory everything is quiet except for the tinny music from the women's transistor radio. Chad tries to strike up a conversation with one of the prettier girls, but she only blushes and laughs, covering her mouth with her hand. He tries out the few Chinese words he has learned from Robert, "Hello" and "How much money?" but this only makes her laugh harder.

We get back on the tour van and the guides take us to another factory, where mechanical looms churn out miles of silk brocade. These machines are incomprehensible, made of steel and ten thousand strands of fine silk thread. These hulks of metal devour coded sheets of bamboo, which are key-punched with some magical, mystical formula that the machines can read and weave into the fine, swirling patterns. Silent women move amid the din and the machinery and the rows of green lamps that hang from the ceilings, checking to see that the miles of cloth are free from blemish. In the gift shop we buy a lot of cloth and scarves.

"Can you believe these prices?" Mrs. Edward says. "Can you imagine what these would cost in a department store back home?" We are paying two and three American dollars for silk squares. I buy one for Maura and one for my mother; one is pale blue and the other is peach. I do not know which one I will give to whom. I don't get one for myself because I don't seem to wear scarves anymore. But I did pick up two tiny woven baskets with lids from the bamboo factory and I am very happy about this. In the van I take them out and look at them, nice and empty.

. . .

THE NEXT DAY it rains, but we go to the zoo anyway. It is a rather interesting spot where beautiful trees and bamboo line the paths, but the animals are confined in horrible green cages.

"Look at that, it's dreadful, simply dreadful," Joyce proclaims. "These conditions are unbelievable. I'm going to write a letter to the ministry of whatever that deals with this. It's absolutely horrible." She begins scribbling something in her notebook.

Sichuan Province is the home of the giant panda, so we dutifully visit several of the miserable creatures, which apparently are being kept indoors because of the weather. The cubs are housed in sad, solitary confinement, looking bored out of their skulls, damp and utterly dejected. They loll about on the concrete floors and stare at us dully. No wonder they have such problems getting these creatures to procreate in captivity, I think. This is such a dreadful atmosphere, who would be in the mood?

Our guide shows us something called a lesser panda, which looks rather like an overgrown red raccoon. We also see the golden monkey, which actually appears to be a moving wet mop.

The best part about the zoo is that for fifty Chinese cents a woman in a little white building loans us each a lime-green umbrella, which we twirl around merrily in the rain. And we are thoroughly amused to check out the gift shop, where pellet guns actually are available for sale. There, amid all the pinched-looking stuffed panda toys, are the packages of plastic firearms.

"What could they possibly be thinking?" Joyce gasps.

The rain makes me feel sad. We have been traveling for what seems like months, and fatigue seeps into my bones. I move slowly; my mind has not been feeling any quicker since I arrived in the Beijing airport, sluggish with jet lag and exhaustion. And now this rain darkens my mood.

But it is lovely now that we have moved on to the Dijianyan Irrigation Project nestled in the mountains. Two thousand years ago someone got the bright idea to carve out part of a mountain and divert the Yellow River into Sichuan Province. With bamboo baskets filled with rocks these Chinese created an amazing feat of engineering; this basic concept, for the most part, holds true today even though modern materials are used.

The haze brought on by rain and fog makes me feel as if I am in the land of fairies. The mist makes the grassy, tree-filled hills look filled with sprites hidden just beyond our vision. The rain in the valley reminds me of the painter Tung Yuan, who saturated his brush and filled the paper with wet dots of ink that evoked mist like no one else. The Two Kings Temple, its stones now green-gray with age, rises demurely from the surrounding hills, and its curving Chinese roofline is picturesque in the fog. In the temple compound the air feels safe and holy.

I could live here, I think.

It would be like living in a landscape painting, surrounded by the greenish-gray patina of a thousand brush strokes. I can hear rushing water down in the valley and overhead is the steady movement of leaves and raindrops. Moss and lichen cling to stones and bricks, and the air is thick with wetness.

But if I were to live here, I wonder if I always would have to be sad: There is something about this place that is filled with sorrow. It is not a painful place but one where your heart would have to be muted, I think, to match the light.

At the bottom of the hill we all totter across a thin suspension bridge that is strung across the roaring river. As we scamper across, we peer down through the bobbing wooden slats at the river raging below, which rushes through the narrow passage just downstream from where the water has been diverted. The tremendous sound is dangerous and exciting. What if I fall? What if I fall? Children up ahead jump up and down on the bridge and scream with delight as their small weight sends the bridge rolling and undulating. We scream, cling on to insubstantial ropes. We scream and laugh hysterically, as if we were on some kind of roller-coaster ride.

When I am safe on land again, surefooted on the saturated ground, I want to weep and I don't know why. The day has been filled with melancholy, but there is something luxuriant about it. I feel loose, as if I have no sharp edges; I feel as if all the Earth's shapes have been softened in the mist.

Once again we are on the train. At times I feel I could ride on here forever, that I would be content to have the scape of land and people entertain me as it flows by the window.

Today is exquisite. The fan works, and it rains outside, so as the train passes through the countryside, the coolness and freshness moves freely through the hard-sleeper compartment where we will spend the day on our way to Dazu.

Already the corn is taller than a man, and it tassels. There is much green here: of rice, tree, taro, bamboo. It is almost a tropical lushness and the wetness of the rain saturates the leaves, the atmosphere.

And the mind.

I savor each moment on these trains, for to me they are womblike. The steady *click clack, click clack, click clack* rocks me, lulls me into a mental slumber where my eyes are open but my senses are closed to all distractions. It takes me back to the genesis of being, to a time before this when other lives breathed this air, to a time when I felt safe and warm, when there was no such thing as danger.

But getting *on* the train is another matter.

We had left Chengdu very early in the morning, groggily sitting in the VIP waiting room at the train station, holding boxed breakfasts. Mrs. Barclay had opened hers immediately for inspection: a hard-boiled egg, two bland Chinese rolls made with white flour, a small, discolored orange, and some kind of fried bread with sesame seeds that probably was filled with sweet black-bean paste.

Suddenly, Jim ran into the room, holding a fistful of tickets. "Hello! Hello! We must get on the train. Please hurry!" He sped out toward the platform, and the group jarred into action. Delirious from having to get up too early, we scurried bleary-eyed after Jim, who kept calling over his shoulder, "Please! Please hurry! The train does not stop long!"

In those frantic moments of rushing through the station, of dragging bags along seemingly infinite platforms, I felt I was running for my life. These were the glimmers of a time not restful, of wartime; these were like flashes into my mother's life. It no longer mattered who the enemy was. Everything around me evoked passages of flight, of fleeing for one's own breath. I looked around at the frenzy, the desperate mobs holding suitcases, baskets, cloth bags, and nylon nets of melons, clothes, all their belongings. There was an urgency in their eyes, a desperation in their faces. It was as though this was the last train to Eden, the promised land of the living.

It could have been the last train from Shanghai; we ran through an underground tunnel to the other side of the tracks, to the last open road to the south. I half expected to see belongings strewn by the wayside in the desperate flight: extra bags of clothes, a bundle of rice that became too burdensome.

All this flashed before my eyes. All this in just the few minutes it took to go from the relatively posh VIP waiting room in the Chengdu railroad station to the train bound for Dazu, the train that led away from death.

The drive from the train station to Dazu is very bumpy, over barely existent roads. Dazu seems like a black town made up entirely of small, dark shops selling black products: lumps of coal, blocks of steel, bulbs of dark, purple eggplant. Everything is narrow, a shaded strip of humanity held in the folds of carefully tended green mountains.

This, perhaps, is the way most of the world lives—pockets of people dwelling between a tiny here and there, setting up houses on the same soil as their great-grandfathers, drinking from the same well, never straying far in thought or distance. True, there is Beijing, Tokyo, Hong Kong, London, Bombay, New York. But then there is nearly everywhere else, hidden in the space in between, populated by those who make up generations and whose labors are conscripted to move mountains.

Hidden away in the hills around Dazu are thousands of Buddhist sculptures, sheltered under carefully architectured stone eaves. The figures were carved out of the mountainside, secluded and protected by an elaborate drainage system that spared them from water, wind, and sun. There are also colorful statues of deities and guards; there is the goddess with the 1,007 golden hands who is hidden in a cave. As we walk among the mountains, mugging for pictures by the enormous sleeping Buddha, I wonder if the spirits' eyes follow our every step. I press my hand against the bathtub-size forehead of the prone Buddha and find that the stone is cool and calming.

"Look, Maya, look!" I turn and see Marcus, trying to pose

innocuously next to a row of guards or spirits carved into the mountain. He grins at me, then wipes his face clean, to be properly stonelike. I smile at him but say nothing.

I find myself turning inward, as if being among these spiritual figures makes me pensive, thoughtful. Perhaps I am simply going deaf, immune to all sounds and all discussion. I don't feel nervous, but something, I think, is going to happen.

From Dazu we take a four-hour ride to Chongqing, a bumpy, curving, and cramped trip on which our bag of peanuts burst, sending several pounds of the loose nuts rolling uncontrollably around on the floor. In the van we feel goofy and mildly carsick; this ride is making us light-headed. Robert gets everyone to start singing songs and we all chime in for patriotic American tunes; and even I join in a rousing rendition of "One Hundred Bottles of Beer on the Wall," but we peter out after thirty-seven bottles. (Jim says he has never heard this song before but likes it.) We are tired. Dopey, we look out the windows.

Every bit of fertile land is being used; around us mountains are scored on the horizontal so little plots can be tilled. Corn between the rice paddies. Beans on hills too steep for corn. The bright, big yellow blossoms of melons along the roadside. And again on the next slope: rice, corn, beans, melon. Up and down each hill, each mountain, around every corner and the next. For one hundred fifty kilometers from Dazu to Chongqing, it is this endless repetition.

· · ·

AFTER HOURS OF this, Chongqing is a shock to the senses: hilly, congested, and polluted. Certainly I can no longer be deaf. Everything is a mess, a cacophony of blaring horns and too many people wedged into a hillside perched on the cusp of land where the Yellow and Yangze Rivers meet. In the van we are stunned into silence; no one seems able to speak. This wartime capital of the KMT still looks bombed out in some sections, where thousands dwell in gray concrete buildings stacked haphazardly on the hillside. As we approach from a distance, I think that the city looks impossible—so many tiny, tiny gray buildings perched on the hills like some kind of game played with toy blocks.

. . .

MAYBE IT WAS just van lag, but we feel much better the next morning, after sleeping in beds that did not move or jolt or sway. Chongqing turns out to be the hippest city we've seen to date—we spot girls in denim miniskirts with their coiffures fused into place with hairspray and see that some of the young men have perms. Everything seems very lively and carefree, but then we turn a corner and come upon a group of scrawny and ill-clad men waiting on the street and leaning on their bamboo poles, looking for work, for something to tote.

We go to a workers' village, which is supposed to be a model of modern communal living. We are told that more than three thousand factory laborers live here and have all their needs met within a mesh of a few streets: They send their children to school, can find doctors, and buy their vegetables and meat all within easy walking distance. The village spokeswoman boasts about how well this system works, how happy everyone is here. Jim serves as our interpreter. But we are dubious; everything to us seems too close, too crowded. One room looms near another, voices travel easily, and there is absolutely no privacy.

"What about gossip?" we ask. "Isn't it just too much to live right next to your co-workers? What about theft?"

It's all very good, the spokeswoman tells us. There is little thievery or misbehaving of any kind because everyone knows everybody; do something wrong and all your neighbors will know.

We think about this. It seems suffocating to us, we Americans who hole ourselves up in our private spaces, which are enormous by Chinese standards since whole extended families crowd into two or three rooms. In American cities neighbors hardly speak to one another, let alone know what everyone is cooking for dinner.

There are no bicycles anywhere in Chongqing because of the hills, and their absence is noticeable. It seems strange not to have them around because bicycles are so numerous everywhere else. Here, people travel by foot or bus, climbing steep roads to homes and rooms where solitude and privacy are but words in concept.

. . .

A HAVEN FROM this congestion is the painters' village. We go there on our second day in Chongqing, taking a drive to the river. We stop in front of a cluster of buildings on the water's edge. We pile out of the van, stopping here as we would at any other tourist spot. But already I do not sense that this is a regular pause on the China-in-a-week guided scurry. We stand near the entrance, and it seems very quiet here. I see that we are amid a group of square buildings; some even have verandahs on the water. Giant pots of flowering bushes bloom on the gray pavement.

So here live the modern-day court painters: men and women who paint what the government wants to see, who practice their art as others see fit. There are fifteen artists here who carve wood and wield paintbrushes, producing beautiful, intricate, and politically correct work. We walk in, and immediately I envy their studios—large rooms with windows. Big tables are cluttered with brushes in giant bamboo pots, inkstones, a tray of stone chops with their names carved in them, red inkpads, and paper. I want to touch everything, feel the smoothness of the black inkstones and the soft animal hair bristles of the brush tips. I want to feel the heaviness of the stone chops in my hands, touch the lions and dragons and horses carved in their tops. I want to touch the table, the rough grain, the dents and grooves. I want to swoon; these rooms are so evocative.

. . .

THEY MAKE ME think of the one I love.

I go outside to a stone verandah and look at the gray, cloudy skies over the river. Clusters of little boats churn up and down the water; their rudders weave small, delicate patterns in the wakes. Next to me the little leaves of the potted trees quiver slightly in the breeze. The blossoms are small and delicate, and they are the color of fuschia so perfect I cannot describe it. The stone tiles under my feet are smooth and worn and made of uneven shapes; yet they all match to form a virtually seamless floor.

I feel my eyes grow wet.

This, I think, could have been Alex's life. He might have loved this type of work. In another lifetime, another world, he might have made his home by the river and painted this scene, this landscape. He might have watched these small boats churn up and down the river, perhaps tried to copy the swirling patterns that the rudders left in their wakes. He might have sipped a cup of tea, holding back the black tea leaves that had floated to the surface with the porcelain lid of his tea mug. Sip, sip. Think. Watch the water. Sip.

But this is not his life. He does not live by the riverside; he does not paint. No, instead he is being practical, something he finds rather distasteful. He makes money for his mother, who is a successful merchant in Hong Kong. He takes care of his father, who is ill. He is a good son.

I have not said much about it up until now, but it has often been on my mind. As the days pass here in China, the day comes closer that our trip will end. On our last three days we will be in Hong Kong, so poetically called the "fragrant harbor." I think of those last days more often now. If I find Alex, what would I say? What would that moment be like when he first opens a door and I see him there, standing right in front of me? What would I do?

Yet I do not want to see him; I am frightened of it. I am terrified of running into him on the street, of turning a corner and suddenly finding him there, buying six golden oranges from a vendor.

We leave the artists' colony. A woman and two men follow us down to the van to say good-bye. They say they have lived in the colony for so long that they know no other life. It is pleasant here, they say.

"But don't you feel constrained?" Joyce asks them. "How do you feel about always having to have everything approved?"

They smile at her.

We have been here a long time, they say. We are old. We are happy here.

Joyce does not really understand. But it is time to go. Thank you, we tell them; it is so beautiful here, so peaceful.

. . .

TONIGHT WE LEAVE on a boat that will sail down the Yangze. We will be another day closer to leaving China, another day closer to crossing the border into Hong Kong. My hands are restless, twitching in my lap. I pick at the hem of my shorts. I wish I had a heavy, black inkstone in my hands, smooth and cool. If I did, I would touch it and think of him.

I gaze out the window as we drive to the river.

ALEX

MEN RUN THROUGH my life like a kind of undertow, both gentle and insistent, occasionally unsafe, but always there. This is strange, because my life has been filled with women: There is my mother, who has the tautness and precision of an iron wire, and my sister, who is something of an alter ego—the prettier, smarter, more vampish self I never was. And there have been occasional girlfriends, wonderful friends of childhood and womanhood, with whom I shared trifles, secrets, and sins. Female roommates and fine teachers of both life and academics have been present to set the pace of my days. But for whatever reason it is by men that I keep time; they are the ones who punctuate, who give rhythmic and forward movement to my years. Perhaps that is because they have caused more of a disturbance, have left more chaos in their wake. No woman, not even my mother, has caused me as much pain or joy as a man. There is no happy medium in their presence.

Yes, men run through my life like a rhythm. But when I step away from myself, when I try to tap out the baseline with my fingertips, I cannot remember anything. I sit there, feeling the surface under my hands as if the memory of that rhythm will resonate from somewhere underneath.

Yet all is still.

. . .

TONIGHT ALEX IS on my mind. He is always there, part of that rhythm that keeps running through my head. But tonight he is here with me consciously. I start remembering things, and one thought leads to another and another, and soon half the night is gone. I have not slept.

Perhaps it is the river. Maybe it is the water that keeps me awake and makes my mind wild and alert, searching for stray thoughts. Joyce has fallen asleep a long time ago. I sit up in this narrow ship's bed, push back the green curtains. This is no ocean liner, so the windows are big, the size they would be in any real bedroom on shore. It is mostly dark out there, but my eyes have adjusted to the dullness. I look out at the water, which flutters slightly, moving toward the sea. There is a light nearby and it casts its glow across the river. The scene reminds me of the night that Lance and I drove out of Narrowsburg in the dark, listening to the river run. There was a light then, too, that cast its length upon the water, a narrow strip of whiteness in the night.

My mind dances about, touching on the infinitesimal.

I think of silly, crazy things. Things that have no meaning, no real purpose. I remember that Alex bought me a chocolate ice cream cone in winter; I ate it, laughing, out on the street with hard little pellets of snow coming down. I remember walking to the convenience store at two in the morning because Alex was convinced he had a mouse in his apartment and wanted to buy a trap. I think of a stolen kiss in the library elevator. And of the time we drove to Niagara Falls, which was infinitely touristy and tacky, but was something that Alex had never seen.

And then I think of more foolishness: things that never were, never will be. Toronto, I think. We always meant to drive to Toronto but never did. Silly, silly us; what was our excuse? Too busy, no time? We always meant to go to an orchard in the fall and pick our own apples, straight from the tree. "But look, they're right here in the supermarket, all polished and ready to eat." Another time, another weekend. We never carved a pumpkin, cut its top off, scooped out the guts. It was Thanksgiving before I remembered. I wanted to buy him a pen, one I saw under glass at a fancy stationery store, but I never got it. Did I think it was too much? Did I have to pay the telephone bill; what was it? Was I going to wait for his next birthday?

Things I meant to do for him. Outings we planned but never took. Next year, we said. Another time.

I think of places we never got to see together: the Grand Canyon, Disneyland, the Golden Gate Bridge. I would have liked to have traveled with him, to explore the Western world. To see the Pyramids at Giza. The Eiffel Tower. The statue of David.

But that will not happen.

He's gone from my life now.

Instead, it is simply me here alone in China, sitting on this boat and staring into the dark countryside, unable to see anything.

· · ·

IT'S STRANGE, THE things you miss about a lover.

It's usually the small detail, the most minor and insignificant thing that one day, totally out of the blue, hits you where you stand. It almost never is the grand event—the special anniversary, the expensive meal with steak or lobster. A lot of the time it's not even something you would expect, like making love. The things you remember are far smaller and somehow infinitely more intimate.

One person told me that he remembers walks. He likes to walk, and suddenly, while crossing a street, it comes back to him: This is where he used to walk with so-and-so; this is what he saw with her, and much of it is still the same—the signs of particular restaurants, the stoplight, the furtive quiet of the usually busy avenue after dark. He remembers the sound of their footfalls on the sidewalk, the way it echoed off the cool, silent brick houses. He'll remember the way her hand felt in his, the way she leaned against his shoulder as they walked down the street. He'll remember this and be sad for just a moment. The girl is gone. She was a long time ago, when he was much younger and a bit too eager. He can't even remember exactly what she looked like; she is hazy, and he only remembers strange, independent details, like the slope of her nose or the view of her earlobe from the side. But he remembers where they walked; he remembers the sound of their steps and the weight of her as she leaned companionably into him. He remembers the street because it hasn't changed all that much, considering how he has.

· · ·

AND ME?

I remember cooking with Alex.

I remember him sharpening the blade of the cleaver on a small whetstone and mixing up amazing pans of food with a flourish of chili paste and sugar. I remember him whipping up *whaat dahn*, a smooth bowl of eggs and water that was steamed until it was like a velvet custard. One salted duck's egg was added for flavor, sometimes one of those smelly thousand-year-old eggs for additional zing. But it was soft and smooth and slid down your throat like a cloud. The mere mention of a steaming pot of hot and sour soup was enough to make me swoon, such a meal in itself because so much stuff had been added to it to make it thick, nearly like a stew—tofu, mushrooms, bamboo shoots, a swirl of egg. It was an essentially lightweight and flirtatious dish, with its piquant flavors that teased the palate, spicy hot and a touch of the bitter sourness. Sometimes, when he was cooking, I'd walk behind Alex and wrap my arms around him. The kitchen smelled of his scent and the sharp tang of scallions and ginger sizzling in the oil. A little yin, a little yang. After Alex left, the smell of steamed ginger and sesame oil was enough to break my heart.

We usually cooked well together, he and I. We moved well together in the kitchen, did not get in each other's way. We both worked swiftly, neatly. The human Cuisinarts, we joked. Quickly, all the vegetables cut on the bias and placed in neat blue-and-white bowls and old Cool Whip containers. I never knew where those containers came from, because we never ate Cool Whip.

I always let Alex do the garlic, though. He just smashed the entire clove with the handle of his cleaver, skins and all. *Bang.* Swift chops with the heel of the knife and it was done. I also let him crack the eggs because he could do this with one hand. Whenever I tried to do it, I always got eggshells in the pan. He never did. There is some finesse to it; there was something tender and appealing about the way he gently held the perfectly shaped egg between his fingers and palm, then rapped it with assurance against the side of the pan, letting the slippery white and flawless golden yolk slide effortlessly into the hot oil. There was something oddly beautiful and poetic about this little play of domesticity.

I liked to cook things quickly, without much forethought. I shopped without premeditation, buying whatever was on sale, whatever happened to be in the little Asian market that we frequented. Sometimes it was ong choi, a kind of Chinese green with a pure, clean taste. Sometimes it was those flat pea pods that look like they are encasing a row of painstakingly neat green lentils. I never bought bitter melon because I hated the way it looked and tasted. I almost always bought a package of some kind of noodle because noodles are my favorite. Once, as a joke, I drew a bowl of noodles to represent myself in a book of ill-penned cartoons for an office party.

"What's this?" my mother had asked, pointing at the lopsided bowl with the wavy lines on top that were supposed to illustrate steam. I said it was supposed to be me. Everyone at work called me the Noodle Queen because of all the lunches of leftover noodle dishes I ate at my desk out of Rubbermaid containers. I kept a pair of bamboo chopsticks in my upper right-hand desk drawer specifically for this purpose.

"But you're Chinese," my mother had scolded in Cantonese, wagging her forefinger at me. "You're supposed to eat rice. You know your father, what a big 'rice bucket' he was."

"It's an inside joke, Mother," I'd told her in English. "It's for the office. They'll know what I'm talking about."

"Chinese people eat rice," my mother had insisted.

"Wo zhidao, wo zhidao," I'd said. I know, I know. I'd switched to the Mandarin dialect out of exasperation. English—Cantonese—Mandarin. I am never sure why my mother and I insist on speaking three languages simultaneously, because we never quite understand each other in any tongue, foreign or native. Maybe that's it: We think that somehow versatility in languages will make up for our basic inability to communicate, that slipping from one form of speech to another somehow will bridge the continents of our generations and personalities, will be a salve on the natural wounds that mothers and daughters inflict upon each other.

So it is a joke when as a woman I stand in my kitchen, staring at its contents. There on the shelf is the soy sauce bottled in Guangzhou Province, the one with the red and silver label.

There on the shelves of my kitchen are my mother's legacy: cupboards that looked almost like hers, with the same brands of sesame seed oil, oyster sauce, plum sauce. Nearly identical packages of noodles made from rice flour and some from eggs (except I have more, given my predisposition toward noodle dishes). The exact same yellow-and-brown tin of jasmine tea.

The gargantuan fifty-pound bag of rice on the bottom shelf to the right of the sink was not really mine. That was Alex's. In our little household he was the "rice bucket."

So I stand there, in the reincarnated kitchen of my mother (with glimmers of Alex here and there), surveying my cupboards, my inventory. It is only then, standing there with all my cupboard doors wide open, that I can decide what to cook. I start with the vegetables, because they are the variable in the meal; they are what has been purchased based on availability and price at the market. Something squashlike, such as zucchini, is better stir-fried, perhaps with a bit of chicken, a few wedges of fresh tomatoes in the proper season. If not, I will root around in my cupboards to see if I have something canned. But frozen corn niblets will do, too. Something leafy, like napa cabbage or watercress, is very good in soup. With their delicate taste, they're pleasant in a mild soup, gracefully wilted and dancing in the boiling liquid.

. . .

THE WAY I cooked sometimes drove Alex insane.

He liked to plan, prowling eagerly through twenty-four-hour grocery stores at one-thirty in the morning when hardly anybody was there except creepy men who wore blue-checked flannel shirts and tired women who looked like they worked behind the counters of 7-Elevens. He delighted in dashing into the Asian grocery only minutes before it closed at nine, eagerly bolting through the tiny aisles and creating menus as he darted about.

"Hey, we still have that beef in the freezer, right?" he would say, his eyes scanning the shelves.

Yes, we still did.

He would start pulling bizarre packages of shriveled, dried fungi from the shelves. I never knew what to do with those kinds of things.

Instead I preferred to make stir-fried dishes and quick bowls of rice noodles just parboiled in pots of leftover chicken stock spiked with hot Thai chili sauce and the zests of limes. Alex liked to cook later in the evenings, making ginseng soup and slow-cooked pots of stewed meats that simmered for hours until the flesh was as soft as a three-minute egg just cracked open.

I don't know exactly what this said about him and me, what deep part of our psyches this symbolized. I studied Freud in my freshman psychology class in college, but I don't remember him saying anything about hot fried noodles.

. . .

THIS IS WHAT I remember about Alex.

And now I am in China, closer to him than ever, standing on the soil of our ancestors' birth, and I cannot feel his pulse in the land. Earlier in this trip I stood inside a temple, painted wildly and ornately in a blaze of geometric orange, blue, red, white, and green shapes. I smelled the incense, thick and potent; I watched the ashes fall into a heap in the offering bowl, saw the smoke trail toward heaven.

"Alex," I had wanted to whisper. "Alex, are you here?"

It's funny, I used to remember everything about Alex. But often now there are days I can't even think of what his face looked like. I have to look in albums, in stacks of photos that lie in a box, unsorted, undated, and unannotated. I didn't keep up with half of the people in the pictures and I've even forgotten some of their names.

There was a time when I could re-create Alex in my mind from head to foot. I remembered the smooth way his skin felt over the bones behind his ears and the small, pale brown mole he had on his left side, right where his elbow hung by his ribs. I knew that it was exactly two of my hand-lengths between his belly button and each nipple; I knew that both of his heels had two deep grooves in them that cracked and split and sometimes bled in wintertime. Alex was an entire head taller than me, and I remember how he used to hold me as we stood, resting his chin on the top of my head. I was just eye-level with his collarbone.

These were the precious and useless things I knew. After he left I would re-create his whole body in my mind, almost have him standing there in front of me. I would talk to him, pray to him, curse him.

"Damn, you, Alex," I scream in my head. "Damn you."

It's easy enough for him to come whistling into my life with a bowl of fried noodles and then leave soundlessly. His life is seamless, even. Undisturbed. And then there's me, an emotional wreck, rusting on the side of state route 585.

I have read wonderful stories, mostly ones that take place in wartime, when a woman meets someone who steals her heart away immediately. He usually is a sailor or a pilot, someone who masters a great hulking chunk of war machinery. But he is gentle and tender, a romantic caught in the winds of war. He brings her bits of chocolate from his military rations; he picks her bouquets of clover from the roadside. They meet, they kiss, perhaps they make a child. And then there is some kind of summons and he's gone—off to fly or sail into the night on great heroic missions. He vanishes. And years later, as this woman (who always is still lovely and thin and wears heels and stockings when she goes to the market) looks down at her little child playing, she truly knows that she will never again love so much.

How soon do you know? I wonder. How soon before you know that the one love of your life already has passed through your arms?

. . .

WE ARE ON a boat on the Yangze. The river is hypnotic. I watch the water, mesmerized by its movements and patterns. That evening the twilight sun had cast a warm glow, turning the river to the color of autumn. We had sailed past the countryside, the low, rolling green that stretched its lips to the very brink of water. We had come upon a long, slim wooden boat. Three men stood at its helm, reaching out and pushing poles into the river bottom to propel it along; a fourth man stood behind them, guiding a long piece of wood that served as a rudder. In the distance the soft peaks of mountains rose against the August sky, like waves turned to stone in the horizon.

The boat has docked for the night. We sail only in daylight so we will not miss any of the magnificent scenery through the three famous gorges of the Yangze.

I leave my bed, gently open the door of our cabin, and stand in the narrow passageway. All the doors are shut, the people holed up in the little private air pockets. It's almost as if no one else is on the boat except for two middle-aged men in white shirts who stand by a window at the far end, smoking cigarettes. It is very late; I do not know why they still are up.

I slide open a window and the cold, dark air rushes in. I squint into the night, lulled by the gentle lapping of the river against the hull, lulled like a child rocked in the arms of an unseen mother. I look toward where we will be traveling, down miles of river I cannot make out, fixing my eyes on the blur of blackness. It is so dark; we are far away from the glow of any cities and the moonlight is faint.

I feel very alone, but the solitude is pleasing. And strangely I feel as if I could stand here forever, braced against this night air. If I am indeed a woman who will never love again, then I am free.

Life holds no disappointment.

It really is very poetic, the way Alex and I met. It was in the fall of my senior year in college, at a party given by some Chinese friends of mine who were from Malaysia. It was a gathering to celebrate the Mid-Autumn Festival. I have never been to a real Mid-Autumn Festival, but I have read about it. The holiday takes place on the fifteenth day of the eighth lunar month, which is usually around late September by our calendar. It sounds so beautiful: People hang out paper lanterns and candles. They eat and celebrate in the moonlight, looking at the constellations. And, most important, they eat moon cakes.

There is a legend about moon cakes that involves espionage and secrecy; a tale that elevates black-bean-paste filling to altogether different heights. The story supposedly took place during the Yuan Dynasty in the 1350s, when China was ruled by northern Mongols (this is one of the very few times in history when China was not ruled by indigenous Han Chinese). The Chinese strategists were trying to overthrow the Mongols, and one of the more clever advisors came up with a plan to seize a particularly important city. The advisor spread a rumor that the Jade Emperor of Heaven was in a rage and was going to send five plague gods to afflict the city with epidemics. But the rest of the rumor was that the people could be saved if they listened to a compassionate immortal who would be sent to help them. The advisor then disguised himself as a sage and passed himself off as this immortal, handing out small cakes to every family in the city. He told everyone that if they ate these cakes at a particular time during the Mid-Autumn Festival, they would be delivered from catastrophe.

So on the fifteenth day of the eighth month, at the appropriate stroke of the watch clock, each family cut open the cake. Inside each cake was a slip of paper instructing the people of the city to revolt and slay the Mongols. The plan worked, with all of the citizens taking to the streets with kitchen knives and wooden sticks.

Apparently, this isn't a true story (facts have a way of interfering with a myth), but still, it is a good legend.

. . .

IT IS THEN very romantic that I met Alex at a party for the Mid-Autumn Festival in the middle of Ohio. The moon is full there, too, even though Ohio is very far away from China; the meteorologists call it the Harvest Moon, and much is made of its size and brightness.

At this party I was standing at a table already laid out with platters of food. On a small card table nearby were the treats—a bowl of wrapped sesame candy, two pans of brownies, a plate of Toll House cookies someone had made, and three boxes of moon cakes that someone else had purchased from the Asian food store.

There was a lot of laughing and the greeting of friends as if they were all long-lost companions. There was the clatter of getting drinks. Some people drank bottles of beer, but others had orange drinks or Cokes.

I saw a tall young man walk in holding a foil pan. He was wearing black jeans and a white T-shirt with the name of our school on it.

"Hey, Marcie!" he said, greeting a girl I knew. He gave her a one-armed hug, balancing the foil pan in the other. I noted that it was a very nice arm.

"Oooh, what did you bring?" the girl named Marcie cooed in Cantonese. She was from Hong Kong. All these people knew one another, all these foreign students from Asia.

"Fried noodles," the boy said.

"Ooh, sounds good." Marcie grinned, switching to English and rubbing her hands together. "You want to put it in the oven? Yes? Okay. It's over there, Alex." She pointed through a door.

"Okay, okay." The boy named Alex nodded, then made his way through the crowd, saying hello to people here and there.

I stood by the table, clutching my diet Coke in the plastic cup, which felt squishy between my fingers. If I held the cup with both hands, I could make the round cup into a square shape where my fingers met. I did this to amuse myself. I smiled around, a little overbrightly. I felt a little weird. All these people I didn't know. Like some sort of nervous vine I clung to the perimeter of rooms, hung on to doorjambs. I didn't want to be too far out in the middle of those spaces, where there was nothing to support me. This was a new, strange event, a social arena in which everyone in the room was Chinese and none of them was a member of my immediate family. The conversations drifted between three languages, but we all resorted to English in a pinch because that was the lowest common denominator.

I found myself talking like they all did: faster and choppier, little words repeated twice. I demurred. I covered my mouth when I laughed, reined in my gestures. I tried to be like all these Chinese girls with their tittering, birdlike laughter. I looked around the room in a perpetual state of awe: all these young people, all of them Chinese with black, black hair (the young women even complimented one another on whose hair was the blackest) and skin as smooth and blemishless as paper. There were a few of us ABCs

252 · Moon Cakes

(American-Born Chinese) from the Midwest; you could tell
who we were because we had tans and a certain sturdiness to
our builds, a sort of corn-fed quality that those raised in Asia
did not.

All through the evening I kept an eye on the young man
named Alex, who seemed to know nearly everyone in the
room. He had such a friendliness about him and was undeni-
ably good-looking: lean, with long limbs and strong hands.
At one point we were briefly introduced, and my insides
clenched for a moment.

"Hurry, hurry, get something to eat," he said, handing me
a Styrofoam plate. "With these guys around there'll be nothing left."

I thanked him awkwardly.

"What was your name again?" he asked, leaning in closer
so he could hear above the surrounding chatter. "Maya?
Doesn't that have something to do with South America? Ru-
ins, right?" He smiled. A very nice smile, slightly off center.
"You don't *look* that old." He smiled again. Then someone
jostled him and he disappeared into another conversation.
"Nice meeting you!" he called after me.

When I got to the food table, which was heaped with
everything from macaroni salad to take-out sushi, I sought
out Alex's fried noodles and took a generous scoop, adding
it to my full plate. Out in the living room, sitting on a folding chair with the plate balanced on my knees, I tried the
noodles first.

Damn, that boy could cook.

I ran into Alex again two days later at the ATM machine.
We arrived at the same time, but he let me go first.

"Oh, no, that's okay," I told him. "I have to find my
card."

"No, no, go ahead." Alex gestured toward the machine.
"I'll wait."

I already was feeling disheveled, and his kindness made me feel worse. I had overslept that morning and missed one of my classes. There must have been a power outage during the night because when I finally did awake with a jolt of panic, my clock-radio was blinking a meaningless "12:00" at me rather menacingly. It was too late to go to class, anyway, so I had decided to stop at the bank. I stood there, rummaging around in my enormous fuchsia canvas bag, trying to find my wallet. It really was nerve-racking having him standing there waiting for me. "You should really go first," I said. "I'm afraid I'm not being very organized about this." Who was I kidding? I never was organized.

"It's all right, I'm not in any hurry." He smiled again, slightly off center.

I finally had to set the bag down on the floor and take off my sunglasses; I was wearing a really dark, round pair that someone once said made me look like Yoko Ono; I did not take this as a compliment. I took out three ragged paperback novels, an Evian bottle deceptively filled with tap water, another pair of sunglasses with green tortoiseshell frames, a Baggie of whole-wheat fig bars, and an address book with a picture of Betty Boop on it. I tossed out another plastic bag with a ball of lavender and rose yarn and my knitting needles; by this time I had started carrying it around with me almost all the time, like a kind of vice.

"Ah, here it is!" I emerged triumphantly with a rather ratty wallet held together by a rubber band. "Sorry I'm taking so long." I shoved the bag aside with my foot and stuck the card in the machine; I withdrew ten dollars.

"All done," I told Alex, a little too sprightly. I gathered my things and had to get up to fetch the water bottle, which was rolling away. Meanwhile Alex punched numbers on the ATM. He did not get any cash but looked at the receipt and put it in his pocket.

"Are you going to campus?" he asked.

I was.

"I'll walk with you then."

The leaves were starting to change, and there was a certain coolness in the air as we walked down the street. Alex asked me what I was studying.

"Oh, nothing very practical," I told him. I was aware of his stride, which was measured, calm, not in a rush.

"And what's this impractical thing? English? Art?"

"Art history." I winced. "And, worse yet, Asian art. Very useful in the unemployment line, I'm sure."

His lips curved into a small, private smile.

"But it's good to follow what your heart thinks," he said. "Too much practicality is not so good."

"What are you studying?"

"Something entirely too practical." He smiled. "Numbers. Systems management."

"Oh."

"But my mother is paying for my education, so I don't have much to say about it." He looked at me, raising his eyebrows in a kind of resignation. I found out later that his father, who was a professor, could not afford to send him abroad without considerable sacrifice. So Alex's mother, from whom he was somewhat estranged, had offered to send him since she was a successful businesswoman. With conditions.

"So, if you could do whatever, what would you do?" I asked.

"Paint," he said without hesitation.

Alex then told me a story about a court painter who had worked for one of the emperors. The emperor told the artist that he wanted a picture of a rooster; the artist said he would begin right away. But a long time passed, years maybe, and the emperor heard nothing from the painter. So one day the emperor went to the painter's home and asked, "Where is the painting of the rooster that I requested?" And without saying anything the artist took out a sheet of paper and

painted a rooster right there, with a few expert strokes. He
presented this to the emperor.

"Why didn't you give this to me before?" asked the emperor. "Why did I have to wait so long for a work that takes
you less than ten seconds to paint?"

Again the artist said nothing. He simply led the way to a
door, which he opened. Inside, piled high to the ceiling,
were thousands of paintings of roosters.

"It took me years to perfect what takes seconds to paint,"
he said.

. . .

I THOUGHT ABOUT this story.

"I'd like to do that," Alex said, putting his hands in his
pockets. "I'd like to learn to paint something perfectly. But
not roosters, though; I don't like birds."

I laughed. "What would you paint?"

"A mountain," he said, sobering. "I want to paint the perfect mountain."

Alex was born, two years before me, right on Hong Kong
island in the shadow of Victoria Peak, which rises up green
and lush like a welt from the center; the island itself is incredibly mountainous and beautiful. To get to where he
grew up you must take a bus or drive a car past Repulse Bay,
which is an amazingly blue crescent that reaches into the
green hillsides. I have seen pictures of Repulse Bay; it looks
like the Caribbean, with beautiful sand and the sea a color
that you cannot imagine exists.

His parents nearly divorced when he was in high school;
it was a gruesome time mixed with equal measures of yelling
and unbearable silences. Although I think his mother was a
dominant force throughout his life, he seldom spoke about
her. Instead Alex's stories of his childhood always were filled
with tales about the places his father took him, the special

treats his grandmother made for him to eat, or the time a favorite auntie sneaked him in to see a kung-fu movie he wasn't supposed to watch. Alex was a much-loved little boy, an elder brother who became an only child at the age of four. His younger brother, Eddy, was nearly three years old when he was stricken with a fever and died. Eddy had been the favorite of their mother, for he was a chubby, laughing child who grinned shamelessly at everyone. Alex, on the other hand, had been the quiet, serious child with a worried expression and large ears that stood out at nearly right angles from his head. After Eddy had been reduced to a pitifully small pile of cremated ashes and buried on the side of a hill, Alex's mother apparently decided that parenting was pointless. She opened a boutique on Nathan Road in the heart of Hong Kong's shopping district, becoming a wildly successful businesswoman and midlevel socialite. Alex's maternal care was left up to his grandmother, who lived with them.

He and I used to joke that perhaps we were attracted to each other because we were orphans after a fashion, missing a parent in one form or another and therefore some sort of crucial element in our own characters. But from the beginning I knew that I was drawn to something in Alex that I could not quite put my finger on, something that was unsaid.

To any casual acquaintance Alex had an easy manner and was quick to make friends. He loved being around people and had an almost manic social schedule in addition to his classes. He was always meeting someone for racquetball, tennis, or bike rides. He never ate lunch or dinner alone but was surrounded by a table of friends. When we were first getting to know each other, he left me breathless just listening to his plans for the day as he darted from study group to happy hour to dinner to a midnight showing of the *Rocky Horror Picture Show*—all with different groups of friends.

But despite his whirl of social obligations, there always seemed to be a remoteness about him, a kind of darkness, perhaps. Sometimes, in the midst of a raucous party when the beer was flowing freely and the stereo was cranked to a near breaking point with the UB40s, Alex suddenly would become very quiet. He would fall back from the crowd, lean up against a wall, and drink deeply from a green bottle.

"Are you okay?" I would scream in his ear above the din.

And he would just nod briefly, almost without moving his head.

We talked about his brother from time to time. Alex didn't remember very much, but he did know that he had been very fond of Eddy. There was a dusty black-and-white photo of the two of them that Alex kept on a shelf next to his bed. The photo had been bleached by the sun, but the brownish images still could be seen: two little boys, in shorts and leather shoes, holding hands on some front step. Eddy was round and smiling and utterly adorable, his eyes disappearing to slits. There was a little furrow between Alex's eyebrows; he looked very concerned about something. It is very strange, but I noticed that in later photos Alex no longer looked so distraught, so fearful. Alex never quite lost that look of seriousness, of intenseness, but the furrowed brow was gone. And in pictures from later years he seemed more relaxed, surrounded by school friends waving goofy party horns or mugging next to someone dressed up as a giant furry strawberry.

Even as a child Alex was a decent person who tried to do the right thing, which isn't so terribly obvious all the time.

Once, when Alex was about eight, he took a package of gum from the store. He liked this gum because it had cartoon pictures of frogs and happy-looking children on the wrappers. The gum was from Japan, and things from Japan always look so nice in their packages. Alex chewed a piece of gum but then felt very bad. He spat the gum out and tried to shape it back into a rectangle like it had been when it was fresh and new. He found the wrapper in the wastebasket and put the gum in it again. It was kind of lopsided, but he hoped that the people at the store wouldn't notice. He sneaked into the store very carefully and put it back. No one saw anything.

But still Alex felt very bad. He felt very guilty. So he told his father, who took him to the store to explain what had happened. The man at the store crossed his arms and frowned very fiercely as Alex told his story. Alex was terrified. He gave the man his money without looking at him, pushing the coins across the counter with his fingertips. The man didn't say anything but rang up the money, *ding, ding!* Alex's father thanked the man and started to lead Alex out of the store.

"Wait!" the man said in Chinese. "Wait a minute." And then he got two new packages of gum from behind the counter. "Take them," he told Alex. "Go on, take them." The man waved the gum at Alex.

The boy took the green and blue packages, which seemed to burn in his palms.

"No, no," Alex's father protested. "Don't be so polite. My son must learn his lesson." He motioned for Alex to give the gum back, but the man refused to take them.

"He has learned his lesson enough," the fierce man said. He smiled. This smile changed his face completely, opened it wide and made him look like a different person altogether.

Alex kept the gum, but it still made him feel bad. He did not eat it but kept it in his drawer in his room for years. The gum became petrified, turned into tiny bricks, but still he did not throw it away.

In his apartment Alex had a studio, which was really a small room not much larger than two closets combined. But the light was good, very bright. He kept the miniblinds pulled up at all times, even at night. There was an overhead fluorescent bulb. I've always hated fluorescent lighting, but it didn't seem to bother him. He would paint on the drafting table. Sometimes I would sit on a small stool and watch him grind sticks of compressed black ink on an inkstone and add water, mixing the liquid blackness with the stony blackness. The bamboo pot was filled with brushes. This pot, made from a section of what must have been an enormous bamboo plant, was so big that I could not even get both hands around the circumference of it.

He always played classical music when he painted. Vivaldi when he was happy. Rachmaninoff when he was feeling pained and reckless. And Chopin, yes. Chopin. Nocturnes, a little night music.

One time, when it was very hot, Alex had me take off my shirt and lie on his bed. He filled the inkstone with ice water and dipped a bamboo brush in it, then straddled my hips and began to write, tracing ancient Tang poetry in Chinese characters on my bare belly. He said the words as he wrote them, speaking Mandarin instead of Cantonese. Mandarin traditionally is the language of scholars and the learned; it is smooth and lyrical, poetic and gentle. If Cantonese can be likened to the guttural harshness of German, then Mandarin is French. The words fell from Alex's lips like a well-loved melody, with the comforting curves of sounds that always rise and fall in the same rhythms.

I closed my eyes and felt the cool, wet brush tip tickle my chest as Alex began to write on my left shoulder, over my breast, and down to my waist in long columns with strong, graceful strokes. The water began to evaporate as the electric fan whirled around and cooled me. I listened as his voice washed over me, intoning words written more than a thousand years ago and committed to memory by the Chinese for centuries:

Chuang qian ming yue guang
Yi shi di shang shuang
Ju tou wang ming yue
Di tou si gu xiang.

Before my bed the moonlight is bright
It makes me think there is frost on the ground
Lifting my head I gaze at the moon
Dropping my head I think of home.

I liked sitting on a stool, watching Alex paint. Once he worked for two weeks drawing three unripe persimmons that he had found at the grocery store. Pages and pages of his fruit renderings were all over the studio—in different compositions, different shades, some more real, others very painterly. He painted the persimmons until the fruit was nearly bursting with ripeness. Then he sliced them up and we ate them; they were too sweet, like apple cider that has been sitting around for too long.

Most of the time Alex worked on landscapes. Sometimes he copied paintings or photographs; other times he would just paint freehand. The painting of landscapes is classical work; certain themes have been around for more than a thousand years. I sat and watched as hills and trees and rivers blossomed on the blank pages; Alex had loose, fluid strokes that fell and arced across the paper. When he held a brush, he was bold, fearless. He knew how the horsehair tips would bend with his touch; he knew how the rice paper would absorb the ink and make an image sharp or hazy. He understood how ink and brush and paper could respond to passion.

He would not give me any of the landscapes. "I'll give you one when I paint the perfect mountain," he told me.

Instead Alex gave me another of his works. It was a hanging vertical hand scroll with a single Chinese character written on it: dream. He had written it swiftly, with an enormous brush; this brush had been partially dry, so the strokes were ragged and harsh. It was a word that looked as if it was in flight, as if it was so anguished that it was tearing itself from the paper. It looked like a cruel word like *hate* or *prison*. The way this word had been rendered did not make it look like an inherently pretty word like *dream*. But it was a wonderful thing.

I still have that hand scroll, rolled up and in an old trunk. A yellow silk ribbon is tied around the scroll; I do not undo it.

I remember a kiss.

Actually, I do not remember the kiss itself but everything surrounding it. I remember standing with my back against a doorway that was white. There were people sitting on fat cushions in the other room, eating lavosh and cream cheese seasoned with dill. There was music and the ceiling fan was slowly spinning, keeping time by revolutions. One, two, three, four . . . endlessly, until you pushed a black button and it stopped.

The floor was wooden, varnished, the color of shiny hot pretzels that have come fresh from the oven of some street-side vendor. I loved this floor. I loved how clean it made the room look, how airy and light.

I was there by the door to the closet, wearing something white. My hair was piled up on my head, lots and lots of black hair twisted into a knot and fastened with a clip that had the ancient Chinese symbol for longevity over and over on it. It is the same symbol that you see all the time on dishes that they have at cheap Chinese restaurants, the endless blue scroll that twirls its way around the rim of a glass plate or bowl. Sometimes these plates and bowls are plastic, but they always have a pink background and the blue scroll that twirls its way around the edges.

I leaned against the closet door. With a wink he looked out the other doorway to see if anyone was looking. They weren't. He came close, wrapping me slowly in his arms.

And then I can't remember any more. I had closed my eyes. A kiss like this is not so much a kiss of passion but of patience. It is feeling, reaching out to brush the other without a sound; it is a whisper without words.

Hello, it says.

Hello, my sweet.

Hello, hello, hello . . .

I could have stood there forever with my back against the closet door, my hair piled high and fastened with a gold clip. I lost myself in the softness of his neck and knew that I could be with him always, that I could wake each morning this way.

Hello, my love.

Hello, hello, hello . . .

Meanwhile the ceiling fan whirled and spun, counting off the numbers of the infinite: One, two, three, four, five . . . around and around.

This kiss that I remember was quite a few years ago, in another city. By then we were very much a pair, Alex and I. We had been with each other long enough that our friends said our names Maya and Alex as if we were one unit. "Let's ask Maya-and-Alex if they want to go see a movie." "Tell Maya-and-Alex to bring paper plates." It wasn't as if we were sappy goons who couldn't be pried apart or anything. It was just that we fit well together and traveled in a pair, like stray dogs.

For then it was enough that we were happy, at least most of the time. I had finished my undergraduate degree the year before and had moved in with Alex while he finished graduate school. I was a research aide at my old university and spent a great deal of time in the library, photocopying things out of dusty books. I did this because it was the only job I could find in that grayish Ohio college town that did not involve waiting tables or flipping burgers. But it really was all right. We had our friends, we went for walks with other people's Irish setters. And we didn't talk about what we would do after Alex finished his degree. We simply chose to ignore what we knew was coming.

. . .

INSTEAD WE FILLED our togetherness with small intimacies. The play of everyday things, however unglamorous, makes up the bulk of any association. But these things need to be done: someone needs to lick stamps, buy scouring powder, pour Drano down the pipes. The occasional houseplant will get aphids and need to be dunked in soapy water. The vacuum-cleaner bags have to be changed. This is the life of the incredibly ordinary, the unbelievably mundane. There really is such a lot of maintenance in our daily lives, so much administrative activity: washing hair, buying dishwashing soap, taking out garbage, fishing burned English muffins out of the toaster, changing batteries in flashlights, smoke detectors, and portable electronic equipment. And that's not even counting car and home ownership. Forget the days of hunting and gathering: Life seems a lot more complicated now than it was when foraging for fungus among tree roots made up a big part of a person's day.

But it is in these small things that our memories can be most potent. To this day I can hardly take a bedsheet out of the clothes dryer without getting sentimental. Alex and I did not have a washing machine in our building, so we had to go to the Laundromat, a chore both of us found annoying and tedious. It was such a loathsome place, stark and overly hot and filled with tacky plastic chairs and people of uncertain character.

Once when we were there a weird woman who looked like a dingy flower child held a Bible pressed nearly to her nose and seemed to inhale the words. Then suddenly she put the Bible down on the bench beside her, picked up a knot of fine pink yarn, and began crocheting furiously. After adding a few rows to what appeared to be an ill-formed potholder, she turned to me with her intensely blue-gray eyes and said, "Hello, you seem like a good person."

I blinked at her.

"Well, thank you." What else could I say?

"I want to give you something," she breathed. "I feel as if I must give you a gift because I've met you." She held the misshapen mass of pink yarn in her palms like an offering.

"Here," she said, thrusting the potholder toward my chin, the crochet needle piercing its center like a slim and lonely chopstick. "Please take it. It's all I have to offer you."

I involuntarily shrank back in my chair and away from the offending pink substance.

"No, really, thank you," I protested feebly, waving my hands in front of me. "I couldn't possibly."

"Please take it," the woman pleaded, her eyes fixed on mine. "I want to give you something."

"No, that's okay," I told her. "I don't need anything, really. Really I don't." I looked around for Alex, but he was at the other end of the Laundromat, sorting whites. Finally I managed to persuade her to keep the potholder.

"Well, I'll leave it right here," she said, patting the chair. "I need to fold my clothes, but if you want to take it, I'll just leave it right here for you. Maybe you're just too shy." She smiled kindly at me and moved away.

I went to where Alex was feeding quarters into a dryer. "Who was that?" he asked, hitting the start button with his fist a couple of times to spur the sluggish machine into action. "What did she want?"

"Oh, she was just some wacko who wanted to give me a potholder," I said quietly, looking over my shoulder.

"A potholder?" He winced. He shook his head, opening the door of another dryer. "Did you take it?"

"No, of course not. She was so weird," I whispered.

"She was probably just trying to be nice," he whispered back.

"Would you have taken it?" I turned to look at the dingy flower-child woman, who was loading her clothes into a gray-green garbage bag and hefting it into a rusted grocery cart like the ones that old ladies take to the supermarket.

Alex shrugged and began taking out the clothes from another dryer. He didn't say anything, but it suddenly occurred to me that he probably would have taken the potholder. He had a small cardboard box filled with a peculiar assortment of objects he had collected over the years—not really normal mementos, such as ticket stubs or postcards, but bizarre things that reminded him of certain instances. Like the two packages of gum that the storekeeper had given him after he had gone with his father to pay for the stolen gum. He had kept a coin that a bum had given him when he saw Alex fumbling in his pockets at a street-corner phone booth and a raffle ticket someone had handed him instead of a coat-check claim. In this box also was the ATM receipt from that day at the bank when he had first really talked to me.

"I didn't have to go to the bank that day," he had told me later. "I just saw you on the street going there, so I went in. It's kind of crazy, right?"

On the far side of the Laundromat I saw the flower-child woman pick up the pink potholder and put it in a grungy batik duffel. I quickly looked away before she could catch me peering at her. I turned to help Alex fold sheets.

He handed me the fitted sheet to our bed because this particular item had always confounded him, and he ended up just balling it up out of exasperation. So I would fold the sheet, turning the corners into themselves, turning the smooth cloth inward as if it were a kind of pastry filled with something sweet. Then we would do the flat sheet together: each of us taking the far corners and shaking out the wrinkles, then walking toward each other and then away, to and fro, in a silly and intimate and lovely dance. Neither of us knew how to dance the way they did in old movies—ballroom dancing with the graceful, eloquent waltz and the steamy tango. This folding of the flat sheet was as close as we ever came, I suppose: This was a domestic two-step under the harsh and perverse glare of the slightly green fluorescent lights, gliding across the cracked linoleum. Even though we both said that we hated doing laundry, there was something indescribably romantic about the Laundromat, where we folded stacks of white Fruit of the Looms, warm from the dryer, and hung socks riddled with static on our shirts so that we resembled a pair of Christmas footwear trees. Our T-shirts came out fresh, free from our sweat and scents, and our towels were like brand new.

· · ·

BUT MUCH OF the trappings of femininity—stockings and pantyhose, slips and camisoles—seem to require obnoxious amounts of hand washing. Alex nearly was frightened out of his mind when one night, soon after we began our domestic life together, he stumbled half awake into the bathroom and somehow got himself tangled up in the forest of slippery and filmy garments that hung like vines from the shower-curtain rod and towel bars. When I heard him cry out, I went to the bathroom and turned on the light and found him trying to extract himself from a swirl of discount-store satin and nylon.

"What *is* this stuff?" Alex said, blinking in the light and looking helplessly about him. "Do women actually wear all this stuff?" A white slip fell down and slithered onto his head and off his shoulders. He tried to bat it away as if it were alive. I started giggling uncontrollably, and Alex swore, pulling pantyhose away from his neck. I picked up all the garments from the floor and threw them in a heap in the bathtub; my hose probably had a million snags, anyway. Then Alex gently looped a black stocking around my neck and drew me to him.

. . .

I FIND IT curious that so many of my memories regarding men are intertwined with domesticity; in a traditional sense one would have predicted that thoughts of home would link sentiment with the women in my life. But neither my mother nor my sister cared much about matters of the hearth; they both always were too busy in the outer, public sphere of their work, the people they knew. When I was a child, it truly was my father who made our house a home: It was he who made the meals that nourished my young body and my sense of security; it was his arms that I sought when tears fell. So perhaps it was only natural that, in later years, my heart warmed to Alex, whose simple rhythms were so evocative and comforting.

My mind is filled with different images of home from so many years, and all of them involve men: I think back and see my father at the ironing board, steaming in the creases of his sleeves while humming to the wailing of women; I recall the rich smell of Lance's sweaters as I hovered near him while he watched the boiling water in the hot-dog pot. And mostly I remember Alex and all the time we spent making our lives fresh again just so we could run about like children and muss it all up. It always brings a small smile to my lips when I think of the time that Alex and I made love in a heap of fresh laundry piled on the bed. To this day the soapy smell of a crisp and dry clean sheet instantly will bring back those moments and I will remember the feel of his hair in my hands.

•

I had moved in with Alex shortly after I graduated from college. About three months later we had our first real (and only) visitor: Alex's father. We both became fiendishly nervous about the impending arrival of our guest and cleaned the apartment obsessively. We washed all the windows and vacuumed meticulously, even behind all the furniture. We put new shelf paper in the kitchen cabinets and scoured the bathroom twice. I reorganized the hallway closet, hiding all my tampons and any incriminating personal items. When Alex's father finally arrived, our hands were chafed and we were utterly exhausted.

He was with us for three weeks. Although we prattled on gaily, we all felt there was a certain weight to this trip. For one thing, no one mentioned that Alex's mother had not come; I was beginning to think that she was like my own mother, someone not to be questioned. Another reason for our discomfort was that we all knew it probably would be the last time that Alex's father would be able to visit the United States easily. He was not well; the old man had some sort of unspecified illness, which I suspected was cancer. And politics made the future uncertain. The year 1997 hovered in the distance like a metaphorical stroke of midnight that would turn gold to ash. If Hong Kong's takeover by the People's Republic of China was one of those crazy Cantonese horror flicks, one could imagine that painted ghosts of all the Chinese emperors would run wildly through the streets of the city, screaming curses in delight and reducing vivid storefronts to splintered glass. But we knew that the real takeover would not be so grand, so splendid and mythic.

. . .

ALEX'S FATHER WAS an adorable man. His head was very round and didn't have much hair left on it. But what there was he parted neatly on the side. Whenever he smiled, his eyes squeezed together and almost disappeared completely, forming thin, bright, happy slits in his head. Alex's father always dressed carefully in a white shirt; beneath it you could see the outline of his undershirt, and he wore gray trousers. In Hong Kong it is often very hot, so he wore sandals even when he taught class. He had them on when he visited us, but he wore white socks underneath the brown leather straps, which gave him a rather odd, nerdish quality.

Alex's father was a sociology professor, a man who learned to become fascinated by the people around him because there were so many of them. I think he lived in some kind of a tenement house when he was a child in Kowloon. When he was a teenager, his family moved to the tall, blanched public housing developments in the New Territories; whole generations of families squeezed into tiny apartments. They had to use communal bathrooms and kitchens.

Alex's father was a quiet man, well loved by his students. I did not imagine that he was an easy professor. He was affable but expected excellence and full attention at all times, as if it was the most natural thing in the world for students to be interested in what he had to say.

We set up a folding foam mattress for him in the living room, with sheets and two blankets and a pillow. I don't think he used the pillow. Alex's father liked to get up very early; we could hear him moving around sometimes, his slippered footfalls whispering across the carpet. We could hear him gently opening the screen door, sliding it slowly so as not to wake us. He stood on the balcony and looked out across the parking lot to a little park, which was so tiny it barely seemed big enough to hold a wooden sign and a bench. It was more like a rest stop for grass. But Alex's father seemed to enjoy this small scene, this little bit of America.

We tried to give him the bed in our room, but he wouldn't hear of it. I'm sure Alex's father was not keen about our living together. After all, he came from a totally different generation.

But he never said anything; he seemed to accept it as if it was the most natural thing in the world, like waiting until it was warm before setting houseplants out on the balcony for fresh air.

· · ·

STILL, HE HAD a way of making me slightly neurotic. I felt that I always was doing something just short of good, that I was just shy of tolerable. He did not look at me with a disapproving eye but with the attitude that, if necessary, I would do. But I didn't want to just "do." I wanted him to like me.

When he first arrived, I had prepared a big pot of jook, or chicken rice porridge, for us to have as a snack when he arrived from the airport. Something simple, I thought. Something tasty but plain at the end of a long journey.

"Oh, how thoughtful," he said as we sat down to our steaming bowls. "Peasant food for the peasants." I thought he grinned a little too broadly as he lifted the spoon to his lips to blow it cool.

"That's right!" I replied overcheerfully. I was mortified. Was I insulting this man who, as a scholar, was clearly far from peasant stock? I glanced nervously at Alex, but he was busily slurping up the thick soup. His father gave no further sign of his opinion as he serenely finished his bowl.

But that was enough to make me squeamish. Perhaps I overreacted. Perhaps I was just nervous about getting to know the father of the man I was living with. After all, I didn't have much experience with fathers, or at least in any sort of adult sense. My most recent experience with a father had involved stealing Q-Tips from his office; clearly this was not current information.

So I worked extra hard to be nice when Alex's father was around. I planned elaborate meals that involved hours of shelling shrimp and shopping for obscure ingredients.

"What's this?" Alex asked me one day, picking up a little bag of hazelnut-size lumps.

"Whole fenugreek."

"Maya, why are you doing this?" Alex asked, surveying a kitchen strewn with vegetables and jars of spices we surely would never use again.

"Your father mentioned that he liked Indian food, so I thought we'd try to make some." I took the fenugreek from him. "Do you think we have to mash this first? Should I get a hammer?"

That night I tried to remain calm as we sat down to dinner. I hoped Alex's father wouldn't notice that there were at least ten mutant and petrified chapatis in the trash; it had taken two batches of dough before I had gotten the hang of it. Whoever would have thought that flour and water could be that fickle? Alex had tried to help me camouflage the chapati rejects under paper towels in the garbage can, but I was still fearful that these early failures would be discovered.

"Interesting." Alex's father nodded as he tasted the curried lamb. "Quite interesting."

What did that mean? I obsessed.

"I had such wonderful food in Bombay," his father said, beginning a raucous tale that somehow involved a sacred cow and a rickshaw driver and ended up with a banquet dinner with the brother of some South Asian dignitary. We all laughed uproariously, but I still had a complex about my chapati. How could my Indian food compete with Bombay's?

Alex was more handsome than his father, and taller, with broader shoulders. I always had thought Alex's hips were exquisite; belts fit well around his slim waist, and trousers fell nicely over his well-shaped buttocks. (Come to think of it, Lance was a particularly pleasant view when seen from the back; it must have been from all that cycling. I suppose I have a weakness for such things.) Although Alex's family was from southern China, he and his father both had the strong facial features of northerners. Their height came from the north as well, influenced by that Mongol blood. But Alex's face was more gentle than his father's, and in the right light he was astonishingly beautiful. Still, Alex felt insecure about his ears and always gave explicit instructions to barbers to somehow cut his hair to minimize the rakish angle at which they protruded from the sides of his head.

. . .

I ENJOYED WATCHING father and son together. We bought a bookcase, "some assembly required," at his father's suggestion, and it was amusing to see the two of them trying to be macho in the living room, peering at a sheet of incomprehensible directions with impossibly unhelpful diagrams. In the middle of assembling the back and attaching the shelves, Alex's father made a sudden pronouncement.

"Why don't you two buy a house," he said without warning, squinting at the instruction sheet. It was more statement than question.

Alex and I blanched.

"Well, we don't have any money," Alex finally said lightly.

"But all this money going into rent. It's a waste of money," his father said. "Buy one cheap, fix it up. I see them in the newspaper every day." He held two pieces of wood together, trying to see how they joined at the corner.

"You know I can't do that sort of thing," Alex said. "We can't even get this bookcase together."

His father chose to ignore this statement.

"No, no, you should do it now, before you have a baby. When you have a baby, you don't have time for anything."

I wanted to keel over.

Alex shot me a glance. "We haven't even talked about getting married yet, Pop. Don't even get started about kids."

"So what's all this?" Alex's father waved a screwdriver around the room. "Everything all set up and you're not getting married?"

"We just thought I'd finish the degree first and then think about it." Alex was digging his toes into the carpet.

"Think about it?" His father waved the screwdriver around some more. "What's there to think about? You like her; she like you. It's okay, right? No problem. That's all, right? What do you need to think about?"

"It's not quite that simple, Pop."

"What's so difficult, I don't understand? Your mother and me, we were introduced. We meet each other a few times, it seems okay, we get married. Very simple. Nothing to think about."

Alex picked up the second sheet of instructions and stared at it. And then, under his breath, he muttered, "Yeah, but you guys hardly speak to each other anymore."

"That has nothing to do with it," his father shot back.

Silence. I wanted to disappear. Why were they just talking as if I weren't there?

"Hand me that bag of brackets?" his father said after a while, peering over the top of his glasses at the instructions. Alex tossed him the plastic bag.

"You know your mother expects you to help her," his father said gently.

"Yeah, I know." Alex sighed.

"She could use the help," Alex's father said, holding up a bracket to the light. There seemed to be something loaded about this statement.

"Yeah, I know."

"She sent you to school."

"I haven't forgotten that." Alex was still looking at the instructions. "Look, Pop, these brackets fit in here." He pointed at the diagram.

His father peered over his glasses at the sheet. "Oh, yes, I see. I see."

Their two heads bent together, they began to confer in earnest about the bookcase. I was really feeling quite ill about the whole discussion by then, so I went into the kitchen to get some orange juice. I poured a tall glass and drank it slowly at the sink, staring at the pattern that the pulp scum left on the side of the glass. No wonder Maura didn't like pulp, I thought; it was pretty disgusting. My temples hurt from drinking the cold juice too quickly. When I went back into the living room, half the bookcase was up.

· · ·

THAT EVENING ALEX and his father took a long walk after dinner, as they often had done. I sometimes went along, but that night I deliberately left them alone. Instead I spied on the two of them from our balcony: two Chinese men strolling down the street with their hands clasped behind them. I noticed how Alex's shoulders were straighter and stronger than his father's; this, I suspected, had quite a bit more to do with youth than mere physique. Their fondness for each other was unmistakable as their heads leaned slightly together in discussion. They paused to admire the flowers growing in a neighbor's yard, and Alex's father cupped a rose between his fingers and drew it to him so that he could smell its fragrance. Then they continued walking, heading down the street.

I felt a little wistful watching them. I thought that it was unfair that I no longer had a father of my own. My own image of my father was so unreal, so colorized, that I sometimes thought that I did not know what was true and what was false. Yes, I did remember a great deal, but was that really the truth? And sometimes it was hard for me to believe that I ever really had a father at all.

As I watched them making their way down the block, I began to feel irritated with Alex's father. Were they talking about me? I wondered. Maybe I should have gone along after all. Why was he being so annoying about the house and marriage thing? Alex and I just had decided to play it all by ear; why did his father have to bring it up? It may not matter to him whether or not he got along with his wife, but it mattered to us. He was being so Chinese. And if Alex's father really didn't like me that much, anyway, why was he still pushing us to get married? It just didn't make any sense. We had lots of time to think about it, right? So what was his hurry?

Before we knew it, it was Alex's father's last evening with us. It didn't seem as though we had done that much—gone out to eat a few times, toured the university, gone for a ride in Amish country. And now he was leaving. He sat in the living room on the couch, watching a home-remodeling show where the hosts demonstrated how people could turn burned-out attics and ancient barns into trendy, color-coordinated living spaces. Alex's father lived in a tiny apartment on the fifth floor of a colorless cement block. He didn't even have any real windows, just sets of those louvers that are speckled so that no one can see inside. I was not sure why Alex's father liked this show so much, but he watched it nearly every evening; maybe he was vicariously experiencing home ownership. He always told us with great interest over dinner how a wall had been knocked down or a young couple had saved eighteen hundred dollars by digging the foundation for a backyard gazebo by hand.

"Look at that," his father had said. "They're blowing in their own insulation."

Alex had been a wreck and distracted all during his father's last day. I had to repeat everything twice because Alex didn't hear anything I said. By midafternoon he had called the airlines three times to confirm his father's flight. He kept offering to drive his father places for last-minute items. To the drugstore for toothpaste? Dental floss? Did he have enough to read on the plane? Did he want to stop at the bookstore?

No, his father said, smiling benignly. He had everything. His one old dark leather suitcase, the edges buffed by travel, was packed neatly and waiting at the front door.

Razors? Listerine? Alex kept asking.

They have Listerine in Hong Kong, his father said. Instead he read the Sunday paper, telling us there were cheap houses on the market, that there were "handyman specials."

"Here," his father said, poking a finger at the paper. "Three-bedroom starter home on quiet street. Eat-in kitchen, one-and-a-half bathrooms, basement."

"That show has gone to your head, Pop," Alex told his father.

All day father and son did this, dancing around the unsaid, sidestepping topics too tender to touch. On this last day it seemed all their unresolved ghosts kept tapping Alex on the shoulder, and he darted around like a fool, trying to swat them away. It was all making me really nervous, but I was trying valiantly not to obsess too much about it. Then, as if in anger, Alex violently overminced an innocent piece of ginger while we prepared dinner. We were making hot fried noodles with chicken and vegetables, spicy garlic eggplant, and a steamed fish.

Alex was not much help. He spilled water as he set a pot of it to boil. He yelled that he couldn't find the garlic even though it was buried under the broccoli in the right-hand crisper of the refrigerator, where it always was. It was getting hot in the kitchen and I turned on the fan in the corner.

Alex cursed as the papery outside shells of the garlic, discarded on the counter, started flying across the stove.

"Go on, talk to him," I said. "I can take care of this."

"No, no, it's faster this way," he said, tearing three cloves of garlic from the bulb.

"I can do this," I said, taking the garlic from his hands. "You go sit with him," I told him gently in Cantonese. "He's going tonight."

His eyes darted over the countertop as if he was looking for something. The water was starting to boil and steam rose on the stove beside him.

He sighed and pushed behind me to get to the sink, where he washed his hands, wiped them on a damp kitchen towel, and walked out. I minced the garlic, added oil to the frying pan. As I put the cakes of dried noodles into the pot of boiling water, I could hear the television click over to the evening news. And then I couldn't hear anything else because the garlic, scallions, and ginger were sizzling noisily in the pan. The fan was whirring and it sent the flaky garlic skins scuttling farther across the countertop. The fan stood still for a moment before oscillating the other way, pushing a wave of steam into the hallway.

The fish had steamed beautifully. It lay there in a flat bowl, the water droplets sparkling on its silver sides, the thin slices of ginger on top soft and wilted. I'd heated oil in the pan until it was very hot and smoking. Using a special pair of tongs, I carefully lifted the bowl out of the pot. Quickly, I lifted up the pan of oil and drizzled it over the fish, which was still so hot that steam smoked off of it. The skin of the fish sizzled and the oil sputtered. The smell was intoxicating. The flesh of the fish crackled and sparkled as I topped it with freshly cut scallions. It was perfect.

•

After dinner we left the dishes on the table. The spine and bones of the fish would still be there when we got back from the airport, lying like a disembodied skeleton on its oval blue and white plate.

The ride to the airport was silent.

We listened to music on the radio, something unthreatening with a lot of violins. The airport was overbright and filled with people in transit, impatient and anxious. Couples lingered in passageways, clinging to each other's arm as if they hoped to take that particular limb along with them for comfort as the plane took off.

At last we came to the gate.

We sat on orange plastic chairs. Alex was between his father and me. I tried to take Alex's hand, but he pulled it away. His father was saying something about what a nice time he had had, how good we had been to him. He was saying that we should come visit him in Hong Kong soon, when it was not unbearably hot. We could go to the beach.

People were starting to get on the plane. None of us moved; there was no use hurrying just to wait in line.

Suddenly his father squinted his eyes and cocked his head, seeking out Alex's face.

"You don't have to wait, you know."

Alex looked up, truly astonished. "What, wait for what?"

"An emergency. Before you come home."

Alex stared at the floor.

"Well, it's time for me to go," his father said, standing up. He turned to me and smiled.

"Ah, loyalty. A curse." He shook his head apologetically and held his arms out for me.

"You take care," I said as I hugged him. "Have a good flight."

And then I stepped aside as father and son embraced.

•

We watched as his father's figure grew smaller and disappeared down the jetway, his white socks seemingly fluorescent underneath his sandals. He turned once, looked for us, and waved. In a few more steps he had vanished around a corner.

We stood, hearts heavy, staring at the place where his father had been.

. . .

IT WAS FOUR months later.

"Alex," I whispered. "Alex."

"Mmmmgh."

"Alex, I need to know."

His head was half buried underneath his beloved, rumpled pillow, which he had had since childhood. By then the pillow was so flat that even plumped to its fullest it was barely an inch high. Alex's back was to me. In the moonlight from the window his skin was the color of ivory and looked young, like a boy's. I inched closer to him, touched the skin at the base of his neck with my nose. I breathed him in; I wanted to remember this. How do you remember a smell? I touched my cheeks against his neck and shoulders, pressed my face into his flesh. And finally I propped myself up on an elbow and took part of his shoulder into my mouth and bit him.

He groaned and mumbled, trying to roll away from me.

"Alex," I whispered again. "I need to know."

"Know wha'? Why are . . . why are you waking me up?" He rubbed his face with his hands and rolled over onto his back. "Wha' time is it?"

"We need to talk."

"Now?" He squinted at the clock-radio. "Maya, it's four in the morning." He pulled his pillow over his head and mumbled something.

"What?" I said, pulling the pillow from his face.

"I said, go back to sleep." He yanked the pillow back.

I wrenched the thing away from him and stared at him.

"Alex, are you going home?"

Blinking, he tried to focus.

"I need to know, Alex. Just tell me."

He let out a long breath between his teeth and propped up his head against the wall.

"I don't know, Maya. Don't ask me now."

"Don't give me that, Alex. You know what you're doing; you're graduating in five months. I just need you to say it. So do it. Just tell me."

We listened to the silence.

"You're going home, aren't you?" I said. "Why don't you just say it?"

Alex stared at the wall, where shadows from the branches outside sprawled across the paint in a pool of blue light. Men, I thought. The great masters of avoidance.

"What did your father say to you?" I pressed on. "He wants you to go back, right? What did he tell you when he was here? And what was all that about getting us to buy a house, huh? What did he say to you?"

Alex rubbed his face with his hands again. Finally he sighed.

"It's more complicated than it seems." He paused. "My mother wants me to get her out of Hong Kong; she wants to transfer her business here to the States and get all her money out."

"But how can you get her out?"

"I have to get a green card."

"But you don't have a job lined up yet, right?" I propped myself up on one elbow. "And what about your father?"

"He doesn't want to leave." Alex sighed. "He's very . . . Chinese. His health is not so good, you know? So he wants to stay. He wants to be buried in China, right? So he won't come."

"So what's the deal with your mother?" I asked. This was really getting convoluted.

"My mother wants to get out as soon as possible."

"And leave your father all by himself?" I gasped.

"He really doesn't mind," Alex said quietly. "They haven't really . . . They haven't been getting along for a long time, anyway, so he figures it's not a big deal, right? He's okay with that. He'd rather stay there by himself than come here. And he's not really by himself—he has all his friends there. They go out, drink tea, play cards. He has his own life there, so it's okay. He figures here he doesn't know any-body."

"Except you."

"Well, right."

"And your mother wants to leave immediately."

"Yes."

"And how is she going to come here?"

There was a long pause.

"She wants me to get married. . . ."

"So you can get a green card?" I was finally beginning to catch on; it was the middle of the night after all.

We listened to the heater roar.

After a while Alex said, "You know, Maya, I'm not going to ask you to go back with me. It's just too much to ask."

"I know."

"It's just too much. Asking someone to leave someplace to go to America is a totally different thing. Even if it's great where you are, you have a chance here. It can be *so hard* there. You have no idea." Alex was speaking each word forcefully, pressing them into the darkness. "You just have no idea."

I thought about this.

"I know. But that's not the point, is it? If we got married, we wouldn't have to live there. You could just bring your mother here."

The heater shuddered to a stop. The silence seemed louder.

"Yeah," Alex said finally. "That's true."

"But you don't want to get married."

A long pause filled up the space between us.

"I can't leave my father, Maya. I don't know, I just can't."

We lay there in the dark.

I found it interesting that I did not offer—insist, really—to go home with him in spite of the difficulties there. I was beginning to understand: He did not want me there.

Besides, I told myself, there was no way I could go. I did not want to go someplace where I looked like everyone else but felt like an alien. I felt no affinity for China, no longing for that peculiar landmass on the other side of the Earth. But America, this land that had once been a frontier of dreams, was different: This was home, and I felt it in my bones. I could not even begin to think of leaving it.

The air was thick and hot; the heat was on full blast again. I suddenly felt exhausted. I put my head in my arms. My eyes hurt. A headache that had been rising crested my temples and eased down behind my ears. It seeped toward the base of my neck and stayed there, pulsing. I started to drift off.

"Alex," I mumbled. "You're a bastard, you know that?"

He bent down and brushed my hair away from my face with his hands. He gathered it up and found an elastic loop on the nightstand and wrapped my hair up. He pushed the last stray strands away with his hands, then touched his lips to my forehead.

He did not speak.

•

I'm not sure how it all happened after that. It was as if time, which had seemed to be on our side, was slipping away faster and faster, picking up speed toward a tangled and unpleasant end. A few months after that talk in the middle of the night, something in me snapped. I could not bear to be around him a moment longer. At the time I was very calm. My circumstances had changed. So I told him I was leaving.

· · ·

ONLY A LITTLE while ago in New York I was reminded of a very distinct incident during that period in my life, which for the most part lies in my memory like a bluish haze. It was a cup that set me off, oddly enough. I saw a green enamel cup in a Manhattan shop, which I liked very much. The cup was very big, made of tin. (That green cup reminds me of the enamel cups that people use here in China except that one was better made. The cups here in China are white and poorly stenciled with pictures of crooked red flowers.) I stood there in the shop for a while, considering whether I should buy that green cup; all the enamelware in the store was only two dollars. Two dollars is not so much for a cup, but I didn't really need another one, so I put it back on the shelf and drifted through the store.

Out on the street I thought of another cup, which wasn't green or enamel at all—but you know how strange your mind can be sometimes, jumping from one thought to another, even though the two thoughts have no connecting thread of logic at all.

I thought of the other cup: my shiny aluminum cup from Thailand that a friend had given me. Thinking of this cup made me sad. This friend had ordered these cups especially for me and Alex because we had liked them so much. They felt so ice-cold when you put cool drinks into them. She had gotten four cups and given one to me and one to Alex.

"Now, when you guys get married," this friend told us,

"I'll just give you the other two cups and you'll have a set. I don't even have to buy a wedding present!" She laughed, and we laughed, too, hugging our new cups.

Our other friends liked to use these cups, too, whenever they came over. They thought drinking out of them was so unusual. And one time, when the cable man came to fix something that was wrong with the wire, I gave him a drink of iced tea out of one of the cups. He was a young black man with beautiful skin the color of a buckeye nut; he liked the cup, too, and he was a total stranger.

Much later, when Alex finally had decided to go home, I went through the apartment and took everything that was mine. I hadn't even decided consciously to leave, but one day I began walking around the living room, pulling my books off the shelves, leaving them on the floor where they fell. I walked into our bedroom, threw open the closet door, and began heaving my belongings on the bed—bags of sweaters, a raincoat still in its dry-cleaning plastic, a box of hats, and stray skeins of yarn. When Alex came home from the university, he found me standing in the hallway closet with tampons, nail polish remover, and bottles of Midol scattered at my feet.

He had an anguished look about him that I chose to ignore. Without a word he began to help me. He found some empty boxes somewhere and started packing things into them. Some things weren't mine, but Alex made me take them, anyway.

"Here," he said, shoving his rice cooker into my hands. "Take it. I won't need it. My father has one."

It was all becoming very horrible, like a divorce.

I took all the better dishes, the vegetable steamer, the reading lamp in our living room, and the bathroom scale. I left the bookcase that Alex and his father had put together; I have no idea what happened to it. I didn't take the futon, either, because it wouldn't fit in the car. I think Alex must have sold it after I left. So now someone I don't know has our bed.

One of the last things I packed was one of the cups from Thailand.

Alex was not in the room then; he must have gone to get something or maybe he left because he didn't want to help me anymore. I don't remember exactly. But I do remember standing there in front of the kitchen cupboards.

I saw the two silvery cups, pretty with little diamond shapes pressed into their sides. Without thinking, I snatched one of the cups off the shelf and wrapped it in newspaper, then shoved it into a box.

Later, when I saw the cup in a new kitchen on its new shelf, it seemed very singular. I thought how nice it would be if it were still part of a pair, side by side with its mate in the kitchen cupboard, to be taken out together and filled with cool drinks. Oh, so ice-cold to the touch! Their silvery sides sweating in the city heat, raining cool, cool drops like a shower.

I sometimes wonder if Alex still has his. I wonder if a new woman drank out of it, held its cold metal in her palms and brought it to her lips. It is odd, but the thought of another woman using that cup does not sadden or anger me. Nor does the thought of her sleeping with Alex, sharing his life. What does make me sad, though, is the thought of those two cups, mine and his, so very far away from each other in their separate kitchens. Alone, with no other drinking vessels like it. Really, they were given as a pair. It is silly, I know. But in my mind I have thought that these cups would prefer to be a pair again.

. . .

YES, IN THE end, I had chickened out. I did not want to put Alex on a plane and watch it hurtling down the runway, pulling itself into the sky and away. So I left first. I packed everything into my old beat-up, navy Cavalier and drove off, leaving him in the driveway of the apartment complex. Out of spite I wanted him to feel what it was like to be left behind. I watched him in my rearview mirror, that tall figure growing smaller, smaller, still waving. Just before I turned into the street, he touched his fingers to his lips.

I wrenched the wheel and lurched into the street, acknowledging nothing.

I drove all the way to New York like a madwoman. I stared straight ahead down the road; my eyes did not wander over the nondescript Pennsylvania scenery. I did not peer into the windows of passing cars to see what was piled up in their backseats or make fun of passengers sleeping with their heads thrown back wildly, their mouths open and flaccid. I had George Winston in the tape deck and listened to the same cassette for nine solid hours, with only two stops to get gas and go to the bathroom. I did not eat but drank three large coffees and a Mountain Dew. By the time I hit eastern New Jersey I was so strung out on caffeine and sheer exhaustion that it was a miracle I did not get into an accident. Fueled only by sheer adrenaline and rage, I maniacally sped into Manhattan and dodged yellow cabs as if I were playing pinball with the Cavalier. I double-parked in front of my sister's apartment building on East Sixty-fifth—much to the annoyance of the doorman, whose wild gesticulations and hollers I ignored—and buzzed my sister. When I got to her door, I stuffed the keys in her hand and said, "Hi. I'm here. You go park it."

After she went downstairs, I wept.

For a while after that I would wake up in the morning, stunned. I would lie there on my sister's couch for long moments before recognizing the beeping of the garbage trucks as they backed up, swallowing trash from the curb.

What had happened?

I couldn't believe that everything was over, so suddenly and so incredibly quickly. Had I really been there in the end, or did I somehow just end up someplace else without him, without anyone telling me? I wondered if I was schizophrenic, if somehow I had another personality who actually experienced my life but continually neglected to inform me of its occurrences over the years—my father, the first man in my life, was dead; Lance, who I thought had been my best friend, had disappeared and then ended up dead; I had graduated from college with an art history degree; the man I loved had gone to the other side of the planet and might as well have been dead. And now I had stopped speaking to my mother and could think of nothing to say to my sister.

What was going on here? How did all of this happen?

I closed my eyes in those early mornings and struggled to keep out any thoughts. I listened to the beeping of the garbage trucks, and perversely they were a comfort to me. They came every morning and beeped underneath my sister's window like some kind of mechanical bird.

At the end I had told him not to write me, not to let me know where he was or what he did. I had his father's address. When the time comes, I told him, I will write you there.

I didn't want to know things. I didn't want to know that he had a girlfriend or, heaven forbid, had gotten married. I didn't want to know that he had forgotten me. In my mind he had walked into the air and vanished after I moved to New York. It was better this way. It has been easier to cope with a kind of death than with a rejection.

That way, I can remember him with tenderness, when he was with me. I can remember the way our knees touched under restaurant tables, the way he kissed my wrists late at night.

•

Soon after the garbage trucks left each morning, my sister would get up and go to the hospital. I do not think she was really awake when she got out of bed; she was accustomed to doing everything in a half-asleep state, trying to get more rest before going back to work. She was a resident in those days; she seemed to be at the hospital all the time. On those early mornings she would shower and leave and not say anything to me as I lay there on her couch, listening to the water drain away.

In the lull after she left, before the light was fully formed in the day, time took on a nightmarish quality. I would lie there, squeezing my eyes shut, trying to go back to sleep. But my mind would run away on its own, seeping into the slivers of the dawn.

Eventually, somehow, there was sleep and strange dreams that I could not remember after waking; there only was the sense that I had been fleeing—running and running for hours.

I do not remember how long I lived like that, suspended in a state of dreams. I do not remember how many mornings I spent in the world of vapors, closed off from what was real and what was not. I did not want to think because I was afraid that if I thought too much, I would lose my mind. It is a strange thing because in Chinese the word for *mind* is the same as the word for *heart*; they are one and the same: *xin*. So, in effect, since my heart was broken, using Chinese semantics my mind would have been broken as well; my grief would have driven me to madness already, so there was no use trying to avoid it.

But I did.

And now, on this trip, everything has risen to the surface. It is so strange: The air seems so rarefied. It is as if I am in a suspended reality, where time and my very person are meaningless. All the thoughts that I never knew existed spring into my mind; old memories appear from nowhere.

. . .

It is the morning of our first full day on the Yangze. I get up from my small bed and look dully around the cabin of the boat. I blink my eyes, and a thought crosses my mind: I wonder if Alex ever has been on a boat. But I know I shouldn't think about such things, not after all this time. I rub my eyes wearily; I am very tired.

Joyce is still asleep. On top of a modest desk is her notebook, which lies open, its pages wrapped around the thick, spiral binding. I cannot read her writing, which is a confusing mass of scribbles in her own form of shorthand. I see clusters of letters like *wht* and *censp*. I pull on my shorts and T-shirt and wash my face, brush my teeth. Then I wander down the hallway of the boat to a small lounge area by a window. The chairs are not very comfortable, but they are plush and red to give that illusion.

I stare out the window, my mind blank. The boat is still docked, and I can hear that some of the other passengers are in the dining room already, beginning their breakfast. There is the clatter of dishes and the slightly sickening smell of fried eggs. There is not much to see outside, just a nondescript bank of grass and a few houses in the distance.

I feel someone leaning against the chair and turn around. It is Marcus.

"Hey," I say to him. "Did you sleep okay?"

He looks sleepy and a little grumpy. "Yeah, I guess so. But I got up really early." He picks at the plush binding on the arm of the chair.

"You got up early? Why did you do that?"

"I dunno." He kicks the wooden feet of the chair, sending little vibrations up my legs. "I'm bored. There's nothing to do around here."

"It'll be better when the boat gets moving," I tell him. "Then there'll be stuff to see."

"I guess." He keeps kicking the chair, which is beginning to get a little annoying. "But I don't wanna look at stuff anymore. I wanna go home."

I look at his small face, which suddenly looks even younger than he is. I know how he feels.

"Yeah, I think we all kinda feel that way," I say. "Traveling is kind of a drag after a while." Marcus will not look up, but I can see the beginning of a scowl forming on his brow. He has a blue baseball cap on backward; I think it says "Cubs" on the other side.

"Yeah, well, I'm bored," Marcus pronounces again. "I wanna go home."

"What would you do if you were at home?"

"I dunno. Lots of stuff. Play games on my computer. Watch TV. Go play with my friends. Stuff like that. Anything. There's nothing to do around here." Marcus gives the chair leg a good kick. "I'm sick of China."

"Well, I'm afraid there's not a whole lot you and I can do about that right now," I tell him. "We're pretty much stuck here for another week unless you can hijack a plane or something."

He seems to consider this a moment, then looks sullen again.

"Are you hungry?" I ask. "Do you want to go to breakfast?"

He shakes his head.

I think I see the crew moving around outside. Before Marcus can start kicking the chair again, I stand up and put my hand on his back, leading him away.

"Come on," I say. "I think they're going to start the boat. Let's go watch."

Marcus follows me listlessly, running his hand along the spindles of a metal railing as he passes, making a rhythmic pinging sound. We push through a pair of glass doors that lead to the outside observation deck and watch as men leap about, gathering ropes and yelling something to one another. Suddenly the whole boat shudders as the engine rumbles to a start.

Marcus's eyes perk up a bit, and he goes to the railing, craning his neck to see as the boat spits out gray smoke from its stack and percolates erratically. We watch as somehow the vessel gathers enough energy to turn into the river. The men are running around on the upper deck, tossing aboard last coils of rope and then leaping on themselves. The boat blasts its horn, and we are on our way, steaming downstream.

The door opens.

"Come, come," Mr. Wong calls to us. "It's time for breakfast."

It is later, and I stare out at the landscape that is China. My mind has been so preoccupied with my memories of Alex lately that it feels stretched beyond its capacity. I close my eyes for a bit and the darkness behind my lids is soothing. I open them again. I look at the mountains rising on both sides of the river, and the sight makes me smile. Who would have thought that one day I would see all this myself, in person? All that time I spent in darkened classrooms, gazing at slides cast upon a white wall, and it never occurred to me that eventually I might see those very scenes with my own eyes.

Of course, who knows where those mountains really were; who knows precisely which bend in the river those ancient Chinese painters chose to re-create on stretches of silk and paper. Those, after all, were landscapes of the mind—versions of reality that followed not the contours of actual geography but those of the painter's heart and spirit.

My eyes follow the curve of stone reaching toward the heavens; they drop to where the stone meets the water, to where there are smaller rocks and plants and reeds.

I look at the river, which is muddy and brown, coursing to the sea. When it reaches the sea, I think, it will turn blue; it will turn thick and heavy with salt.

When I am in Hong Kong, I think, I finally will see the ocean after all this time inland.

. . .

Suddenly, I am overwhelmed by a feeling of wistfulness and I close my eyes again.

Hong Kong. The thought of it makes my heart clench, just for a moment. If a heart could wince, that is the sensation I have beneath my breast: a pinch of the heart, an involuntary flinch.

In less than a week we will leave China; we will cross the border into that famous harbor, to where the one I still love lives. The prospect frightens me. It will be strange enough to walk through those streets knowing that I might be passing down a road that he has stepped on; it will be disarming enough to look out at the sea and be certain that his eyes have looked out at the very same scene.

All that is enough.

The possibility that I might see him there is more than I can begin to grasp. And, moreover, it's more than I want to deal with. I know I am being foolish and silly, but a skittish heart is a difficult thing. I am so well practiced in indecision.

In any case, I think it will be nice to see the ocean. I wish I could stay on this boat all the way there. I close my eyes again and feel the breeze against my face. I let my mind go to nothing and simply listen to the dull roar of the engine, the continuous splash of the water against the boat. I close my eyes and listen to the sounds of the river.

. . .

SUDDENLY, I JOLT in my seat. For an instant all my wayward thoughts from the past few weeks seem to align themselves.

The sea, I think. The river runs to the sea, the river runs to the sea.

Yes, but of course! And all at once, everything seems very clear: I know why I came to China.

My heart beats faster.

All this time I have told myself it was for other reasons: I wanted to see the art; I wanted to see the mountains; I needed to get away from the city.

But no, not really, not really.

I came for Alex. To look for him. Not in the flesh, certainly. I know where to find him, physically, in Hong Kong; I don't have to spend six weeks in a Third World country to do that. No, it is as if I am looking for answers in the leaves at the bottom of a tea bowl: I am looking for traces of the world that formed him, that built his spirit. I am looking for all the threads of a story that began thousands of years ago in lost dynasties and that now lead up to him.

I am trying to figure out what it was in his Chinese heart that lured him away from me.

At first I did not know what I was doing.

I thought the answer to why he left me was in New York. So I looked for clues there, but not consciously. I thought I was just restless; I could never keep still.

I walked and walked. From Wall Street to the fragrance shops in the West Village. Then to Chinatown, where sticky roast pork hung in the windows and steamed the glass. I hunted in the train stations, deep and smelly and horrifying in their blackness, but where people played beautiful instruments and collected coins in old velvet cases.

I looked for him in coffee shops. Didn't he used to like coffee shops? Or was that Lance? In those New York coffee shops I always felt a little sick, where there was always a feeling of plenty, of too much: trays and trays of cakes and lovely little tarts all encased in their paper cups; piles of uniformly shaped cookies and biscuits; heaps of rolls covered with poppy seeds and onion flakes. So much food with sticky centers and gooey middles.

I looked for the threads of him hidden somewhere in the anise biscotti, behind beautiful foil boxes of chocolates and truffles; I thought they might be entwined in the gold cords and silver elastics. Disguised in the crackle of cellophane and the rustle of tissue.

I found nothing in New York.

I thought the secret was hidden from me and the dirty men on street corners; it eluded groups of teenage boys and girls who traveled in packs after dark. I thought he hid from the ear-piercing screech of trains as they squealed to their dreadful stops, expelling people onto the platform, inhaling more passengers in great, steaming clots; inside, the people lay flattened against one another, hanging onto the straps like pale carcasses on hooks.

And after a while I gave up, numbed by all the fury in the city.

But then, out of the blue, I decided to go to China.

China, yes! It makes so much sense now; I cannot believe it has not occurred to me before. I came to the land where for us time began because I am looking for what made him Chinese. Is it some special ingredient? Some particular mark on the personality gene? Is it something in the air? The water? What is it that made him rush back here to Asia, kowtowing to ancestors long dead?

So I look surreptitiously, so no one in my tour group will notice. I am so sure it is here. Earlier in this trip I looked in the corridors of an old stone temple. Out its windows with no glass were rice paddies, green like fields of emeralds. We climbed the stairs to the top. Up and up and up . . . Through the cool passageways where we felt it was necessary to whisper. We could almost hear the shuffle of cotton and silk against the worn stone from centuries ago. A thousand million footfalls had softened, smoothed, and darkened the edges of those steps. We could pretend that a thousand million hearts had been broken on those stairs; ten thousand wishes had been cast into the tureens thick with burning incense. How many stolen kisses were taken from these balconies? How many sly embraces? There I looked for answers. My mind raced.

I look for those traces of him every day. This is why I have been so restless. I think they are hidden in the streets, under the table skirts of sidewalk vendors: Tall tales and skinny ones, whispered ones and operatic ones. Tales captured on the wisps of cigarette smoke, trailing toward the heavens. Nearly every Chinese man smokes, so think of how many stories that is! I think that these tales must be sweet and brutal, fecund, nearly rancid in the moist summer heat.

I look everywhere, because who is to know from where the secret tales of him will emerge? Open a glass pot in the state-run friendship store and will they fly out and dart about the room? Will they flutter wildly, like startled birds caught between the front door and the screen? Like ghosts, both happy and sad, contented and haunted, they float just above our conception of reality, of fixed space.

I look and listen. Stupidly, I think I must be like a dog that can hear sounds beyond the range of humans. I think I must be like a bat that can sense vibrations in the air. . . .

So this is it. I know why I am here.

I am looking for what it means to be Chinese, because it was Alex's Chinese loyalty that brought him back to this side of the Earth. I am looking for that pull of home, that strange call he heeded.

And now I realize it is the same call that my own father listened for night after night, hidden within the plaintive cries of his Cantonese opera tapes. But for my father it was a sound that brought him home in mind only. It was a home that he had left willingly and that most likely had been cruel.

. . .

I AM ON a boat in China. I look out at the mountains and the water.

I think of the scenes that Alex had painted, those vivid landscapes rendered in descending shades of gray. I look out at the swirling, muddy waters and turn my ears into the gentle wind. I strain my ears and listen, listen for what I think I am supposed to hear.

DOUBLE

HAPPINESS

IT IS A while later; I do not know how much time has passed. I sit, breathless, on the deck of the boat.

I blink, stare at the trees on shore as if I have never seen such plants before. My rush of thoughts has left me winded. My head feels strange. I look around me. I need to rest for a while.

I stretch my neck. Suddenly I feel relieved. My mental sojourn has quelled some of my anxieties as to why I am in the middle of China right now, floating around on a river. I go inside to the bar and ask for some orange soda. It's warm, but I am getting used to this. I take my glass outside and go to the railing of the observation deck, sipping the soda slowly; it is too sweet, but I am getting used to that, too.

Chad comes out and stands next to me.

"Hey," he says. "See anything interesting? Any dead bodies?"

I shake my head. Everything he says has a way of being annoyingly inappropriate.

"They say we're gonna see the first gorge in the next hour or so."

I nod, not wanting to encourage any more conversation. He pulls out a bag of M&M-type candies from his shirt pocket. "Want some?" he asks, tearing open the bag. "I got them from our hotel in Chongqing, so they're probably really shitty, but what the hell. Chocolate's chocolate, right?"

He pours some of the candy-coated pellets into my hand. I taste a few; he's right, they're not very good, a little bit chalky and stale. When Chad figures out that I'm not being terribly verbal, he drifts away to chat with our tour guide, Jim, who is at the other end of the deck.

I gaze into the water and my mind wanders, but without threat. I think fondly of my father; he brings a smile to my lips. I think of Alex and smile as well, but with a touch of regret. The two are men I will love forever, and somehow their memory is tied irrevocably to this strange land. Oddly, Lance fits here, too, for he links the two, serving as the passageway from one to the other. I do not know what China means to the others in my tour group—perhaps it is the country exotic, the land of silk and spice, of ivory and fine-boned women. For me, however, this place is where it all began: This is where the men I loved most were conceived, both in flesh and spirit. And for that alone I always will be respectful.

We now are on the waterways, on the tributaries that lead through the heart of China. This is how a person most likely went from place to place; this is where women sent their men off to war, those women who in classical paintings eternally stood at the riverside by a brushwood fence, looking downstream from where their lovers would never return.

The others in the group are standing at the deck railing, looking at the first of three gorges that we will pass on our three-day cruise down the Yangze. The mountains loom up on either side of us, sheer cliffs of rock that plummet into the water; this is not the Grand Canyon of the American West, but the sight is still breathtaking.

It has been raining. It rained continuously last night; it

drove down in sheets, making the water roar past our boat as we docked for the night. It had been rather exciting to travel in the rain, to feel lost and adrift on our miniature sea yet know that we were only on the river and relatively safe.

Suddenly someone is yelling, pointing to the brown river that is like a swirling stream of chocolate milk.

"Look!" Joyce yells. Everyone rushes to the starboard side, to look to where she is pointing. "It's a body!"

"That's not a body," Mr. Barclay says. "It looks just like a log."

The shape is moving swiftly toward us; in a flash it passes: A bloated carcass, pale and splotched like a pig, is already out of clear sight. We see no head, no feet, no horns, no hooves. But we all see the white underpants, still on the body of an otherwise naked man facedown in the water.

"Oh, my God," Joyce says. "Oh, my God." Her hands are shaking as she raises them to cover her mouth, which will not close but hangs open as if she wants to say something else.

"Shit, Maya," Chad says to me. "I was just *kidding* about the dead bodies. . . ."

The crowd bursts into nervous chatter. Who was that? Do you think anyone knows? Should we tell the captain? Mrs. Edward has put her arms around Joyce and is leading her inside; Joyce's hands still are clasped over her mouth, and she walks as if she has no sea legs.

I stand there, mute, dumb, staring at the swirling water. I stare, half expecting the body to be there again, to rise from the depths. I look at the swollen banks, feeling a little dizzy.

All of a sudden the river seems pregnant. It has that overfull, bloated look, appearing to swell past the high-water marks. The river seems somehow hormonally out of kilter, unable to control some strange wildness that wells up within it. The river rushes through the gorge, speeding faster and faster, an enormous volume of water forcing its way through the narrow passageway of stone. Little cyclones swirl in the river, sucking down leaves and twigs and bits of plastic; there seem to be hundreds of the cyclones in sight now, as if the river bottom were lined with hundreds of little drains sucking all the water away.

Jim comes out to tell us there have been terrible floods in the past two days in central China; we are lucky to have missed them. And he tells us not to worry about the man in the water; there's no telling where he was washed away from. We are silent. We realize we are not in America; no one will go rushing out to try to locate that body, to find the family to whom that man belonged. There is no law-enforcement agency that is that well organized to undertake such a task, no network in place to take care of such matters.

Within the next twelve hours three more bodies are spotted floating in the Yangze—two more men clad in their undershorts and facedown in the water, one faceup and wearing black pants. All are swollen, blown up like pigskin balloons used to float rafts. This seemingly docile river can turn face, can suddenly turn wild; no wonder it is called the "sorrow of China."

. . .

BY NOW THE waters have turned relatively calm, gently taking us through the mountains, past fantastic rocks worn down by time. We travel through the Three Gorges of the Yangze, down the waters that have carried countless Chinese through the dynasties.

From the boat we can see the people of the river. The men have beautiful backs and shoulders, forged by a lifetime of pushing bamboo oars through the water. Even the little children are dark from time spent outside on the water, looking for lovely patterned rocks and small fish. We can tell that they are not afraid of the river; they balance themselves easily on small boats and in the shallows, splashing each other playfully. We see a man who has a small bowl in his hands, which he uses to scoop water from the river and pour over his head. We pass a group of women sitting on their haunches at the bank, washing bundles of clothing in large enamel basins. For the people of the river the water is everything; it is like a kind of mother earth, the source of all things good and evil.

It is our second day on the river. Our ship is named *The Three Gorges*, a veritable *Love Boat* complete with a sharp and savvy cruise director, Peter, a tour leader, Mr. Chu, and a fully stocked bar that has three plates of cookies and crackers for us to snatch as we go onto the sightseeing deck. Other than the gruesome sight of the bodies in the water, I am beginning to enjoy our little cruise. It's nice not to be rushing around from one sightseeing spot to another. It's pleasant just to sit and not move. I need this rest, and for the first time since we came to China I am beginning to feel a little relaxed, less manic. But I also am feeling a little weak; all this traveling has made me tired. And, more than that, I am emotionally exhausted: I am glad to have figured out my motives, however unwitting, for coming to China. But it will take a little while to get used to the idea.

I have taken to standing outside on the sightseeing deck. This morning after breakfast I stood out there for what seemed like hours, staring into the water, which was soothing to watch and hear. I gazed at the swirling patterns of the river around rocks and plants. I liked to see the point of the boat pushing through the water, making an inverted V in the surface for miles and miles. Around the banks the water whorled and was the color of milky coffee. I felt placid but not necessarily at ease. I hoisted myself up over the edge of the railing, bending over the top of it so that my feet were dangling, like a child's. After a while Mrs. Petersen came out to wrap one of her scarves around my head.

"It's so breezy out here, honey," she told me as she knotted the silk square at my throat. "You don't want to catch your death of cold."

. . .

IT IS SUNNY now, and we stop at one of the cruise's main ports of call, Ghost City. We must make an exhausting climb of more than 500 steps to see the wooden figurines of brightly colored spirits. I am mesmerized by the display of the East and West hells, depicting people being boiled, speared, sliced, bludgeoned, burned, poisoned, eaten, and likewise tortured to death for various unforgivable transgressions during their lives. I think children are brought here to frighten them into good behavior. The faces of the damned are carved into eternal, gaping screams; blood drips from their wounds into red pools. Evidently, "Chinese torture" is no carefree idiom. I have heard how people were killed by being forced to eat bowls of food embedded with bamboo splinters (which would shred the victims internally, causing them to hemorrhage to death) and by slicing (in which the doomed were cut alive into tiny pieces like so much filet).

It's cool up in the mountains, but I start to sweat and feel chilled. All these ghosts and demons are beginning to unnerve me. I nod to the others and say I must sit down for a moment; I'm tired from the climb. I will catch up. Robert offers me water; Marcus asks if I need first aid. No, no, it's nothing, I tell them. I just want to sit for a while. They drift on, looking at three massive wooden carvings of spirits perched on the hillside overlooking the river.

I find a bench and sit, thinking of the damned in their torturous hells. In one facet of Chinese belief there are twelve levels of hell; the sinner is sent to a punishment befitting his or her earthly crime. At one level is a giant wok, where the damned boil in oil; there's nothing like being stir-fried for all eternity.

I think of how this world is so different from the one I know so well. I think of my apartment, my cats, and of a bicycle I had when I was a child, the one with the white banana seat. That world of my childhood and that place where I now live are nothing like this, the China of a dozen hells. My mind begins to take off, scampering through the folds of my life, which at times has felt so convoluted. My thoughts take me to a place I have not wanted to go to.

Disjointed images flash in my head, then vanish.

I think of my father eating breakfast; he is chewing oatmeal, reading the newspaper. Then I see Maura sitting in John's lap, giving him a kiss, nibbling on his ear. I think of Lance riding down a hill on his bicycle; I am fixated on his elbow, motionless as his legs pump past, pedal, pedal, legs moving so fast I cannot even make them out. I imagine Alex at his drafting table, wielding a huge brush, sodden with ink; all the blackness is dripping onto the paper. I see bodies, swollen and nameless, floating down the river, one after another. I think of my mother sitting at her dressing table, touching perfume to her exquisite neck. I see a cleaver falling *wap!* into the flesh and bone of a chicken, already dead, already plucked and half cooked; the head and neck fall off. There is blood on the chopping block, blood on the knife. Blood from the mouths of the damned in Ghost City, screaming silently into eternity. There is blood in the toilet. So much blood.

I am chilled. I look down; my fingertips are blue.

My thoughts run and run and I cannot seem to stop them. For years I ran, but what had that gotten me? So now there are all these loose thoughts jumbled in my head, rushing, rushing.

All this running away, all this running around, and what is it all for? Run all the way to China and what do I find but me. Gotcha. You're It.

What's behind Door No. 3? What's the million-dollar

question? What has been the question that follows like a curse, hovering, nipping at the heels of dreams? Yes, yes, so I am here to find out what it means to have a Chinese heart, but there's more, always more. There's that question, there all along, that I pretended not to notice.

. . .

IN MY MIND this question has been like a whispered prayer, counted on a string of beads.

Do I go?

Do I go to see Alex? In Hong Kong? After all this time the thought of seeing him is unbelievable. I'd rather have him in the abstract image of dreams and memories . . . he is so unclear that way, so unreal. I never have to deal with what is real then, what is not.

Aiya, Alex.

Everything he does not know; all the sorrow he left behind, and I never said a word. I was so stupid. I bundled up my weeping heart and tried to hide it away. But all the tears seeped out and now it's all a mess—water, water, everywhere, and still my throat is dry and tight. I cannot speak. I cannot even think of letting the words drop from my mouth, one and then another, in his presence. Really, it is no small question whether I go to see him in Hong Kong because the real question is: Do I tell?

Do I tell?

Yes, the real question is: Do I tell him that he had a son?

. . .

A LITTLE BOY. A second image of the one I loved. For me this was a double happiness, a double blessing.

Am I crazy, cruel, for not telling Alex? But the boy was not even supposed to *be*. So innocent, yes! So unknowing. But conceived just before his father left. And me. Ashamed.

I told no one. Except my sister. That is why I went to

New York. Wonderful and terrible New York, where I knew no one but her.

I waited.

What to do, what to do? The days went by. The weeks. All those early mornings I lay cold and sick on my sister's couch; I could not think clearly. But I tried to think. I prayed, although I hadn't prayed in years. I was so indecisive. I was running out of time to decide about anything.

I meant to tell him, really. But the longer I didn't tell him, the worse it became. I couldn't just tell him over the phone, could I? Long distance? Still, not to say anything seemed more dishonest.

I began to swell, just a little.

But then, late in my third month, something happened. I bled. I could not stop. So much redness everywhere. They pulled the baby from me one dull morning just before the dawn.

I am sure it must have been a boy. A son, just as his father also was a son: a double happiness. And now a double sorrow.

Gone. So how could I tell him then? How can I tell him now? How can I tell him he had a son but I let him die?

He was gone before I even had a chance to comprehend his being here at all. His was a half-life that lasted what seemed like only a breath, a mere exhalation. A blink.

And then there was nothing.

Only an empty space where all my joy had been.

There was a time, after the child, that I sat motionless in a chair for three days, hobbled by my guilts and sorrow. I was like a woman in feudal China who had bound feet. A woman like that would have been taken as a child and had her toes turned under, her foot bent in half and wrapped in strips of cloth. Her mother did this, or perhaps a nursemaid.

"Do not cry," the elder woman would say as day by day

she crushed the tiny feet in her hands, "I'm doing this for your own good." A girl with small feet would most likely qualify for a better marriage to a richer man. A girl with tiny feet—a girl with three-inch "golden lotus" feet—was considered to be a thing of beauty. Never mind that her feet had bled and rotted and were twisted and deformed; never mind that she could not run to save her life and could only walk with the help of a handmaid. That was the point: She took tiny steps like a child and could not stray far.

But me, what of me? My sister had helped me get my own apartment, a sublet. I sat in it, motionless in a chair with my full-size feet, yet still I hobbled myself. I could not move. I sat holding my empty belly, so stricken with grief that I could not cry. For hours and hours I sat in a rattan mamasan chair, curled up like an infant with my big feet tucked under my thighs. The cats climbed into my lap and I stroked them, combed their fur with my fingers until I was covered with great mounds of loose hair that I did not sweep up. I set out an open box of cat food on the floor for my poor, confused pets. For days I did not change before collapsing into bed and I would sleep in a swirl of feline fur. In the late morning I would lie there, unable to move, my feet weighted as if all my grief had sunk in the night and settled in my toes, heels, and ankles. My mind was numb.

On day I wanted to drink.

There was nothing in the apartment but cheap sherry that had been used for cooking. I sat, curled up with my leaden feet beneath me, and drank the saccharine liquid straight from the bottle. The taste was vile, but I enjoyed this sensation. My head reeled and my cheeks burned from the alcohol that ran straight through my empty stomach and into my blood. I barely made it to the kitchen sink, where I vomited a bitter flood into a pile of dirty dishes. I forced four orange-colored peanut-butter-and-cheese crackers into my mouth and chewed, made myself swallow. The room spun as I staggered to my bed, wiping my mouth with the backs of my hands; the cats fled from me.

The next day I made myself get up and clean the kitchen. I put on rubber gloves and doused the reeking sink with bleach and turned the hot water on full-blast. I did the dishes and swept the worst of the cat hair into a giant garbage bag. I changed the cat litter. I stripped the bed, put down fresh sheets, and heaped my dirty linen and clothes in one corner of the room to be dealt with later. I took a hot, hot shower that lasted forever. When I came out, dripping, steaming, and pink, my feet were swollen and wrinkled. I looked in the mirror and wept.

My sister is the only one who knows my shame, and I think this gives her an emotional leverage over me, which is disturbing. I worry that one day, at a crucial moment, she forcibly will hold her knowledge over me; usually it is the ones we love who possess the greatest ability to devastate us.

She and I do not speak of what we know. In our silence we paper over the truth. I do small favors for her, give her little attentions. She does not ask for them, but I do these things just in case; she knows how grateful I am, truly. She was very kind at the time. So now I feel I must never cross her; I never will speak ill of John, although I dislike him immensely. I will be a good sister-in-law.

We have created another house of ghosts.

Someone is calling to me. I look up. It is Jim, the tour guide. We are leaving, he tells me. I stand up slowly, feeling a little faint. Jim comes over, takes my arm.

"Are you all right?" he asks.

I blink at him, look away. Yes, just a little tired, I lie.

He opens his flight bag, gets out a small jar of Tiger Balm. "Here," he says, "put this here." He taps his temples, holds out the open jar. I rub on the cure-all ointment; it has a pungent, herbal smell, a smell I associate with my mother. I tell him thank you.

Jim takes my arm again to help support me, but I tell him that I will be all right. We walk slowly down the hill together, down the 500 steps that lead away from the city of ghosts.

So this is it, I think. This is what it all has come to.

I walk down the steps slowly. I dare not look away from my feet; I am afraid I will trip. I am shaking just a little.

"Take your time, take your time," Jim says. He tries to take my arm again, gently, and again I pull it away from him.

No, no, I'm okay, I say to him.

I do not say that I don't want to be touched, especially by a man, just now.

We walk down the steps, one foot at a time. I stare at the stones, look at the smoothness, where thousands of other feet have worn them down. I see a pebble; I see some stray grass growing through the stones. One foot down, then another. For some reason I think of Lance, but only of his feet: one red-sneakered foot, one blue. Oh, Lance.

We reach a stopping point. I lean against a low stone wall. From this vantage point we can see our boat docked at the riverside. The sun is bright, and it has become incredibly beautiful out today. But the water is the color of ash, gray and brown.

Jim and I continue walking. He is being very kind. He doesn't ask me anything more. Just walks with me to make sure I am doing all right.

So this is it, I think again.

All the way to China and here it is: all my ghosts, all my guilts are here as well. Hello, they say. Surprise, we got here first! We're having fun, why aren't you? And they laugh and laugh; the joke's on me.

•

"What's the matter, are you okay? Do you have a fever? What's wrong?"

I push away from the crowd of my well-meaning tour group. No, no, it's nothing, I say; I just want to lie down. I'll be fine; I have a headache. Someone thrusts a bottle of aspirin in my hand. Joyce follows me to our cabin; she is hovering around and I want to hit her, make her go away. She fusses with the curtains, my pillows. She gets me water, makes me swallow the aspirin tablets. Finally she leaves. At last.

I close my eyes.

The boat shudders violently as the engine starts, and we leave the shore of ghosts. I sleep, dreamless.

. . .

IT IS THE next day.

At breakfast I eat enormous amounts. I am starving; I did not have dinner last night. I eat two bowls of rice porridge and three of those small, bland steamed buns. Everytime the lazy Susan on our table spins around, I take what rotates in front of me: spoonfuls of scrambled eggs, a bit more preserved tofu, and a few more boiled peanuts for the porridge. Tea, more tea. Oddly, a plate of thin white toast arrives; it is so strange to see sliced bread because I have not encountered it for weeks. I take two pieces, have more eggs. Finally I am full and feel much better, but I am still spent.

. . .

NOW WE ARE on a tributary of the Yangze, riding a small boat with a dreadful motor. We are told our bigger boat will not fit through this narrower, shallower passage. But the scenery is supposed to be good.

They stop the boat and let us out onto a beach of sorts. It is all rocks, a narrow shore that runs to the base of the steep but low mountains. We put our hands in the water; it is very cool. And strangely clear.

"Look at the rocks!" Mrs. Yamamoto says. "Look at all of them!"

We pick up the stones. They are stunningly beautiful— layers of quartz and sandstone layered together like exquisite petits fours. Good enough to eat. A brilliant white crystal. A dull, dark gray one that turns shiny black when you dip it in water. Some are reddish. Light gray. Yellow. We pick and choose stones, fill our hands and pockets with the pressed sand.

I find two stones, black and flat and round. Two, exactly alike. I squeeze them in my hand, hold them like a memory of another two.

We get back on the small boat. The motor roars and sputters as we leave the inlet. The boat vibrates horribly, shaking us, making our teeth chatter and our minds go numb. We cruise slowly toward the main boat, which is moored on the Yangze. I take the stones out and look at them. This is the dust of China, pressed into flat disks, worn to these perfect shapes by the running of the river. The water has washed all the corners away, washed away the harshness. But then I think of the men whose bodies we saw floating in the river; I cannot forget them. The river did that, too.

I look out the open window and squint into the sunlight. I stare dully at the water, which is taking all our sadness to the sea.

We have docked. The cruise is over, and we are leaving the water. But it seems soggy here; apparently it has rained for days. I am sad to be leaving the boat. I have become accustomed to the way it rocks, to the way the scenery passes by. I have gotten used to watching the patterns in the river, the curves of the mountains as they flow downstream with us. A group of men meets us at the riverside; some of them seem very old. They are here to carry our luggage up an enormous hill to the road, where a van waits for us. We gape in disbelief as the men tie two or three suitcases on each side of their bamboo poles. I have to struggle with my lone bag; I cannot imagine carrying six times its weight.

"My bag is too heavy," Mrs. Barclay protests, trying to stop him. "Don't carry it with all these others; you'll hurt yourself." But a gaunt old man with several teeth missing just waves away her words and grins. He staggers under the weight; the pole looks as if it will bite into his neck and snap it. But he steadies himself, his calf muscles twitching. Then he begins climbing up the hill on the dirt path, keeping the tremendous weight in perfect balance.

We gape some more, feel terribly guilty.

"It's okay, it's okay," the cruise director tells us. "They do this every day. It is their job." But we still feel bad.

. . .

WE FLY INTO Wuhan on CAAC (which, we were told, should stand for Chinese Airlines Always Cancel instead of whatever aviation name it purports to have).

It rains.

Our guide says it has rained for seven days here in Wuhan, but the hardest was the day before yesterday. Actually, everywhere is wet in China, as water pours from the skies, swelling rivers and dams. We find out that China is in the throes of one of the worst floods ever and that a thousand are dead.

Truly, the water is everywhere here; we did not leave it when we departed from the Yangze. It washes up over sidewalks, drips off umbrellas, gushes out of drainpipes. People wear plastic sandals and rain ponchos draped over their bicycles. Dead fish wash up on the banks of the tranquil East Lake and float on the pavement in water ankle-deep. But we are thankful for the water because it breaks the heat, which would otherwise have been unbearable this time of year. It is as if the heavens opened in part to spare us from the oppressive hotness, but something went wrong and people drowned.

We go to a painting factory, where I find out that the workers copy paintings of landscapes and flowers with passionless precision. We walk through a series of small rooms and a dozen or so people are seated at tables, copying mountains like the alphabet. I am so disappointed. Crushed. All those lovely watercolors, cranked out by communist drones who put in eight hours a day re-creating deadness on paper. We did not stay long there as there was so little to see and no one in our group wanted to buy anything.

As we stand outside the factory, waiting for the driver to open the door of our minibus, I see a little boy standing by a nearby doorway, watching us. He is very small, perhaps not more than two years old. He is wearing little blue trousers and a slightly grubby T-shirt with a cartoon picture of a cat on it. His eyes are steady, serious, and he studies us without blinking. He is holding something in his hand, but I cannot make out what it is. I look at his face again and realize he is staring right at me; he's utterly adorable, with dumpling cheeks, and something in me is very sad all of a sudden. When we have all boarded the minivan, the driver starts the engine and we head toward the main street; I look out the window. The little boy is still there, watching.

I can't take much more of this, I think.

I'm sick of traveling and tired from lugging too much emotional baggage around. I need a porter for all this. That would be nice. I smile at the thought, which amuses me a bit as we drive on through the streets.

These days in China seem filled with sorrow. There are times when everything seems too much, when I can't help but gather sadness from the streets, adding to my own parcels of guilt. I am beginning to wonder if Chinese and Catholics share some kind of cosmic kinship; we both conduct so much of our daily transactions in shaded currencies of feeling bad, of falling short, of not living up to a kind of divine perfection. There are a thousand rules for proper conduct and a million ways to fail them.

So as we take a tour through the streets of Wuhan, I pull sadness in through the minibus window, adding to my own burden. But this is the way it is: To be Chinese, I am beginning to think, is to accept the difficulty of being human. There is happiness, of course, and joy and good fortune. And working hard is a good thing. But there also is bitterness and deep sorrow, and to be Chinese means to swallow them whole, because that is the way of the living; it is part of the deal for staying on this side of death.

We drive on.

I see a young girl, a young woman really, with her hair tied back, at the market. She stands under a tarpaulin stretched across some poles, her face red from the scorching heat that rises from a pool of oil in a giant wok. She is frying lumps of dough; I do not know what they are.

I see another woman, young, wearing gold-rimmed glasses, reading a book in the government department store. She is sitting behind a counter lined with tin cups and plates, plastic kitchenware in bright yellow and red.

At the outskirts of Wuhan I see another woman, her hair tied in a blue bandanna, her pant legs rolled up to the knees. She is barefoot; her shins and calves are a mess of bruises and insect bites. She holds a plastic tub of dirty wash water, then pitches it beside a building, where the ground is muddy and rancid with effluent and waste.

My heart is filled with sorrow when I see these women.

"I'm sorry, I'm sorry," I want to say to them. I'm sorry that I took your place.

I think about the randomness of birth, of how the seeds of

our souls grow in the wombs of our mothers. We have no choice in the lives that await us when we emerge, wet and slick, from the safety of those inner seas.

I see a woman washing clothes on rocks at the banks of a river brown with silt. She could be me, I think. But solely by the lottery of fate I was born to parents on American soil, and I feel guilty at my good fortune.

I look at this woman, squatting on the riverbank, and I want to weep. For in reality she *is* me. She is my sister; the blood of China runs through her as it does through me.

I turn my head.

I cannot watch this life from which I was spared.

. . .

ALEX'S WORDS COME back to me, what he said about life being so hard in Hong Kong. You have no idea, he said. You just have no idea.

If I had gone to Hong Kong, I would not have had to wash clothes at a riverbank; I would not have stood in the hot sun all day hawking small things off a makeshift table. But it still would have been hard, and I now know for sure that I could not have withstood it.

This—all this—was the kind of life my father had left behind and chosen to forget. He had not wanted to remember the hunger and brutality. When one is desperate, when one is pushed to the edge, it is amazing what one person can do to another in a time of scarcity. Like too many rats in a cage, killing one another one by one. It is that incredible will to survive, above all else. Now, it is no longer wartime, but too many memories of it remain here.

My father made another life and filled it with new, more pleasant memories. He did not demand much from his days; for him a day without fear was probably enough. Food on the table, a roof over one's head. That sort of thing. But in creating such a life of ease for me, my days became filled with a kind of emptiness, especially when he no longer was there to occupy them with his good nature.

I used to think that my father had no past, but I now see that that is not so. It still is here, all of it. There may not be that awful famine anymore; there may not be death at every turn. But the memory of it remains, and that is enough.

Before I know it we are in the air again, flying south, like birds in winter. Except that it is the dead of summer. Every day we wake up in disbelief, look at our American, pampered, air-conditioned selves and say peevishly to one another, "It is *so* hot," as if this is a surprise, as if we had expected it to change from yesterday. We are all getting tired. Sheepishly, I crave a glass of cold milk, a bowl of cottage cheese; we have had no dairy products in a month. Chad pulls out a roll of Chinese toilet paper, which looks and feels like pink crepe paper, from his knapsack.

"I'll be glad when I don't have to lug this around all the time," he says. We all know what he means. We crave flush toilets, hand soap, disposable paper towels. We are tired of hoarding bottled drinking water. We want French fries with a lot of ketchup, a Snickers bar, a bagel with lox. We want to be able to read street signs again; we want to watch bad American television.

. . .

INSTEAD, WE FLY south into the center of Guangdong Province, and outside the plane I can see how incredibly green it is. Here it is, I think: This is from whence I came. This is the countryside in which all my ancestors are buried, thousands of pounds of bones now gone to dust. I cannot say that I feel a sense of home, yet strangely this scene also does not seem so foreign.

As soon as we get off the plane, it is as if I can hear again. I suddenly understand the small chatter of people around me in the streets, in their uncouth, guttural tones of Cantonese. After checking into our hotel, which is garish and grandiose (but which has lovely bathrooms with soft white toilet paper), we go for a walk through the streets. The tourist commercial center around our hotel seems so Western compared to where we have been. There are glass storefronts with sleek displays of watches and cameras and strands of pearls. Everyone is dressed in professional urban chic, with pressed white shirts and stylish dresses. But later we go to the marketplace and the scene changes: raw meat hangs on vulgar hooks in the open air; plastic tubs swirl with silvery eels that swim frantically in circles. A man blows his nose directly onto the street by pressing a finger to his left nostril and exhaling violently through his right.

This is the giant Chinatown.

This is the China that lives in the mind of every American, for Canton, now Guangzhou, is the land that bred the owners of chop-suey restaurants and laundries, where sweet-and-sour pork and the entrepreneurial spirit are commonplace. I look around and see: It is gauche. It is the place where pathetic, miserably scrawny cats, rabbits, dogs, hedgehogs, and chickens sit in wire cages outside the front stoops of eateries, waiting to be chosen for death. It is where the fish seller will slit open the silver belly of a carp and show the beating heart to prove its freshness to the customer. It truly is the home of a people who will eat anything with four legs that doesn't resemble a table. It is loud with the sound of too many people speaking too much in too small a space. Guangzhou is the underside of the Chinese belly, what you find when you flip it over like a rock: busy, crawling, squirming, and dirty, but very much alive with the vibrancy that only exists in the darkness away from the eyes of emperors old and current.

There is little to see or do in Guangzhou. We are not taken around to see many so-called famous scenic or historic spots, no great feats of nature. Instead, we are taken shopping, to the government Friendship Stores, which are crowded with tourists who have taken day trips from Hong Kong into China. I look at these people and wonder if they believe that this is all there is to China. Guangzhou is a place of humanity and money, where silver changes hands as swiftly as the people put on different faces for the transactions. Yet it is thoroughly unabashed and honest about its mercantilism. It never tries to be something it isn't. And it knows it is better off than virtually anywhere else in China.

But while it is honest about its success, it is not charmed by it. The people are rude and indifferent because there is nothing to be gained by politeness and attentiveness. The Western face holds no mystery; it is only the owner of a fat wallet. And for a bit of that they will give the servile smile and let you believe in the quaint myths of Oriental exotica. But not for long, because there is money to be made elsewhere.

It is hot tonight in Guangzhou.

The city steams.

Joyce has gone for a swim in the hotel pool. I have turned off the air conditioner because it is too loud. Oddly enough, in these last days in China I don't want the sounds of this world to be drowned out by the dull roar of Western comfort. I open the window and the still-warm heat rolls in, thick and slightly rancid, smelling of overripe mangoes and fish. I hear men talking outside. They are discussing something, but I cannot make out their words because of the traffic. Instead, I just hear their percussive consonants, the pointed sounds of Cantonese. The men speak loudly over the traffic, two and three voices at once. What are they debating? I wonder.

I lean out my window and stare down at the busy street. The stores are still open. A light but steady flow of cyclists are still in transit. A bus roars to a stop across from the hotel, expels a scattering of passengers onto the sidewalk. Its doors shut with a snap, then the bus heaves itself up and pushes down the street.

I look down at the men. They are sitting on old vegetable crates on the sidewalk, smoking. Some have their legs crossed delicately at the knee, like women. One sits with his legs spread apart and rests a hand on each knee as if he is trying to push his legs into the ground. They all are wearing black trousers and white shirts, with white dishtowels knotted at their waists. I think they probably work at one of the restaurants that cater to tourists.

Three of them are young, but not too young like boys. They are very lean; I think that my hips must be bigger than theirs and this embarrasses me. Their sleeves are rolled up to their elbows, and I can see the sinews of their muscles, which are taut even as they sit, holding their cheap Chinese cigarettes between two fingers. They are not very attractive men, too thin, their faces filled with bones. Still, I find them collectively beautiful, sitting there on the sidewalk on vegetable crates.

The man sitting with his legs open is older. He has on a white T-shirt, worn thin with age. He is fatter than the others; his paunch presses into his shirt, spills over his belt onto his pants. His face is full, too, and he looks tired. Not merely from the day's work, though, but from years of it. Decades of it. He swipes his forehead with the back of his right hand, still holding a cigarette, then returns the hand to his knee. He looks as if he is holding up his entire upper body with those hands. If he removed them, he would probably collapse, give up. Ask the gods to take him back, recycle his tired soul and give it to someone else.

The men have stopped talking.

They just sit and smoke, stare down at the sidewalk. A young girl in a plain dress walks by, carrying a basket of something green and leafy with white stems. In America her dark pants might be called clam diggers, I think. But here in China they are just short, several inches above her ankles. Her light-colored shirt picks up the light of the kitchen as she passes the door. Her sandals slap the sidewalk. She walks past the men, not looking at them. They do not seem to look at her either. But when she has passed, one of the younger men slowly turns his head and nonchalantly gazes after her, watching her ponytail bob as she walks away, *slap, slap, slap* on the sidewalk. He turns his head away from her, back toward the kitchen door. He gets up off the vegetable crate, takes one more pull on his cigarette, which he has smoked down to the last half-inch, to where he can barely hold it. He throws the cigarette down on the pavement. Steps on it.

One by one the other men finish their smokes without a word. Pitch the butts into the street or in the gutter. They get up and go back inside to the kitchen, vanishing from my sight and into their lives.

I pull my head in from the window, shut it. Listen to the muffled sounds of the street through the window. So much of my trip to China has been like this—observing life through glass. We have not gotten to talk to many Chinese, gotten to know them. Most of that is by design: All foreign tours are supervised by government agencies and we will see only what they want. And especially in bigger cities like Beijing, people still are hesitant to speak to outsiders. It was not that long ago that to do so was to court danger.

For a little while I stand there watching the passing traffic, but little interests me now that the men have gone in. An old man hobbles by with a cane. A cluster of modernly dressed young people pass, chatting animatedly. Another bus makes a stop.

I am getting too warm. Tiny drops of sweat form on my forehead and nose, my upper lip.

I pull the drapes and turn on the air conditioner, which roars to life with a clatter, then evens out to an obnoxiously loud hum. I stare at the burgundy drapes, think of the China I have just blocked out. In this room I could be in any Holiday Inn in the world. I could be in a Howard Johnson's in Illinois were it not for the thermos bottle of hot water and the tiny complimentary tube of toothpaste with green Chinese characters on it.

I look around the perfect, sanitized room and miss China already.

. . .

Joyce is still not back.

I take out the stones that I took from the river and look at them: smooth and dark, warm from being in my pockets against my thighs. It is amazing to think that the river formed them; they are so perfect, so round. I tap their sides together and the sound is small but high, near the upper reaches of an octave. I take one stone in each hand, but this feels strange. It is better to have them together in one palm.

I am beginning to think that I have ended up with less than I started with. As a child I did not think this was possible. I thought a person grew up and only got more—more presents, more toys, more friends. I thought life was supposed to be cumulative, that over the years the things and people in your life would add up to be a bigger number, like in the inchworm song:

> Two and two are four,
> Four and four are eight,
> Eight and eight are sixteen,
> Sixteen and sixteen are thirty-two.
> Inchworm, inchworm,
> Measuring the marigolds. . . .

I did not know that you could add things together and somehow end up with less. One by one I have stacked up the years of my slender life, and year by year there is less to count. I have little to show for my loss of innocence.

I feel the stones in my hand, rub them between my fingertips.

I think of everything that never was.

I imagine all those lives that were not lived, beginning with my father, who never saw my sister and me grow to womanhood, who never knew us as more than children, bits of flesh cleaved from his own. He never saw us graduate in our dark caps and gowns or met the men we loved. And he never will hold a grandchild in his arms.

I think of Lance and all his possibilities, drowned like a litter of newborn pups. He never was a philosopher who walked about in a tweed jacket with dark suede patches at the elbows; he did not become a ragged and moody poet who wrote in a garret. When he died, all of his brightness was in half blossom, lovely and magnificent even then, with all that wonderful spirit. True, there will be no more pain for him, but there also never again will be the hope of joy.

And there is seldom a day that passes that at some point I do not think of Alex. I was a person made whole by being split in two: I gave one half to him, but then he left with it. I do not know if there is a way to get that back.

Ultimately, I most feel the loss of the one who did not survive to breathe of this world. He is the one who had no chance at childhood, at being human. He died before birth; his tiny life was blessed and brief.

I sit in this hotel room, which is filled with soft, human comforts. Nice, plush beds. A gleaming mirror. A desk made of smooth, dark wood. But the colors of the carpet, the drapes, and the bedspread remind me of wine that has been left out for too long: It is saturated in burgundy but holds no warmth.

· · ·

THE DAY AFTER tomorrow we will be leaving China.

I had thought I would be glad. I had thought I would be thrilled to be back at home again, with my cats and all my things. I had fantasized about eating an entire pan of bread pudding; I had dreamed about staying in bed and not moving for an entire week. I would order pizza and have it delivered right to my door. I would watch hours of *I Love Lucy* reruns.

But now the thought of leaving China makes me sad. I have no desire to be back in New York. When I return, my sister will be getting married, and I want no part of that excessive pageant. If I could stay away, I would.

This country has been very strange; its effect on me must have been very subtle. I do not know when I began to love China, when I began to soak in her landscape like a luxuriant, curative balm. All I know is that as I sit here, on the brink of departing, I cannot bear to leave.

THE SEA

WE LEAVE GUANGZHOU by train for the Shenzhen Special Economic Zone, a kind of "instant noodle" town—just add capital and there you go; you have a city. This morning we travel like locals, riding in the third-class hard-seat cars. True to form, the stationmasters oversold the number of tickets, and a dozen passengers on each car are left to stand in the aisles, clinging to the backs of the wooden benches or sitting down on bundles strewn along the narrow passageway. All the windows are open and hot air blows freely through the cars, making this seem like a kind of teenage road trip.

But no one seems very festive on this train; everyone is tired, like commuters just trying to get home after a long day. The group across the aisle listlessly plays cards for a while, but the wind keeps blowing the cards all around the car. We catch a five of diamonds and a queen of spades and give them back. The other people thank us without smiling and put the deck away. One of their party, a young woman in a pink floral dress, is sleeping as she stands, resting her head on a satchel that is precariously balanced on the back of the wooden bench. Finally a young man in her group gets up, offers her his seat. She blinks, then sits down. In a moment she is slumped onto the arm of the man next to her, her head nodding in time to the train.

. . .

ONCE IN SHENZHEN we check into a hotel that is so new that there is no running water in our rooms.

"Don't worry, don't worry," the concierge says. "It will be all right when you get back." We leave for our outing, dubious. Mrs. Yamamoto unearths a box of little moist towelettes from somewhere in her suitcase and passes them around to us. We dab at our faces and necks with the little towels, which smell like astringent. They are cooling but leave a sticky feeling, and everyone just wants to wash their hands.

. . .

WE ARE TAKEN to a place called Splendid China, a beautifully landscaped park filled with all the architectural and natural wonders of China reproduced in miniature. A lot of Hong Kong and Taiwanese tourists come here just to say they've stepped foot on mainland China; that way they can see all the sights without having to travel anywhere. It is all here: the Temple of Heaven, the Great Wall, the Forbidden City—even the Yangze River with mounds of stone that are supposed to represent the three gorges.

The heat is stifling as we walk listlessly through the flowered gardens, sucking down chrysanthemum drink from little boxes. It is so hot we can barely breathe; the heat presses in on us from all sides and I think we would melt if we stood in one spot for too long. We gaze bleary-eyed at the pristine replicas of all these sights; we have seen the real things already and these models look like Lego renderings. Dr. Theodore wants to take a group photo by the miniature Great Wall, which is barely two feet high. We pose wearily. He fiddles with a bunch of lenses, a light meter. *Snap.*

"Thanks!" Dr. Theodore says cheerily. "I want to prove that I saw all of China, even the fake version."

Suddenly I realize with horror that I've forgotten about Renee's picture.

"Oh, my God," I say to no one in particular.

"What?" Joyce says. "Is something wrong?"

"No, I just almost forgot something," I tell her. "But it's okay. Never mind."

For weeks I have been carrying around Renee's tiny photo, which I slipped into my wallet behind my health insurance card, but I have not taken it out to show her anything. I struggle with my bag and find her tiny image. I strategically drift away from the rest of the group; I don't want anyone to see me doing this.

"Sorry, buddy," I say to Renee telepathically, hoping my apology reaches New York via mental airwaves. "I forgot. But we're still in China, so don't be mad, okay?"

I check around me surreptitiously. No one is looking.

I hold her picture up. "See?" I whisper. "This is the Great Wall, and this one looks in better shape than the real one, which is getting pretty old, you know." I wave Renee around. "This is it, can you see it? This is China."

Now it is nearly twilight.

The light is wonderful at this time of day, when the afternoon has not quite given up. The air seems very golden.

I stand on a hill in Shenzhen and look out across the water. I squint into the sun. Here on this point of land is where everything comes together. Everything merges here. All the yesterdays flow into tomorrows like water coming onto the sand. This is where all my grandfathers and grandmothers were born, a hundred generations before me, a thousand blood kin I do not know. In the distance is Hong Kong, where we will go tomorrow.

Earlier a woman had walked by on the street. "Look!" Mrs. Barclay pointed out. "She looks just like you."

I turned.

And so did she. Our eyes met for that infinite second, and in that glance we saw ourselves. We were sisters, cousins; we were one and the same.

. . .

NOW I STAND on the hill in Shenzhen, overlooking the sea. I am standing at the edge of China, which is like being at the end of the Earth. I think of stepping out on the water, which looks so thick with salt that it would support the weight of a woman. But I know that it will not. So instead I think of walking out into the water, into the shallows, where the warm water would lap around my ankles. I think of walking out farther, up to my knees, where the pull would be stronger. The sand would be less sure under my feet there; it would be soft, giving way beneath every step. I think of raging waves upon the shore; I think of how I would look, walking into the water in a long dress, with my hair blown all about me. I think of how the white of my dress would turn to gray in the water of the sea. The sound of the waves would be like a roar, crashing on the sand. The waves would come up and reach out . . . out just a little farther, a little farther yet—for that extra bit of shoreline only a grain away. Then the waves would pull back suddenly, taking everything with it in its wake, swallowing it back into the sea.

. . .

BUT THAT IS only my imagination.

Instead, everything here is flat, placid in this nightmarish heat.

I look around my feet.

I find a shard of stone under a nearby tree; with its sharp corner I dig with the point, cutting through the thick and stubborn grass, which clings ferociously to the soil. I have to use the shard of stone as a saw, tearing away at the dry roots. My hands are so dry that they hurt; dirt cakes under my nails. I keep digging away with my primitive tool.

Finally the space is made. It is a depression the diameter of my cupped palms and about as deep.

It is to be a shallow grave.

From my pocket I take the two stones from the river, smooth and warm in my hand. I feel how hard they are, how light. I raise them to my lips, kiss them; I touch my lips to their smooth sides.

Then I lay the stones, side by side, in the earth. I carefully sweep back the crumbs of soil, put the broken clods of grass on top. Press down.

Ashes to ashes. Dust.

The Chinese believe it is good to be buried on a hill facing south and facing water. The view is good. The hill protects the dead from cold northern winds and from bad spirits. A proper funeral also would have had a band procession with whining stringed instruments and the clanging of gongs. Pretend paper money, paper houses, and all kinds of paper riches would be set on fire—with the idea that the smoke would take all these things to heaven for a splendid afterlife for the dead.

But everything is quiet. And I have no incense to light, no offerings except my sorrow.

. . .

I STAND UP and stare at the sea.

Some Chinese immigrants, no matter how long they stay in America, want to return to their homelands to die. It is the custom of some to have their bones or ashes transported back to their villages, to their places of birth, for burial.

Now, I think, my flesh is here also, on this hill overlooking the sea and protected from those eternally cold northern winds. When I decided to come to China, I did not know I did so with intent.

I find my wallet in my satchel, take out Renee's picture. I turn her face to the sea.

Look, Renee, I say softly. Look how beautiful it is. Can you see? This is the land where all my hopes were born. And this is the sea onto which they were all cast off.

ANDREA LOUIE is a first-generation Chinese-American who grew up in Ohio. She was a reporter for the *Akron Beacon Journal* but left her secure, sensible job to become a full-time novelist. She now lives in New York City, where she temps to pay the rent and writes to feed her soul. *Moon Cakes* is her first novel.